VOCABULARY FOR THE COLLEGE-BOUND STUDENT

By HAROLD LEVINE

Author of
English: A Comprehensive Course
Comprehensive English Review Text
Vocabulary for the College-Bound Student
Vocabulary for the High School Student
Vocabulary Through Pleasurable Reading, Books I and II
Vocabulary and Composition Through Pleasurable Reading,
    Books III, IV, V, and VI

Dedicated to serving

AMSCO

our nation's youth

When ordering this book, please specify:

either

R 118 W

or

VOCABULARY FOR THE COLLEGE-BOUND STUDENT, WORKBOOK EDITION

AMSCO SCHOOL PUBLICATIONS, Inc.

315 Hudson Street　　　　　　　　　　**New York, N.Y. 10013**

Purchase Date_____ Cost_____

STUDENT	DATE ISSUED	DATE RETURNED

Student assumes responsibility for this text
Give it excellent care.

PREFACE

The primary aim of this book is to provide help—but help with *understanding*—for high school students seeking to enlarge their vocabulary. It is designed to help them whether their goal is college admission, or better employment opportunities, or overall self-improvement.

A companion aim is to assist busy English teachers interested in enriching instruction through direct teaching of vocabulary. The book attempts to do this by providing vocabulary materials and procedures that have proved successful in the classroom.

Teachers know that, as students read more, they gradually expand their vocabulary. They also know that such expansion is usually incidental or, more appropriately, accidental, unless the teacher deliberately provides for the learning of specific words. There is therefore strong reason for teachers to supplement reading as a means of vocabulary growth by mounting direct attacks upon vocabulary. This volume provides resources for such attacks.

Absent from these pages is a feature often found in vocabulary publications—long lists of un-related words, skimpily defined, and with few or no illustrative sentences. Strange words inade-quately taught can only bewilder the student.

As explained in Chapter I, this book organizes vocabulary study by teaching words in groups, *each group consisting of words related to one another in some meaningful way.*

Chapter II uses the grouping principle of the *central idea.* Each of its twenty-five word groups is organized around a different idea, such as *health, praise, height, smell,* etc.

Chapter III teaches twenty-five groups too, but this time the unifying concept is a Greek root, such as PHIL meaning "love," and MIS meaning "hate"; or a Greek prefix, such as HYPER meaning "over," and HYPO meaning "under."

Chapter IV does the same with Latin, but on a much larger scale because of Latin's greater influence on English.

Chapter V teaches a group of notable words descended from the myths and history of the Greeks and Romans.

Chapter VI deals with several groups of Anglo-Saxon origin. In some of these, Anglo-Saxon-derived words are presented side by side with Latin-derived words of similar meaning.

Chapter VII teaches groups of words adopted from French. Each group is organized around a separate topic, such as *conversation, food, dress,* etc.

Chapters VIII and IX do the same with loanwords from Italian and Spanish, respectively.

Chapter X teaches students how to expand their vocabulary further by showing them how to form derivatives. It helps them, for example, to convert *plausible* to *implausible, plausibly, im-plausibly, plausibility, implausibility,* etc. In so doing, it provides a review of some useful spell-ing rules.

Chapter XI discusses and analyzes the officially released sample vocabulary questions for four widely given pre-college examinations:

1. Preliminary Scholastic Aptitude Test (PSAT)

2. Scholastic Aptitude Test (SAT)

3. National Merit Scholarship Qualifying Test

4. New York State Regents Scholarship Examination

Chapter XII, *Dictionary of Words Taught in This Text,* is intended as a tool of reference and review.

The pronunciation of each new word is supplied. The system of indicating pronunciation based on Webster's New Students Dictionary, copyright 1964 by G. & C. Merriam Co., Publishers of the Merriam-Webster Dictionaries, is used by permission.

Throughout the volume, the author and editors have attempted to reinforce learning by abundant illustrative sentences, varied exercises and drills, and cumulative reviews. Many of the exercises have been patterned after the types of vocabulary questions encountered in pre-college tests.

Nothing in the organization of this text should prevent teachers from starting with whatever chapter they may wish, in accordance with their students' needs. The directions have been kept simple so that, after brief motivation in class, the students may proceed on their own. Periodic discussion of one or more groups of words from any part of the text will provide enrichment in any grade of high school English. Since vocabulary growth is a gradual process, it is urged that this text be introduced as early as possible in the high school course.

Teachers may also want to recommend this book to the college-bound student working by himself to prepare for scholarship and college-admissions tests.

The student who uses this book, whether an "independent" or a member of a class, should understand that correctly answering test questions about a word does not necessarily prove that he has really learned it. To make a newly met word his own, he must *use* it in his speaking and writing. This is the surest way of incorporating that word into his permanent vocabulary.

—H.L.

CONTENTS

CHAPTER I. THE IMPORTANCE OF VOCABULARY TO *YOU*

CHAPTER II. BUILDING VOCABULARY THROUGH CENTRAL IDEAS

CHAPTER III. WORDS DERIVED FROM GREEK

CHAPTER IV. WORDS DERIVED FROM LATIN

CHAPTER V. WORDS FROM CLASSICAL MYTHOLOGY AND HISTORY

CHAPTER VI. ANGLO-SAXON VOCABULARY AND ITS ENRICHMENT THROUGH LATIN

CHAPTER VII. FRENCH WORDS IN ENGLISH

CHAPTER VIII. ITALIAN WORDS IN ENGLISH

CHAPTER IX. SPANISH WORDS IN ENGLISH

CHAPTER X. EXPANDING VOCABULARY THROUGH DERIVATIVES

CHAPTER XI. SAMPLE VOCABULARY QUESTIONS IN PRE-COLLEGE TESTS

CHAPTER XII. DICTIONARY OF WORDS TAUGHT IN THIS TEXT

CHAPTER I

THE IMPORTANCE OF VOCABULARY TO *YOU*

VOCABULARY AND THINKING

Words stand for ideas. Words are the tools of thought. If your word power is limited, you are necessarily a limited thinker, since you can neither receive ideas nor communicate with others except within the confines of your inadequate vocabulary. Unless you broaden your vocabulary, you will be unable to do the thinking that success in life demands.

VOCABULARY AND COLLEGE ADMISSION

Quite properly, college admissions officers will be interested in the extent of your vocabulary. Research has established a close correlation between vocabulary and intelligence. A good vocabulary, therefore, will identify you as a student of superior mental ability. It will suggest, too, that you have done wide reading, since reading is the principal way of developing a good vocabulary. In the college entrance and scholarship tests you are likely to take, you will find vocabulary a major ingredient. If you have any doubt about this, see Chapter XI, where sample questions from several widely given pre-college tests are reprinted and analyzed.

VOCABULARY GROWTH THROUGH READING

Persons who read widely gradually build up extensive vocabularies, especially if they have a curiosity about words. This curiosity, compelling them to regard every unfamiliar word as a breakdown in communication between author and reader, sends them thumbing through the dictionary. Should you, too, develop such word curiosity, you will be assured a lifetime of vocabulary growth.

Though reading is the basic means of vocabulary growth, it is a relatively slow means. For the college-bound student who has not yet achieved a superior vocabulary, reading needs to be supplemented by a direct attack that will yield comparatively rapid growth—and that is the purpose of this book.

LEARNING VOCABULARY THROUGH THIS BOOK

This book will involve you in a four-pronged attack on vocabulary.

Attack #1: Learning Vocabulary in Groups of Related Words

Vocabulary growth that evolves from reading has one serious disadvantage: it is poorly organized. The new words you encounter as you read usually bear little relationship to one another. This, of course, does not mean that you should think any the less of reading as a means of vocabulary building. It does, however, suggest that you may achieve relatively rapid vocabulary growth by studying *organized groups of related words.*

In the "central-ideas" chapter you will find twenty-five groups of related words. Each group presents words revolving about one idea—*joy, sadness, flattery, age, relatives, reasoning,* etc. The new words are further explained in hundreds of illustrative sentences that have one feature in common: they present new vocabulary in such context as will make the meaning obvious and easy to remember.

Attack #2: Learning Vocabulary Derived From Greek and Latin

The principle of the lever has enabled man, using relatively little effort, to do a great amount of work. You can apply the same principle to learning vocabulary. If you study certain productive Greek and Latin prefixes and roots, you can gain word leverage. Each prefix or root adequately understood will help you to learn the many English words it has produced. In the Greek and Latin chapters, you will meet important prefixes and roots, each with numerous English offspring.

Rounding out the attack on Greek and Latin are two briefer chapters. One will teach you useful English words derived from classical (Latin and Greek) mythology and history. The other, dealing with the interplay of Latin and Anglo-Saxon, will contribute further to your word hoard.

Attack #3: Learning Vocabulary Borrowed From French, Italian, and Spanish

Since English has borrowed heavily from French, you are sure to encounter adopted French words in books, newspapers, and magazines. Such words are considered a part of our English vocabulary and are often key words in the passages in which they occur. Not to know the meanings of common French borrowings is therefore a serious vocabulary deficiency.

The French chapter presents more than one hundred twenty commonly used loanwords, divided into small, easy-to-learn groups. To give you confidence in your understanding of each word, care has been taken to make the definitions and illustrative sentences as helpful as possible. You will find similar treatment in the briefer chapters on important Italian and Spanish loanwords.

Attack #4: Learning to Form Derivatives

Suppose you have just learned a new word—*fallible*, meaning "liable to be mistaken." If you don't know how to form derivatives, all you have added to your vocabulary is *fallible*—just one word.

But if you know how to form derivatives, you have learned not one but several new words. You have learned *fallible* and *infallible; fallibly* and *infallibly; fallibility* and *infallibility*, etc.

Chapter X will teach you how to form and spell derivatives so that you may know how to add many new words to your vocabulary whenever you learn one new word.

"EXERCISING" NEW VOCABULARY

Muscular exercise is essential during your years of physical growth. Vocabulary exercise, too, is essential in your periods of word growth.

To learn new words effectively, you must put them to use early and often. The challenging drills and tests in this book will give you abundant opportunities for varied vocabulary exercise. But you should do more on your own.

In your reading and listening experiences, be conscious of vocabulary. Take the initiative on suitable occasions to use new vocabulary in speaking and writing. Such follow-up is a *must* if you are to make new words securely yours.

CHAPTER II

BUILDING VOCABULARY THROUGH CENTRAL IDEAS

One helpful way to build your vocabulary is to study groups of related words. According to this method, you may first take up a group of new words dealing with "joy"; then another group dealing with "sadness," etc. You will soon discover that studying several related words at one time can be much more profitable than studying lists of unrelated words.

This chapter presents twenty-five groups, each consisting of words relating to a unifying central idea. Under each central idea there are many important new words dealing with that idea, together with definitions and illustrative sentences. These sentences have been specially constructed to help you fix in mind the definition and use of each new word.

Despite all this assistance, you will not achieve the results made possible by this book unless you *apply yourself*. Expanding your vocabulary is a rewarding but *challenging* task. It calls for sustained effort and imagination. Here are a few suggestions that will enable you to get the most out of this chapter.

1. Pay careful attention to each illustrative sentence. Then construct, at least in your mind, a similar sentence using your own context.

2. Do the abundant drill exercises thoughtfully, not mechanically. Review the words you miss.

3. Deliberately *use* your new vocabulary as soon as possible in appropriate situations—in chats with friends, class discussions, letters, and compositions. Only by *exercising* new words will you succeed in making them part of your active vocabulary.

1. JOY, PLEASURE

WORD	MEANING	TYPICAL USE
bliss 'blis	perfect happiness	The young movie star could conceive of no greater *bliss* than winning an "Oscar."
blithe 'blīth	merry; cheerful; happy	In *blithe* company it is easy to be gay.
buoyant 'bȯi-ənt	1. cheerful 2. able to float	We need your *buoyant* companionship to lift us from boredom.
complacent kəm-'plās-ᵊnt	self-satisfied	From your *complacent* manner, I should judge you are pleased with your final grades.
convivial kən-'viv-ē-əl	1. fond of eating and drinking with friends 2. jovial	Our *convivial* host hates to dine alone.
delectable di-'lek-tə-bəl	very pleasing; delightful	The food was *delectable;* we enjoyed every morsel.
ecstasy 'ek-stə-sē	state of overwhelming joy; rapture	If we win the championship tomorrow, there will be *ecstasy;* if we lose, gloom.
elated i-'lāt-əd	in high spirits; joyful	Except for my little sister, who misses the old neighborhood, the entire family is *elated* with the new house.
frolicsome 'fräl-ik-səm	full of merriment; gay; playful	The clown's *frolicsome* antics amused the children.

gala 'gā-lə	characterized by festivity	The annual Mardi Gras in New Orleans is a *gala* carnival of parades and merriment.
jocund 'jäk-ənd	merry; cheerful	Our neighbor is a *jocund* fellow who tells amusing anecdotes.
jubilation ‚jü-bə-'lā-shən	rejoicing	On election night there usually is *jubilation* at the campaign head-quarters of the victorious party.

2. SADNESS

ascetic ə-'set-ik	1. shunning pleasures; self-deny-ing 2. person who shuns pleasures	The *ascetic* Puritans rigidly sup-pressed many forms of recrea-tion.
chagrin shə-'grin	1. embarrassment; mortification 2. disappointment	Imagine my *chagrin* when I learned that I had not been invited to the party!
compunction kəm-'pəŋ(k)-shən	1. regret; remorse 2. misgiving; qualm	Miss Jones had no *compunction* about failing the track star, as he had not done his work all term.
contrite kən-'trīt	showing deep regret and sorrow for wrongdoing; deeply penitent; repentant	Believing the young offender to be *contrite*, the dean decided to give him another chance.
dejected di-'jek-təd	sad; in low spirits; depressed	We are elated when our team wins, but *dejected* when it loses.
disconsolate dis-'kän-sə-lət	cheerless; inconsolable	The mother could not stop her *dis-consolate* son from sobbing over the loss of his dog.
disgruntled dis-'grənt-ᵊld	in bad humor; displeased	From her *disgruntled* expression I could tell she was not satisfied with my explanation.
doleful 'dōl-fəl	full of sorrow; mournful; dolorous	The refugee told a *doleful* tale of hunger and persecution.
glum 'gləm	moody; gloomy; dour	As they emerged from the confer-ence, both statesmen were *glum* and refused to talk to reporters.
lamentable 'lam-ən-tə-bəl	pitiable; rueful	He described the *lamentable* hard-ships of the three miners trapped in the underground chamber.
maudlin 'mȯd-lən	weakly sentimental and tearful	After presenting a couple of *maud-lin* numbers, the quartet was asked to sing something more cheerful.
nostalgia nə-'stal-jə	1. homesickness 2. yearning for the past	Toward the end of a vacation away from home, we usually experience a feeling of *nostalgia*.

pathetic pə-'thet-ik	arousing pity	Despite his *pathetic* condition, the crippled lad had a ready smile.
pathos 'pā-thäs	quality in events or in art (literature, music, etc.) that arouses our pity	The young seamstress who precedes Sydney Carton to the guillotine adds to the *pathos* of A TALE OF TWO CITIES.
pensive 'pen-siv	thoughtful in a sad way; melancholy	Unlike his gay classmates, the new pupil was *pensive* and shy.
plight 'plīt	unfortunate state; predicament	Numerous offers of assistance were received after the *plight* of the distressed family was publicized.
poignant 'pȯi-nyənt	painfully touching; piercing	One of the most *poignant* scenes in MACBETH occurs when Macduff learns that his wife and children have been slaughtered.
sullen 'səl-ən	ill-humoredly silent; gloomy; morose	The *sullen* youngster would not tell why he had not done the assignment.
throes 'thrōz	anguish; pangs	Fortunate are those who have never experienced the *throes* of separation from a loved one.
tribulation ˌtrib-yə-'lā-shən	suffering; distress	The time between the final examinations and the announcement of the marks is a period of real *tribulation* for most students.

3. STOUTNESS

burly 'bər-lē	stout; husky and rough	Extra-large football uniforms were ordered to outfit our *burly* linemen.
buxom 'bək-səm	plump and attractive	By the side of her lean city cousin, the farm girl looked radiant and *buxom*.
cherubic chə-'rü-bik	chubby and innocent-looking; like a *cherub* (angel in the form of a child)	Your well-nourished nephew, despite his *cherubic* face, can be quite mischievous.
obese ō-'bēs	very fat; corpulent; portly	Prince Hal describes the *obese* Falstaff as a "huge hill of flesh."
pudgy 'pəj-ē	short and fat	My tall, athletic brother was rather *pudgy* as a child of ten.

4. THINNESS

attenuate ə-'ten-yə-ˌwāt	make thin; weaken	Photographs of President Lincoln reveal how rapidly the cares of leadership aged and *attenuated* him.

II. BUILDING VOCABULARY THROUGH CENTRAL IDEAS   **5**

emaciated i-'mā-shē-ˌāt-əd	made unnaturally thin	*Emaciated* by his illness, the patient found that his clothes would no longer fit.
haggard 'hag-ərd	careworn; gaunt	*Haggard* from their long ordeal, the rescued miners were rushed to the hospital for treatment and rest.
lank 'laŋk	long and thin; slender	Every basketball team longs for a *lank*, agile center who can outleap his rival.
svelte 'svelt	slender; lithe	Ballet dancers observe a strict diet to maintain their *svelte* figures.

5. FLATTERY

adulation ˌad-yə-'lā-shən	excessive praise; flattery	True leaders can distinguish sincere praise from blind *adulation*.
blandishment 'blan-dish-mənt	word or deed of mild flattery	Suitors often use terms of endearment, flowers, and similar *blandishments*.
cajole kə-'jōl	persuade by pleasant words; wheedle	Sister *cajoled* Dad into raising her allowance.
curry favor 'kər-ē fā-və(r)	seek to gain favor by flattery	The candidate tried to *curry favor* with the voters by praising their intelligence and patriotism.
fulsome 'fùl-səm	offensive because of insincerity; repulsive; disgusting	How can you endure the *fulsome* praises of your subordinate who lauds your every decision, right or wrong?
ingratiate in-'grā-shē-ˌāt	work (oneself) into favor	By raising her hand for every question, the new pupil tried to *ingratiate* herself with the teacher.
lackey 'lak-ē	slavish follower	The monarch could never get a frank opinion from the *lackeys* surrounding him, for they would always agree with him.
obsequious əb-'sē-kwē-əs	slavishly attentive; fawning	The *obsequious* subordinates vied with one another in politeness and obedience, each hoping to win the manager's favor.
sycophant 'sik-ə-fənt	parasitic flatterer	*Sycophants* live at the expense of vain, rich men who enjoy flatteries.
truckle 'trək-əl	submit servilely to a superior	Some people, unfortunately, gain promotion by *truckling* to their supervisors.

fester 'fes-tə(r)	form pus; rankle; rot; putrefy	When a wound *festers,* it becomes inflamed, swollen, and painful.
hypochondriac ˌhī-pə-'kän-drē-ˌak	person morbidly anxious about his health, or suffering from imagined illness	The *hypochondriac* often interprets a normal condition as a symptom of serious illness.
immunity im-'yü-nət-ē	1. resistance (to a disease) 2. freedom (from an obligation)	Most people acquire life-long *immunity* to German measles once they have had that disease.
lesion 'lē-zhən	injury; hurt	The slightest *lesion* on a tree's bark, if left untended, may kill the tree.
malignant mə-'lig-nənt (*ant.* **benign**)	1. threatening to cause death 2. very evil	An emergency operation was scheduled to remove the *malignant* tissues.
morbid 'mȯr-bəd	1. gruesome 2. having to do with disease	In describing his illness, he discreetly omitted the *morbid* details.
pestilential ˌpes-tə-'len-shəl	1. morally harmful 2. pertaining to a pestilence	Parents, teachers, and spiritual leaders have attacked certain comic books as *pestilential.*
regimen 'rej-ə-mən	set of rules to improve health	After the operation I had to follow a *regimen* of diet and exercise prescribed by my physician.
salubrious sə-'lü-brē-əs	healthful	Southern Florida's *salubrious* climate attracts many convalescents.
sebaceous si-'bā-shəs	greasy; secreting fatty matter	The *sebaceous* glands in the skin secrete an oily substance essential for skin health.
therapeutic ˌther-ə-'pyüt-ik	curative	The visit by his children had a *therapeutic* effect on the hospitalized patient.
toxic 'täk-sik	poisonous	Operating a gasoline engine in a closed garage may cause death, as the exhaust fumes are dangerously *toxic.*
unguent 'əŋ-gwənt	salve; ointment	Frank's skin irritation was relieved after he applied the *unguent* prescribed by his physician.
virulent 'vir-(y)ə-lənt	1. extremely poisonous; deadly; venomous 2. very bitter	Some insecticides and weed killers contain arsenic, a *virulent* substance.
virus 'vī-rəs	1. disease-causing organism too small to be seen through a microscope 2. corruptive force	Polio is caused by a *virus,* an organism visible only through the electron microscope.

8. PRAISE

acclaim
ə-'klām

welcome with approval; applaud loudly

I did not enjoy that novel although it was *acclaimed* by several leading reviewers.

encomium
en-'kō-mē-əm

speech or writing of high praise; tribute

Lincoln's "Gettysburg Address" is, in part, an *encomium* of those who fought at Gettysburg.

eulogize
'yü-lə-ˌjīz

praise; extol

The police commissioner *eulogized* the patrolman for his alertness and bravery.

laudable
'lȯd-ə-bəl

praiseworthy; commendable

The bus driver's *laudable* safety record evoked high praise from his superiors.

laudatory
'lȯd-ə-ˌtȯr-ē

expressing praise; eulogistic

Most of the critics wrote *laudatory* reviews of the new film; only one found fault with it.

plaudit
'plȯd-ət

(used mainly in the plural) applause; enthusiastic praise

Responding to the *plaudits* of her admirers, the singer reappeared for an encore.

9. DEFAMATION

calumnious
kə-'ləm-nē-əs

falsely and maliciously accusing; defamatory; slanderous

Witnesses who heard the *calumious* attack offered to testify in behalf of the slandered person.

derogatory
di-'räg-ə-ˌtȯr-ē

expressing low esteem; belittling; disparaging

On examining the culprit's permanent record card, the dean found few laudatory comments but several *derogatory* ones.

imputation
ˌim-pyə-'tā-shən

1. insinuation
2. accusation

You have tried to besmirch my character with the cowardly *imputation* that I have robbed the poor.

libel
'lī-bəl

false and defamatory printed (or written) statement

We shall certainly sue the newspaper that printed this *libel* against our company.

malign
mə-'līn

speak evil of; vilify; traduce

I cannot bear to hear you *malign* so good a man.

slander
'slan-də(r)

false and defamatory spoken statement; calumny

The rumor that I was discharged is a vicious *slander*; the fact is that I resigned.

stigma
'stig-mə

mark of disgrace

With the *stigma* of a prison record, the ex-convict had difficulty in finding employment.

stigmatize
'stig-mə-ˌtīz

brand with a mark of disgrace

A youngster naturally resents being *stigmatized* by a nickname like "Fatty."

10. JEST

banter
'bant-ə(r)

playful teasing; joking; raillery

The retiring employee was subjected to gentle *banter* about his coming life of ease.

caricature
'kar-i-kə-ˌchù(ə)r

drawing, imitation, or description that ridiculously exaggerates peculiarities or defects

The Class Night skit that drew the loudest plaudits was a *caricature* of the first day in high school.

droll
'drōl

odd and laughter-provoking

The pupil's composition had the *droll* title "On Eating Crackers in Bed."

facetious
fə-'sē-shəs

1. in the habit of joking
2. said in jest without serious intent

Our *facetious* club president has a way of turning almost every comment into a joke.

flippant
'flip-ənt

treating serious matters lightly

Don't be so *flippant* about the need for studying; it is a serious matter that may affect your graduation.

harlequin
'här-li-k(w)ən

buffoon; clown

The *harlequin's* clowning endeared him to all.

hilarity
hil-'ar-ət-ē

noisy gaiety; mirth; jollity; glee

The laughter and shouting resulted in the entry of the principal, curious to learn what all the *hilarity* was about.

irony
'ī-rə-nē

1. species of humor whose intended meaning is the opposite of the words used
2. state of affairs contrary to what would normally be expected

In *irony,* the basketball players nicknamed their 6'6" center "Shorty."

jocose
jō-'kōs

given to jesting; playfully humorous; jocular

Some columnists write in a *jocose* vein; others are inclined to be serious.

levity
'lev-ət-ē

lack of proper seriousness; trifling gaiety; frivolity

During the assembly program George kept giggling, a *levity* for which his teacher scolded him later.

ludicrous
'lüd-ə-krəs

exciting laughter; ridiculous; farcical; absurd

Pie-throwing, falling down stairs, and similar *ludicrous* antics were common in early film comedies.

parody
'par-əd-ē

humorous imitation of a serious writing

The Washington press corps entertained the Chief Executive with a *parody* of a Presidential message to Congress.

sarcasm
'sär-ˌkaz-əm

sneering language intended to hurt a person's feelings

Instead of helping, he offered such *sarcasm* as "You have made your bed; now lie in it."

II. BUILDING VOCABULARY THROUGH CENTRAL IDEAS   13

sardonic sär-'dän-ik	bitterly sarcastic; mocking; sneering	Villains are often portrayed with a *sardonic* grin that suggests contempt for others.
satire 'sa-ˌtī(ə)r	language or writing that exposes follies or abuses by holding them up to ridicule	Jonathan Swift's GULLIVER'S TRAVELS is a brilliant *satire* on mankind's follies.
travesty 'trav-ə-stē	imitation that makes a serious thing seem ridiculous; mockery	That a notorious criminal should escape trial because of a technicality seems like a *travesty* of justice.

EXERCISES

EXERCISE 7. Each word or expression in column I has an ANTONYM (opposite) in column II. Insert the *letter* of the correct ANTONYM in the space provided.

COLUMN I	COLUMN II
_____ 1. mark of honor	(A) laudatory
_____ 2. susceptible	(B) poisonous
_____ 3. nontoxic	(C) halcyon
_____ 4. treat (someone) as unimportant	(D) doleful
_____ 5. hilarious	(E) levity
_____ 6. derogatory	(F) stigma
_____ 7. turbulent	(G) encomium
_____ 8. seriousness	(H) lionize
_____ 9. denunciation	(I) condemn
_____ 10. extol	(J) immune

EXERCISE 8. Write the *letter* of the word NOT RELATED in meaning to the other words in each group.

1. (A) joking (B) sportsmanship (C) banter (D) teasing (E) raillery _____
2. (A) improve (B) recuperate (C) impute (D) recover (E) convalesce _____
3. (A) imitation (B) caricature (C) parody (D) lesion (E) travesty _____
4. (A) satire (B) applause (C) plaudit (D) encomium (E) commendation _____
5. (A) rot (B) putrefy (C) fester (D) rankle (E) molt _____
6. (A) defamation (B) libel (C) virus (D) calumny (E) slander _____
7. (A) vulture (B) parrot (C) mimic (D) ape (E) copy _____
8. (A) sarcastic (B) mocking (C) sardonic (D) eulogistic (E) sneering _____
9. (A) healthful (B) salubrious (C) benign (D) therapeutic (E) environmental _____
10. (A) nag (B) mare (C) badger (D) harass (E) annoy _____

EXERCISE 9. In the space provided, write the *letter* of the word or expression that has most nearly the SAME MEANING as the italicized word.

------ 1. *Astringent* rebuke   (A) mild   (C) undeserved
                         (B) friendly   (D) stern

------ 2. Effective *antidote*   (A) harlequin   (C) remedy
                         (B) punishment   (D) precaution

------ 3. *Derogatory* comment   (A) unfair   (C) congratulatory
                         (B) belittling   (D) false

------ 4. *Benign* ruler   (A) healthful   (C) kindly
                         (B) aging   (D) tyrannical

------ 5. *Ironical* development   (A) contrary to expectation   (C) discouraging
                         (B) very sudden   (D) unfortunate

------ 6. *Festering* slums   (A) decaying   (C) poverty-stricken
                         (B) crime-ridden   (D) spreading

------ 7. Utterly *farcical*   (A) hopeless   (C) irresponsible
                         (B) incompetent   (D) absurd

------ 8. Prescribed *regimen*   (A) rules   (C) dose
                         (B) medicine   (D) enforcement

------ 9. *Venomous* fangs   (A) vigorous   (C) dangerous
                         (B) virulent   (D) pointed

------ 10. *Halcyon* atmosphere   (A) cloudy   (C) calm
                         (B) noisy   (D) clear

EXERCISE 10. Write the *letter* of the word (or set of words) which, if inserted in the sentence, would agree most closely with the thought of the sentence.

1. In crime reporting, newspapers withhold the names of offenders under sixteen so as not to _____ them.
   (A) popularize   (C) stigmatize   (E) traduce
   (B) libel   (D) slander

2. DON QUIXOTE, a _____ novel by Cervantes, ridicules exaggerated notions of chivalry.
   (A) satirical   (C) historical   (E) eulogistic
   (B) sentimental   (D) realistic

3. The _____ currently being exhibited in the _____ have attracted numerous students of ornithology.
   (A) apes . . aviary   (D) monkeys . . apiary
   (B) parrots . . apiary   (E) vultures . . aviary
   (C) bees . . aviary

4. For his laudable feat, the astronaut was _____ by the citizens of his hometown.
   (A) badgered   (C) maligned   (E) caricatured
   (B) parodied   (D) lionized

5. Winston Churchill _____ the heroes of the Battle of Britain in this memorable _____: "Never was so much owed by so many to so few."
   (A) congratulated . . travesty   (D) acclaimed . . tribute
   (B) defended . . encomium   (E) extolled . . oration
   (C) vilified . . plaudit

II. BUILDING VOCABULARY THROUGH CENTRAL IDEAS   **15**

EXERCISE 11. In each sentence fill in the missing letters of the incomplete word. Each dash stands for one missing letter.

1. At the dedication ceremony, the mayor will e _ _ _ _ _ _ _ the hero for whom the school is being named.

2. If a notation of Richard's cheating during the examination is made on his permanent record card, it may s _ _ _ _ _ _ _ _ _ him for the rest of his school days.

3. It is i _ _ _ _ _ _ _ that the severely paralyzed lad should have the name Hale, which means "healthy."

4. The biochemist claimed that the substance has t _ _ _ _ _ _ _ _ _ _ _ properties useful in the treatment of diseases of the lungs.

5. F _ _ _ _ _ _ _ _ remarks on solemn occasions are entirely inappropriate.

6. The child, having accidentally swallowed the poison, was promptly administered a suitable a _ _ _ _ _ _ _ and then rushed to the hospital.

7. Several newspaper editors commended the governor for his l _ _ _ _ _ _ _ efforts to prevent the strike.

8. Beneath the outer layer of the skin are the s _ _ _ _ _ _ _ _ glands, which secrete oil to lubricate the skin and the hair.

9. Many a life has been saved by the timely surgical removal of a m _ _ _ _ _ _ _ _ _ growth.

10. Though responsible for the fatal collision, the envoy could not be arrested because of diplomatic i _ _ _ _ _ _ _ .

EXERCISE 12. Write the *letter* of the word that best completes the analogy.

1. *Invalid* is to *hypochondriac* as *real* is to _ _ _ _ _ _ .
   - (A) sickly
   - (B) genuine
   - (C) healthful
   - (D) imagined
   - (E) impossible

2. *Birds* are to *ornithologist* as *poisons* are to _ _ _ _ _ _ .
   - (A) bacteriologist
   - (B) pharmacist
   - (C) toxicologist
   - (D) physician
   - (E) coroner

3. *Waste* is to *scavenger* as *dirt* is to _ _ _ _ _ _ .
   - (A) oil
   - (B) parasite
   - (C) cleanser
   - (D) ant
   - (E) weed

4. *Photograph* is to *caricature* as *fact* is to _ _ _ _ _ _ .
   - (A) drawing
   - (B) exaggeration
   - (C) sketch
   - (D) truth
   - (E) description

5. *Laughter* is to *ludicrous* as *sorrow* is to _ _ _ _ _ _ .
   - (A) dolorous
   - (B) droll
   - (C) facetious
   - (D) jocose
   - (E) flippant

11. WILLINGNESS—UNWILLINGNESS

WORD	MEANING	TYPICAL USE
alacrity ə-'lak-rət-ē	cheerful willingness; readiness; liveliness	An ideal class is one which pupils attend with *alacrity* and leave with reluctance.
aversion ə-'vər-zhən	strong dislike; repugnance; antipathy	Philip's *aversion* to work led to his dismissal.
loath 'lōth	unwilling; averse; disinclined; reluctant	We were *loath* to leave our friends, but Dad's transfer to California left us no choice.
volition vō-'lish-ən	will	Were you discharged or did you leave of your own *volition?*

12. HEIGHT

WORD	MEANING	TYPICAL USE
acclivity ə-'kliv-ət-ē (*ant.* declivity)	upward slope	The sharp *acclivity* compelled us to drive in low gear.
acme 'ak-mē	highest point; pinnacle; summit	With the painting of the MONA LISA, Leonardo da Vinci is generally believed to have reached his *acme* as a painter.
apogee 'ap-ə-jē (*ant.* perigee)	1. farthest point from the earth in the orbit of a man-made satellite or heavenly body 2. highest point	At its *apogee* the satellite was 560 miles from the earth, and at its perigee 150 miles.
climactic klī-'mak-tik (*ant.* anticlimactic)	1. arranged in order of increasing force and interest 2. of or constituting a *climax* (point of highest interest)	Notice the *climactic* order of ideas in this sentence: "Swelled by heavy rains, brooks became creeks, creeks rivers, and rivers torrents."
consummate kən-'səm-ət	perfect; carried to the highest degree	The pilot guided the liner into its berth with *consummate* skill.
eminence 'em-ə-nəns	1. high rank 2. lofty hill	Raised suddenly to an *eminence* for which he was ill qualified, the new executive could not get along with his subordinates.
ethereal i-'thir-ē-əl	1. of the heavens; celestial 2. airy; delicate; intangible; tenuous	Charles was told by his employer, "Get rid of your *ethereal* notions and come down to earth."
exalt ig-'zȯlt (*ant.* humiliate)	1. lift up with joy, pride, etc.; elate 2. raise in rank, dignity, etc.; extol; glorify	My parents were *exalted* by the news that I had been admitted to Arista.
precipice 'pres-ə-pəs	very steep, overhanging place; cliff	The climbers had to make a lengthy detour around an insurmountable *precipice.*

precipitous pri-'sip-ət-əs	1. steep as a precipice 2. hasty; rash	We descended from the summit in low gear, using our brakes all the way, since the road was so *precipitous*.
preeminent prē-'em-ə-nənt	standing out above others; superior	As a violinmaker, Stradivarius remains *preeminent*.
sublimate 'səb-lə-‚māt	1. redirect the energy of a person's bad impulses into socially and morally higher channels 2. purify	With the aid of dedicated social workers, energies that now find release in gang fights can be *sublimated* into wholesome club activities and sports.
sublime sə-'blīm	elevated; noble; exalted; uplifting	Visitors to the Grand Canyon are uplifted and refreshed by its *sublime* scenery.
vertex 'vər-‚teks	farthest point opposite the base, as in a triangle or pyramid; apex	The *vertex* of the largest Egyptian pyramid was originally 482 feet from the base.
zenith 'zē-nəth (*ant.* **nadir**)	1. highest point; culmination 2. point in the heavens directly overhead	His election as President marked the *zenith* of his long career in politics.

13. LOWNESS, DEPTH

abject 'ab-‚jekt	1. deserving contempt 2. sunk to a low condition; wretched	For your *abject* submission to your tyrannical associate we have the utmost contempt.
abyss ə-'bis	bottomless, immeasurably deep space	The sudden death of his closest friend threw Tennyson into an *abyss* of despair.
anticlimax ‚ant-i-'klī-maks (*ant.* **climax**)	abrupt decline in dignity or importance at the end; comedown; bathos	Jane Austen used *anticlimax* with comic effect when she described a mother who in the same breath inquired about her daughter's "welfare and poultry."
chasm 'kaz-əm	deep breach; wide gap or rift	Prospects for a settlement became remote, as the *chasm* between the rival parties deepened.
declivity di-'kliv-ət-ē (*ant.* **acclivity**)	downward slope	The hill was ideal for beginning skiers because of its gentle *declivity*.
dregs 'dregz	1. most worthless part 2. (usually plural) sediment at the bottom of a liquid	Gamblers, thieves, and hoodlums are among the *dregs* of society.
earthy 'ər-thē	1. coarse; low 2. of or like earth; worldly; not spiritual	Though satisfied with your helpers' work, we do not care for their *earthy* humor.

humble 'həm-bəl	1. of low position or condition 2. not proud; unpretentious; modest; courteously respectful	Despite his *humble* origin, Lincoln rose to the highest office in the land.
humiliate hyü-'mil-ē-ˌāt (*ant.* **exalt**)	lower the pride, position, or dignity of; abase; degrade; mortify	Rose feels I *humiliated* her in class today when I said her answer was wrong.
humility hyü-'mil-ət-ē	freedom from pride; humbleness; lowliness; modesty	Boasters and braggarts need a lesson in *humility*.
menial 'mē-nē-əl	low; mean; subservient; servile	Many college students do *menial* work as bus boys and waiters to help pay their tuition.
nadir 'nā-də(r) (*ant.* **zenith**)	lowest point	Hopes of the American Revolutionary forces were at their *nadir* in the bitter winter of 1777-78 at Valley Forge.
plumb 'pləm	get to the bottom of; ascertain the depth of; fathom	Sherlock Holmes amazes readers by his ability to *plumb* the deepest mysteries.
profound prə-'faund	very deep; deeply felt; intellectually deep	Einstein's theories are understood by relatively few because they are so *profound*.
ravine rə-'vēn	deep, narrow gorge worn by running water	Survivors of the plane that crashed in the mountain *ravine* were rescued by helicopter.

14. RELATIVES

filial 'fil-ē-əl	of or like a son or daughter	The youngest daughter looked after her ailing father with *filial* devotion.
fraternal frə-'tərn-əl	of or like a brother	There was much *fraternal* affection between the brothers; they loved one another.
genealogy ˌjē-nē-'äl-ə-jē	a person's or family's descent; lineage; pedigree	The *genealogy* of every American but the Indian can be traced back to an immigrant.
gentility jen-'til-ət-ē	1. good manners 2. aristocratic birth; membership in the upper class	George Bernard Shaw's PYGMALION shows how a cockney flower girl quickly acquires the *gentility* necessary to pass as a duchess.
kith and kin 'kith; 'kin	friends and relatives; kindred	Because he married in a distant state, the soldier had few of his *kith and kin* at the wedding.
maternal mə-'tərn-əl	of or like a mother	The kindergarten teacher has a kindly, *maternal* concern for each pupil.

nepotism	favoritism to relatives by those in power	Whenever a President appoints a relative to a government position, the cry of *nepotism* is raised by the opposition party.
'nep-ə-ˌtiz-əm		
paternal	of or like a father	The molding of a child's character is an important *paternal* obligation.
pə-'tərn-ᵊl		
progenitor	forefather	Adam is the Biblical *progenitor* of the human race.
prō-'jen-ət-ə(r)		
progeny	offspring; children; descendants	Josiah Franklin's *progeny* numbered seventeen, the fifteenth being a lad named Benjamin.
'präj-ə-nē		
sibling	one of two or more children of a family	Eileen has three *siblings*—two younger brothers and an older sister.
'sib-liŋ		

15. SMELL

aroma	pleasant odor; bouquet	What a smoker may describe as a rich tobacco *aroma*, a nonsmoker may consider a disgusting stench.
ə-'rō-mə		
fragrant	having a pleasant odor; odoriferous; odorous	A florist's shop is a *fragrant* place.
'frā-grənt		
fusty	1. stale-smelling; musty; moldy	To rid the unused room of its *fusty* smell, we opened the windows and let the fresh air in.
'fəs-tē	2. old-fashioned	
incense	substance yielding a pleasant odor when burned	Ancient Greek and Roman worshipers often burned *incense* to please their gods.
'in-ˌsens		
malodorous	ill-smelling; stinking; fetid	Brewing coffee makes a kitchen aromatic; boiling cabbage makes it *malodorous*.
mal-'ōd-ə-rəs		
noisome	1. offensive to smell; disgusting	Buses discharge *noisome* exhaust fumes that can make one sick.
'nȯi-səm	2. harmful; noxious	
olfactory	pertaining to the sense of smell	Because of their superior *olfactory* sense, bloodhounds can pick up the trails of fleeing criminals.
äl-'fak-t(ə-)rē		
pungent	1. sharp in smell or taste; acrid	As she sliced the onions, the *pungent* fumes made her eyes tear.
'pən-jənt	2. biting; stimulating	
putrid	1. stinking from decay	An occasional rinse with a soapy solution will keep garbage cans free of *putrid* odors.
'pyü-trəd	2. extremely bad; corrupt	
rancid	unpleasant to smell or taste from being spoiled or stale	If butter or fish has a *rancid* odor, it is unfit to eat.
'ran-səd		
rank	1. having a strong, bad odor or taste; offensively gross or coarse	When threatened, a skunk protects itself effectively by emitting a *rank* odor.
'raŋk	2. extreme	

reek 'rēk	1. emit a strong, disagreeable smell 2. be permeated with	Even after the fire was extinguished and the tenants were allowed to return, the building *reeked* of smoke.
scent 'sent	1. smell; perfume 2. get a suspicion of	The room was fragrant with the *scent* of freshly cut lilacs.
unsavory ˌən-'sāv(-ə)-rē	1. unpleasant to taste or smell 2. morally offensive	Mother traced the *unsavory* odor to a decaying onion in the vegetable bin.

EXERCISES

EXERCISE 13. In the space before each word or expression in column I, write the *letter* of its correct meaning in column II.

	COLUMN I	COLUMN II
------	**1.** spicy	(A) abyss
------	**2.** most worthless part	(B) high rank
------	**3.** chasm	(C) humility
------	**4.** consummate	(D) precipitous
------	**5.** disinclined	(E) dregs
------	**6.** humiliated	(F) loath
------	**7.** descent	(G) pungent
------	**8.** eminence	(H) lineage
------	**9.** hasty	(I) humbled
------	**10.** freedom from pride	(J) perfect

EXERCISE 14. Write the *letter* of the word NOT RELATED in meaning to the other words in each group.

1. (A) contemptible   (B) abject   (C) reluctant   (D) wretched   (E) low   ------

2. (A) putrid   (B) unsavory   (C) menial   (D) fusty   (E) malodorous   ------

3. (A) children   (B) offspring   (C) scent   (D) progeny   (E) descendants   ------

4. (A) vertex   (B) apex   (C) climax   (D) acme   (E) base   ------

5. (A) rank   (B) position   (C) gross   (D) offensive   (E) coarse   ------

6. (A) abyss   (B) precipice   (C) eminence   (D) peak   (E) cliff   ------

7. (A) modesty   (B) humility   (C) unpretentiousness   (D) pride   (E) humbleness   ------

8. (A) unwillingness   (B) repugnance   (C) antipathy   (D) aversion   (E) alacrity   ------

9. (A) rift   (B) acclivity   (C) breach   (D) ravine   (E) gorge   ------

10. (A) servile   (B) paternal   (C) obsequious   (D) submissive   (E) subservient   ------

EXERCISE 15. Fill each blank with the most appropriate word or expression selected from the vocabulary list below.

VOCABULARY LIST

maternal	progeny	exalted
rancid	bathos	kith and kin
attraction	aversion	chasm
gentility	delectable	humiliated
filial	climax	declivity

1. Janet's _____ to the water made her dread our swimming class.

2. It is only natural that we should be _____ by our successes.

3. Mother's Day gives children an opportunity to show their _____ devotion.

4. The gripping suspense at the _____ of the play held the audience breathless.

5. As we came down the steep _____, the speed of our car increased sharply.

6. The meal was wholesome and delicious except for the butter, which was _____.

7. Strangers are often more considerate toward a child than his own _____.

8. Coming as it did after three excellent skits, the rather dull final act produced an effect of

_____.

9. Your companion's earthy manner of speaking suggests that he has no _____.

10. I felt _____ when the marks were posted, since I had not passed the test.

EXERCISE 16. Write the *letter* of the word that means the SAME as or the OPPOSITE of the italicized word.

_____ 1. *profound*
(A) earthy
(B) shallow
(C) corrupt
(D) damp
(E) noxious

_____ 2. *pedigree*
(A) genealogy
(B) pinnacle
(C) nepotism
(D) perigee
(E) apogee

_____ 3. *zenith*
(A) drop
(B) rise
(C) nadir
(D) gain
(E) setback

_____ 4. *sibling*
(A) uncle
(B) nephew
(C) aunt
(D) sister
(E) cousin

_____ 5. *noisome*
(A) quiet
(B) mild
(C) loud
(D) disgusting
(E) calm

_____ 6. *glorification*
(A) gentility
(B) volition
(C) humiliation
(D) dislike
(E) incense

_____ 7. *acrid*
(A) deep
(B) pungent
(C) steep
(D) bottomless
(E) rash

_____ 8. *preeminent*
(A) degrading
(B) astringent
(C) superior
(D) mortifying
(E) abasement

_____ 9. *unbrotherly*   (A) cowardly   (C) flippant   (E) ethereal
                           (B) filial   (D) fraternal

_____ 10. *sublimated*   (A) postponed   (C) unrelated   (E) purified
                           (B) plumbed   (D) extended

EXERCISE 17. Which of the two terms makes the sentence correct? Write the *letter* of the correct answer in the space provided.

1. A genealogist may help you learn more about your _____.

            (A) progenitors   (B) descendants

2. To a writer, winning the Nobel Prize means achieving the _____ of literary fame.

            (A) perigee   (B) pinnacle

3. The employer cannot be accused of nepotism, since none of his employees is _____ him.

            (A) critical of   (B) related to

4. Mr. Myers was _____ to recommend Audrey for the medal because of her laudable record in his class.

            (A) eager   (B) loath

5. The ideas in the following quotation are arranged in _____ order: "Tony has been an excellent outfielder, our most dependable hitter, and the best all-around player on our team."

            (A) climactic   (B) anticlimactic

EXERCISE 18. Write the *letter* of the word-pair that best expresses a relationship similar to that existing between the capitalized word-pair.

_____ **1.** INFINITE: END

    (A) wealthy : money   (C) abysmal : bottom   (E) delectable : delight
    (B) blithe : happiness   (D) contrite : repentance

_____ **2.** AUDITORY: HEARING

    (A) keen : observing   (C) tactile : tasting   (E) irritable : feeling
    (B) gustatory : touching   (D) olfactory : smelling

_____ **3.** VERTEX: TRIANGLE

    (A) peak : mountain   (C) slope : base   (E) index : preface
    (B) summit : foot   (D) hill : ravine

_____ **4.** PROGENY: PROGENITOR

    (A) root : branch   (C) genius : protector   (E) orchestra : conductor
    (B) river : source   (D) bricks : house

_____ **5.** FETID: FRAGRANT

    (A) imperfect : consummate   (C) shallow : profound   (E) reeking : aromatic
    (B) humble : pretentious   (D) fresh : stale

16. AGE

WORD	MEANING	TYPICAL USE
adolescent ˌad-ᵊl-'es-ᵊnt	growing from childhood to adulthood; roughly, of the teenage period	In their early *adolescent* years, boys and girls usually attend junior high school.
antediluvian ˌant-i-də-'lü-vē-ən	1. antiquated 2. belonging to the time before the Biblical Flood (when all except Noah and his family perished)	Compared with today's streamlined jets, the plane the Wright brothers flew in 1903 seems *antediluvian*.
archaic är-'kā-ik	1. no longer used, except in a special context 2. old-fashioned	An *archaic* meaning of the word "quick" is "living," as in the Biblical phrase "the quick and the dead."
callow 'kal-ō	1. young and inexperienced 2. unfledged (too young to fly)	A prudent executive cannot be expected to entrust the management of his company to a *callow* youth just out of college.
contemporary kən-'tem-pə-ˌrer-ē	1. of the same period or duration 2. person who lives at the same time as another	The English Renaissance was not *contemporary* with the Italian Renaissance; it came two centuries later.
crone 'krōn	withered old woman	The *crone* warming herself by the fire was once an attractive young woman.
decrepit di-'krep-ət	weakened by old age	Several *decrepit* inmates had to be carried to safety when the home for the aged was evacuated during the fire.
defunct di-'fəŋ(k)t	dead; deceased; extinct	The *defunct* corporation and the Acme Lumber Company, which is still in business, were both founded in the same year.
forebear 'fȯr-ˌbe(ə)r	forefather, ancestor	Her *forebears* on her father's side had settled in New Jersey before the Civil War.
hoary 'hȯr-ē	1. white or gray with age 2. ancient	Santa Claus is usually portrayed as an elderly, stout man with a *hoary* beard.
infantile 'in-fən-ˌtīl	of or like an infant or infancy; childish	A child may revert to the *infantile* act of thumb-sucking when he feels insecure.
inveterate in-'vet-ə-rət	1. firmly established by age; deep-rooted 2. habitual	From their forefathers, Americans have inherited an *inveterate* dislike of tyranny.
juvenile 'jü-və-ˌnīl	1. of or for youth; youthful 2. immature	Books for grade-school children are usually located in the *juvenile* section of the library.

longevity län-'jev-ət-ē	1. long life 2. length of life	Methuselah is renowned for his *longevity;* according to the Bible, he lived for 969 years.
mature mə-'t(y)ů(ə)r	1. full-grown; ripe 2. carefully thought out	Though an excellent worker, Ronald was not appointed manager as he was only twenty-three; the employer wanted a more *mature* person in that position.
nonage 'nän-ij	legal minority; period before maturity	On his twenty-first birthday, the heir assumed control of his estate from the trustees who had administered it during his *nonage.*
nonagenarian ,nō-nə-jə-'ner-ē-ən	person in his 90's (Note also **octogenarian,** person in his 80's, and **septuagenarian,** person in his 70's.)	George Bernard Shaw, among his many other distinctions, was a *nonagenarian,* for he lived to be 94.
obsolescent ,äb-sə-'les-ᵊnt	going out of use; becoming obsolete	Our firm's machinery is *obsolescent;* it will have to be replaced within the next two years if we are to meet competition.
obsolete ,äb-sə-'lēt	no longer in use; out-of-date	The modern refrigerator has replaced the icebox, now *obsolete.*
patriarch 'pā-trē-,ärk	1. venerable old man 2. father and ruler of a family or tribe 3. founder	Practically all of the *patriarch's* children, grandchildren, and great-grandchildren attended the celebration of his eightieth birthday.
posthumous 'päs-chə-məs	1. published after the author's death 2. occurring after death	Only two of Emily Dickinson's poems were published before her death; the rest were *posthumous.*
primeval prī-'mē-vəl	pertaining to the world's first ages; primitive	From the exposed rock strata in the Grand Canyon, scientists have learned much about *primeval* life on this planet.
primordial prī-'mȯrd-ē-əl	1. existing at the very beginning 2. elementary; primary; first in order	Man's *primordial* conflict with his environment has continued to the present day.
pristine 'pris-,tēn	in original, long-ago state; uncorrupted	A diamond in its *pristine* state as it comes from the mine looks altogether different from the diamond in a lady's ring.
puberty 'pyü-bərt-ē	physical beginning of manhood or womanhood (at about age 14 for boys and 12 for girls)	Among the changes in boys at *puberty* are a deepening of the voice and the growth of hair on the face.
puerile 'pyů(-ə)r-əl	foolish for a grown person to say or do; childish	Some seniors think it's fun to throw objects at passing cars, but I consider it *puerile.*

senile 'sēn-ˌīl	showing the ⸋⸋kness of age	Grandfather no longer has the energy he used to have. He often forgets things. He has become *senile*.
superannuated ˌsü-pər-'an-yə-wāt-əd	retired on a pension; too old for work	Many who at 65 are compelled to join the ranks of the *superannuated* may be more productive than younger employees.
venerable 'ven-ər-ə-bəl	worthy of respect because of advanced age, religious association, or historical importance	At family reunions our *venerable* grandmother, now past 80, is accorded the greatest respect.
veteran 'vet-ə-rən	1. person experienced in some occupation, art, or profession 2. ex-member of the armed forces	In his bid for reelection, the mayor, a *veteran* of twenty years in public service, cited his opponent's lack of experience.
yore 'yȯ(ə)r	(always preceded by *of*) long ago	In days of *yore* there was trial by combat; today, we have trial by jury.

17. SOBRIETY—INTOXICATION

abstemious ab-'stē-mē-əs	sparing in eating and drinking; temperate; abstinent	Employers usually do not hire known alcoholics, preferring personnel who are *abstemious* in their habits.
carousal kə-'raú-zəl	jovial feast ⸋ ⸋nking party	While the enemy was celebrating Christmas Eve in a merry *carousal*, Washington and his troops, quite sober, crossed the Delaware and took them by surprise.
dipsomania ˌdip-sə-'mā-nē-ə	abnormal, uncontrollable craving for alcohol; alcoholism	An organization that has helped many persons to overcome *dipsomania* is Alcoholics Anonymous.
inebriated in-'ē-brē-ˌāt-əd	drunk; intoxicated	Captain Billy Bones, *inebriated* from drinking rum, terrified the other patrons of the Admiral Benbow Inn.
sober 'sō-bə(r)	1. not drunk; temperate 2. serious; free from excitement or exaggeration	The motorist's obligation to be *sober* must be emphasized in driver-training programs.
sot 'sät	person made foolish by excessive drinking; drunkard	Don't ask a *sot* for directions; consult someone whose mind is clear.
teetotaler 'tē-'tōt-ᵊl-ə(r)	person who totally abstains from intoxicating beverages	Former dipsomaniacs who are now *teetotalers* deserve admiration for their courage and will power.

18. SEA

bow
'bau̇
(*ant.* **stern**)

forward part of a ship; prow

A search from *bow* to *stern* before sailing disclosed that no stowaways were on board.

brine
'brīn

1. salty water
2. ocean; sea; the deep

Brine can be converted to drinking water, but at high cost.

doldrums
'dōl-drəmz

1. calm, windless part of the ocean near the equator
2. listlessness

Becalmed in the *doldrums*, the sailing vessel was "As idle as a painted ship/Upon a painted ocean."

flotsam
'flät-səm

wreckage of a ship or its cargo found floating on the sea; driftage

Flotsam from the sunken freighter littered the sea for miles around.

jetsam
'jet-səm

goods cast overboard to lighten a ship in distress

Jetsam washed ashore indicated that frantic efforts had been made to lighten the ship's cargo.

jettison
'jet-ə-sən

1. throw (goods) overboard to lighten a ship or plane
2. discard

The pilot of the distressed plane *jettisoned* his surplus fuel before attempting an emergency landing.

leeward
'lē-wərd
(*ant.* **windward**)

in the direction away from the wind

To get out of the wind, we chose deck chairs on the *leeward* side of the ship.

marine
mə-'rēn

of the sea or shipping; nautical; maritime

Marine interests favor increased subsidies to shipbuilders as a way of enlarging our merchant fleet.

starboard
'stär-bərd
(*ant.* **port**)

right-hand side of a ship when you face the bow (forward)

When a ship follows a southerly course, sunrise is on the port and sunset on the *starboard* side.

19. CLEANLINESS—UNCLEANLINESS

carrion
'kar-ē-ən

decaying flesh of a carcass

Vultures fed for several days on the air-polluting *carrion* left by hunters.

contaminate
kən-'tam-ə-ˌnāt

make impure by mixture; pollute

Many of our rivers are being *contaminated* by sewage and industrial wastes.

dross
'dräs

1. waste; refuse
2. scum on the surface of melting metals

When you revise your composition, eliminate all meaningless expressions, repetitions, and similar *dross*.

expurgate
'ek-spər-ˌgāt

1. remove objectionable material from a book; bowdlerize
2. purify

In his FAMILY SHAKESPEARE (published 1818), Bowdler *expurgated* Shakespeare's works, removing words and expressions that he considered improper for reading aloud in a family.

immaculate
im-'ak-yə-lət

spotless; absolutely clean; pure; faultless

With some water, a cloth, and a little energy, a dirty windshield can be made *immaculate*.

offal
'ä-fəl

1. waste parts of a butchered animal
2. refuse; garbage

Sea gulls hover about wharves where fish is sold, waiting to scoop up any *offal* cast into the water.

purge
'pərj

1. cleanse; purify
2. rid of undesired element or person

If elected, the candidate vowed he would *purge* the county administration of corruption and inefficiency.

slattern
'slat-ərn

untidy, slovenly woman

A *slattern* is usually as careless about her housekeeping as her personal appearance.

sloven
'sləv-ən

person habitually untidy, dirty, or careless in dress, habits, etc.

It is difficult for a person who is immaculate to share a room with a *sloven*.

sordid
'sȯrd-əd

filthy; vile

As soon as the athlete received the bribe offer, he informed his coach of the *sordid* affair.

squalid
'skwäl-əd

filthy from neglect; dirty; degraded

The neglectful owner of the *squalid* tenements was ordered to have them cleaned at once on pain of fine and imprisonment.

sully
'səl-ē

tarnish; besmirch; defile

The celebrity felt that his name had been *sullied* by the publicity given his son's arrest for speeding.

20. NEARNESS

adjacent
ə-'jās-°nt

lying near or next to; bordering; adjoining

Alaska is *adjacent* to northwestern Canada.

approximate
ə-'präk-sə-mət

nearly correct

The *approximate* length of a year is 365 days; its exact length is 365 days, 5 hours, 48 minutes, and 46 seconds.

contiguous
kən-'tig-yə-wəs

1. touching
2. near; adjoining

England and France are not *contiguous;* they are separated by the English Channel.

environs
in-'vī-rənz

1. districts surrounding a place
2. suburbs

Many of the city's former residents now live in its immediate *environs*.

juxtaposition
ˌjək-stə-pə-ˈzish-ən

close or side-by-side position

Perfumed soap may impart its scent to foods in *juxtaposition* with it.

propinquity
prō-ˈpiŋ-kwət-ē

1. kinship
2. nearness of place; proximity

Disregarding *propinquity*, the executive gave the post to a highly recommended stranger rather than to his own nephew.

EXERCISES

EXERCISE 19. Each word or expression in column I has an ANTONYM (opposite) in column II. Insert the *letter* of the correct ANTONYM in the space provided.

	COLUMN I	COLUMN II
_____	1. full-fledged	(A) descendant
_____	2. vigorous	(B) abstinent
_____	3. forebear	(C) filthy
_____	4. right	(D) callow
_____	5. intemperate	(E) bow
_____	6. windward	(F) maturity
_____	7. nonage	(G) inveterate
_____	8. immaculate	(H) leeward
_____	9. stern	(I) decrepit
_____	10. not habitual	(J) port

EXERCISE 20. Write the *letter* of the word NOT RELATED in meaning to the other words in each group.

1. (A) immaturity (B) adolescence (C) senility (D) nonage (E) childhood _____
2. (A) cleansed (B) tarnished (C) expurgated (D) sublimated (E) purged _____
3. (A) boredom (B) doldrums (C) inactivity (D) listlessness (E) longevity _____
4. (A) sordid (B) sober (C) abstinent (D) temperate (E) abstemious _____
5. (A) venerable (B) aged (C) patriarchal (D) hoary (E) convalescent _____
6. (A) antiquated (B) archaic (C) obsolescent (D) obsolete (E) antediluvian _____
7. (A) port (B) bow (C) tow (D) stern (E) starboard _____
8. (A) original (B) habitual (C) primitive (D) pristine (E) uncorrupted _____
9. (A) carouser (B) sot (C) alcoholic (D) teetotaler (E) dipsomaniac _____
10. (A) unsullied (B) slovenly (C) defiled (D) squalid (E) besmirched _____

EXERCISE 21. In the space provided, write the *letter* of the word that has most nearly the SAME MEANING as the italicized word.

_____ 1. *Unexpurgated* edition
  (A) abbreviated
  (B) uncut
  (C) purified
  (D) bowdlerized

```
------    2. Jefferson's forebears       (A) contemporaries      (C) ancestors
                                          (B) rivals              (D) followers

------    3. Defunct princess            (A) dead                (C) intemperate
                                          (B) infantile           (D) slatternly

------    4. Inveterate latecomer         (A) strange             (C) juvenile
                                          (B) extinct             (D) habitual

------    5. Sober estimates              (A) approximate         (C) exaggerated
                                          (B) calm                (D) inaccurate

------    6. Venerable patriarch          (A) founder             (C) monument
                                          (B) martyr              (D) philosopher

------    7. Jettisoned cargo             (A) surplus             (C) discarded
                                          (B) wrecked             (D) loaded

------    8. Primordial rights            (A) inherited           (C) elementary
                                          (B) secondary           (D) royal

------    9. Surface dross                (A) waste               (C) dregs
                                          (B) flotsam             (D) polish

------   10. Contiguous plots             (A) sordid              (C) noxious
                                          (B) contagious          (D) touching
```

EXERCISE 22. Fill each blank with the most appropriate word selected from the vocabulary list below. (Hint: For a clue to the missing word, study the italicized expression.)

VOCABULARY LIST

juxtaposition	puberty	primeval
obsolescent	abstemious	dross
squalid	puerile	obsolete
senility	immaculate	nonage
longevity	jetsam	carrion

1. Aunt Matilda thinks it *childish* for grown-ups to yell and boo at ball games. She cannot understand their _____ behavior.

2. When an individual distinguished for his *length of life* is interviewed by the press, he is usually asked for the secret of his _____.

3. The horse-drawn carriage has long been *out of date*. It became _____ with the invention of the automobile.

4. In the hospital, every room was *spotless*. The corridors, too, were _____.

5. During his *legal minority,* the young monarch had heeded his advisers, but, once past his _____, he took absolute personal control.

6. The school physician can easily distinguish those eighth-graders who are at *the physical beginning of manhood (or womanhood)* from those who have not yet arrived at _____.

7. The two mischievous lads occupied desks in *a side-by-side position.* Such _____ gave them ample opportunity to create disturbances.

8. Jackals feed on *the decaying flesh of a carcass.* Kites, hawks, and buzzards also subsist on _____.

9. By studying fossils, scientists have established many facts *pertaining to the world's first ages* and have learned a great deal about _____ plants and animals.

10. When pedestrians track in mud from *dirty* streets, the custodial staff has to mop the halls and stairways frequently to prevent them from becoming _____.

EXERCISE 23. Write the *letter* of the word (or set of words) which, if inserted in the sentence, would agree most closely with the thought of the sentence.

1. A struggling artist knows that _____ recognition will not help him battle poverty.

    (A) contemporary   (C) sober   (E) posthumous
    (B) ample   (D) fulsome

2. At _____, Grandfather, with a powerful handshake, vigorous stride, and wiry figure, is in excellent condition for an octogenarian.

    (A) 73   (C) 91   (E) 78
    (B) 84   (D) 69

3. _____ and _____ are in relatively close proximity.

    (A) Vermont . . . Rhode Island   (D) Alaska . . . Hawaii
    (B) Maine . . . Maryland   (E) Pennsylvania . . . South Dakota
    (C) Florida . . . Texas

4. Anyone whose room is as untidy as Ralph's must be a (an) _____.

    (A) crone   (C) sot   (E) nonagenarian
    (B) adolescent   (D) sloven

5. The new commander, a staunch believer in sobriety, would not tolerate _____ in any of his subordinates.

    (A) disrespect   (C) inebriation   (E) frivolity
    (B) propinquity   (D) bantering

EXERCISE 24. Write the *letter* of the word that best completes the analogy.

1. *Drought* is to *rain* as *doldrums* is to _____.

    (A) sea   (C) sails   (E) wind
    (B) calm   (D) sunshine

2. *Refrigerator* is to *chill* as *brine* is to _____.

    (A) moisten   (C) spoil   (E) spill
    (B) preserve   (D) fill

3. *Employed* is to *salary* as *superannuated* is to _____.

    (A) bonus   (C) pension   (E) commission
    (B) wages   (D) royalties

4. *Banana* is to *peel* as *carcass* is to _____.

    (A) offal   (C) game   (E) carrion
    (B) meat   (D) hunter

5. *Front* is to *rear* as *bow* is to _____.

    (A) leeward   (C) port   (E) starboard
    (B) prow   (D) stern

21. REASONING

WORD	MEANING	TYPICAL USE
analogy ə-'nal-ə-jē	likeness in some respects between things otherwise different; similarity; comparison	An *analogy* is frequently made between life and a candle, since each lasts a relatively short time and is capable of being snuffed out.
arbitrary 'är-bə-ˌtrer-ē	proceeding from a whim or fancy; capricious; despotic	Salary increases should depend on an employee's record rather than on some official's *arbitrary* decision.
arbitrate 'är-bə-ˌtrāt	decide a dispute, acting as *arbiter* (judge); submit a dispute to an arbiter	When the opposing claimants asked me to *arbitrate,* it was understood they would abide by my decision.
axiomatic ˌak-sē-ə-'mat-ik	self-evident; universally accepted as true	A principle long considered *axiomatic* is being questioned by economists—that the Federal government must balance its annual budget.
bias 'bī-əs	1. opinion formed before there are grounds for it; prejudice 2. predilection; partiality	Prospective jurors with a *bias* for or against the defendant were not picked for the jury.
bigoted 'big-ət-əd	intolerant; narrow-minded	It is futile to argue with *bigoted* persons; they hold stubbornly to their prejudices.
cogitate 'käj-ə-ˌtāt	think over; consider with care; ponder	Since the matter is important, I must have time to *cogitate* before announcing my decision.
criterion krī-'tir-ē-ən (*pl.* **criteria**)	standard; rule or test for judging	Colleges usually follow these *criteria* in selecting their students: scholarship, character, and extracurricular record.
crux 'krəks	most important point; essential part	Skip over the minor points and get to the *crux* of the matter.
deduce di-'d(y)üs	derive by reasoning; infer	From the fact that the victim's wallet and jewelry were not taken, we *deduced* that robbery had not been a motive for the murder.
dilemma də-'lem-ə	situation requiring a choice between two equally bad alternatives; predicament	Trapped by the flames, the guests on the upper stories faced the *dilemma* of leaping or waiting for an uncertain rescue.
dogmatic dȯg-'mat-ik	asserting opinions as if they were facts; opinionated; asserted without proof	If you keep saying the plan will not work without offering proof, you are being *dogmatic.*

eclectic e-'klek-tik	choosing (ideas, methods, etc.) from various sources	In some matters I follow the progressives and in other matters the conservatives; you may consider me *eclectic*.
fallacious fə-'lā-shəs	based on a *fallacy* (erroneous idea); misleading; deceptive	For centuries men held the *fallacious* view that the sun revolves around the earth.
fallible 'fal-ə-bəl	liable to be mistaken	Umpires occasionally make mistakes; like other human beings, they too are *fallible*.
heterodox 'het-ə-rə-,däks (*ant.* **orthodox**)	rejecting regularly accepted beliefs or doctrines; heretical	Political dissenters in dictatorships are often persecuted for their *heterodox* beliefs.
hypothetical ,hī-pə-'thet-i-kəl	supposed; having the characteristics of a *hypothesis,* a supposition made as a basis for reasoning or research. (If supported by considerable evidence, a hypothesis becomes a *theory,* and eventually, if no exceptions are found, a *law.*)	The detective investigated each employee because of a *hypothetical* notion that the robber had received "inside" information.
illusion il-'ü-zhən	misleading appearance; false impression; misconception	Barbara had thought that no college student could be dishonest, but the theft of her textbooks shattered that *illusion*.
indubitable in-'d(y)ü-bət-ə-bəl	certain; incontrovertible; indisputable	The defendant's confession, added to the witnesses' testimony, makes his guilt *indubitable*.
orthodox 'ȯr-thə-,däks (*ant.* **heterodox**)	generally accepted, especially in religion; conventional; approved	Boys are required to wear ties in schools that insist on *orthodox* dress.
paradoxical ,par-ə-'däk-si-kəl	having the characteristics of a *paradox* (a self-contradictory statement which may nevertheless be true)	It is *paradoxical* but true that a teacher may be taught by his pupils.
plausible 'plȯ-zə-bəl	superficially true or reasonable; apparently trustworthy	To people of ancient times the notion that the earth is flat seemed *plausible*.
preposterous pri-'päs-t(ə-)rəs	senseless; absurd; irrational	The choice of Stella for the leading role is *preposterous;* she can't act.
rational 'rash-ə-nᵊl	1. able to think clearly; intelligent; sensible 2. based on reason	Man is *rational;* animals have little power of reason.
rationalize 'rash-ə-nᵊl-,īz	devise excuses for one's actions, desires, failures, etc.	The fox in the fable *rationalized* his failure to get at the grapes by saying that they were sour.

sophistry ˈsäf-ə-strē	clever but deceptive reasoning	Imagine the *sophistry* of that child! He denied having a water pistol because, as he later explained, he had two.
specious ˈspē-shəs	apparently reasonable, but not really so	The contractor's claim that his men have an average experience of five years is *specious*; he has had twenty years of experience, but his three assistants practically none.
speculate ˈspek-yə-ˌlāt	1. reflect; meditate; conjecture 2. buy or sell with the hope of profiting by price fluctuations	Space exploration may solve a problem on which we have long *speculated*—whether or not human life exists elsewhere in the universe.
tenable ˈten-ə-bəl	capable of being maintained or defended	An argument supported by facts is more *tenable* than one based on hearsay.

22. SHAPE

amorphous ə-ˈmȯr-fəs	shapeless	At first my ideas for a term paper were *amorphous*, but now they are beginning to assume a definite shape.
concave kän-ˈkāv (*ant.* **convex**)	curved inward, creating a hollow space	In its first and last quarters the moon is crescent-shaped; its inner edge is *concave* and its outer *convex*.
contour ˈkän-ˌtu̇(ə)r	outline of a figure	The *contour* of our Atlantic coast is much more irregular than that of our Pacific coast.
distort dis-ˈtȯrt	1. twist out of shape 2. change from the true meaning	A company that speaks of the "average experience" of its technicians may be *distorting* the truth, as some of them may have had no experience.
malleable ˈmal-yə-bəl	1. capable of being shaped by hammering, as a metal 2. adaptable	Copper is easily shaped into thin sheets because it is very *malleable*.
rotund rō-ˈtənd	1. rounded out; plump 2. full-toned, as a *rotund* voice	A *rotund* figure is usually a sign of overweight.
sinuous ˈsin-yə-wəs	bending in and out; winding; serpentine	Signs that forewarn motorists of a *sinuous* stretch of road usually indicate a safe speed for negotiating the curves.
symmetrical sə-ˈme-tri-kəl (*ant.* **asymmetrical**)	balanced in arrangement; capable of division by a central line into similar halves	This badly misshapen bumper was perfectly *symmetrical* before the accident.

23. IMPORTANCE—UNIMPORTANCE

grave
'grāv

deserving serious attention; weighty; momentous

The President summoned his cabinet into emergency session on receipt of the *grave* news.

nugatory
'n(y)ü-gə-,tȯr-ē

trifling; worthless; useless

My last-minute cramming was *nugatory;* at the examination, I didn't remember a thing.

paltry
'pȯl-trē

practically worthless; trashy; piddling; petty

I complain not because of the *paltry* few pennies I was overcharged but because of the principle involved.

paramount
'par-ə-,maủnt

chief; above others; supreme

A mother's *paramount* concern is her children's welfare.

relevant
'rel-ə-vənt

bearing upon the matter in hand; pertinent

The prosecutor objected that the witness' testimony had nothing to do with the case, but the judge ruled that it was *relevant*.

24. MODESTY

coy
'kȯi

pretending to be shy

Annabelle's shyness was just a pretense; she was being *coy*.

demure
di-'myủ(ə)r

1. falsely modest or serious; coy
2. grave; prim

The girls giggled behind the teacher's back, but as soon as he turned around they looked *demure*.

diffident
'dif-əd-ənt

lacking self-confidence; unduly timid; shy

Why is it that students who should be the most confident about passing are usually the most *diffident?*

modest
'mäd-əst

1. not thinking too highly of one's merits; unpretentious; humble
2. decent

Joe got the highest mark in the test, but he is too *modest* to mention it.

staid
'stād

of settled, quiet disposition; sedate

The boy wanted to get away from his *staid* elders to rejoin his exciting companions.

25. VANITY

brazen
'brāz-°n

1. shameless; impudent
2. made of brass or bronze
3. harsh-sounding

Two persons in the audience were smoking in *brazen* defiance of the "No Smoking" sign.

egoism
'ē-gə-,wiz-əm

conceit; selfishness

By assuming full credit for our committee's hard work, the chairman has disclosed his *egoism*.

ostentatious ˌäs-tən-'tā-shəs	done to impress others; showy; pretentious	Parked next to our staid family car was an *ostentatious* red convertible.
overweening ˌō-və(r)-'wē-niŋ	thinking too highly of oneself; arrogant; presumptuous	After his initial victories, the *overweening* pugilist boasted that he was invincible.
pert 'pərt	too free in speech or action; bold; s~~~~~	When the principal asked Marie to apologize, she replied with a *pert* "Never!"
vain 'vān	1. conceited; excessively proud 2. empty; worthless	Oscar boasts about his marks to everyone, even strangers. I have never seen such a *vain* person.
vainglorious vān-'glȯr-ē-əs	excessively proud or boastful; elated by vanity	*Vainglorious* Ozymandias had these words inscribed on the pedestal of his statue, now shattered: "Look on my works, ye Mighty, and despair!"

EXERCISES

EXERCISE 25. In the space before each word or expression in column I, write the *letter* of its correct meaning in column II.

COLUMN I		COLUMN II	
------	**1.** asserted without proof	(A)	gravity
------	**2.** curved outward	(B)	rationalization
------	**3.** importance	(C)	brazen
------	**4.** conventional	(D)	untenable
------	**5.** excuse for failure	(E)	dilemma
------	**6.** change from the truth	(F)	orthodox
------	**7.** shameless	(G)	distortion
------	**8.** predicament	(H)	dogmatic
------	**9.** indefensible	(I)	irrational
------	**10.** unable to think clearly	(J)	convex

EXERCISE 26. Write the *letter* of the word NOT RELATED in meaning to the other words in each group.

1. (A) deceptive	(B) infallible	(C) erroneous	(D) fallacious	------
2. (A) bold	(B) immodest	(C) pertinent	(D) impudent	------
3. (A) intolerance	(B) prejudice	(C) impartiality	(D) bias	------
4. (A) concave	(B) buxom	(C) rotund	(D) corpulent	------
5. (A) unrelated	(B) impertinent	(C) rude	(D) irrelevant	------
6. (A) petty	(B) piddling	(C) paltry	(D) prim	------
7. (A) specious	(B) unpretentious	(C) illusory	(D) sophistical	------

8. (A) preposterous   (B) vain   (C) proud   (D) conceited   _____

9. (A) shy   (B) diffident   (C) arrogant   (D) coy   _____

10. (A) indisputable   (B) axiomatic   (C) incontrovertible   (D) hypothetical   _____

EXERCISE 27. Fill each blank with the most appropriate word selected from the vocabulary list below.

VOCABULARY LIST

axiomatic	analogy	saucy
dilemma	staid	hypothesis
theory	paradox	dogmatic
nugatory	illusion	speculating
sophistry	relevant	ostentatious

1. Scientific research usually begins with a(an) _____.

2. Grandmother and Grandfather look dignified and _____ in their wedding picture.

3. Jack never wears any of his medals because he doesn't want to appear _____.

4. On a sinking ship, all considerations except the paramount one of saving the lives of the passengers are _____.

5. When exasperated with my little brother, I call him a "snake," but Mother doesn't like the _____.

6. It is _____ that the shortest distance between any two points on a plane surface is a straight line.

7. As we were discussing tomorrow's picnic, Dinah interrupted with a (an) _____ question about the weather forecast.

8. The proprietor faces the _____ of going into bankruptcy or seeing his debts mount further.

9. _____ always involves risk, as prices fluctuate.

10. What I had been reasonably certain was a ship approaching on the horizon turned out to be a mere _____.

EXERCISE 28. Write the *letter* of the word that means the SAME as or the OPPOSITE of the italicized word.

_____ 1. *coyly*   (A) selfishly   (C) courteously   (E) indubitably
                      (B) bashfully   (D) arbitrarily

_____ 2. *heretic*   (A) believer   (C) heir   (E) rival
                      (B) veteran   (D) eclectic

_____ 3. *winding*   (A) heterodox   (C) serpentine   (E) narrow
                      (B) precipitous   (D) misleading

_____ 4. *vanity*   (A) tolerance   (C) prejudice   (E) bigotry
                      (B) bias   (D) worthlessness

_____ 5. *shapeless*   (A) sinuous   (C) momentous   (E) morbid
                      (B) deductive   (D) amorphous

_____	6. *impudent*	(A) serious	(C) fallible	(E) respectful
		(B) capricious	(D) egoistic	
_____	7. *criteria*	(A) symmetry	(C) decisions	(E) outcomes
		(B) standards	(D) criticisms	
_____	8. *paramount*	(A) steep	(C) piddling	(E) rocky
		(B) overweening	(D) paradoxical	
_____	9. *analogy*	(A) crux	(C) hypothesis	(E) axiom
		(B) dilemma	(D) similarity	
_____	10. *adaptable*	(A) callow	(C) malleable	(E) plausible
		(B) unattached	(D) demure	

EXERCISE 29. If the italicized word is *correctly* used in the sentence, write *C* in the space provided. If *incorrectly* used, write *X*.

_____ 1. Myra carefully cut the apple into two exactly *asymmetrical* halves.

_____ 2. The assertions of a person who is known to be prejudiced are quite likely to be *opinionated*.

_____ 3. A digest magazine may be called *eclectic* because its articles are chosen from various publications.

_____ 4. A true sportsman will always *rationalize* his defeat and praise the winner's superior performance.

_____ 5. Anyone who would dare to push his way into the bus ahead of the people waiting on line is surely *brazen*.

EXERCISE 30. Write the *letter* of the word-pair that best expresses a relationship similar to that existing between the capitalized word-pair.

_____ 1. CONTOUR: STATUE

    (A) shadow: body   (C) peak: mountain   (E) original: imitation
    (B) coastline: island   (D) area: surface

_____ 2. CRUX: ARGUMENT

    (A) title: book   (C) core: apple   (E) costume: actor
    (B) bridge: river   (D) door: house

_____ 3. CONCAVE: CONVEX

    (A) bowl: platter   (C) cup: saucer   (E) building: dome
    (B) bulge: dent   (D) cavity: swelling

_____ 4. HYPOTHESIS: TRUTH

    (A) supposition: fact   (C) deceit: honesty   (E) guess: blunder
    (B) proof: conclusion   (D) folly: wisdom

_____ 5. ERROR: RATIONALIZATION

    (A) mistake: correction   (C) guilt: admission   (E) failure: excuse
    (B) fault: merit   (D) weakness: ignorance

CHAPTER III

WORDS DERIVED FROM GREEK

A great revival of interest in ancient Greek and Latin civilizations took place in England in the years 1500-1650, a period known as the Renaissance. At this time numerous ancient Greek and Latin words and their derivatives were incorporated into our language. This process of language growth has continued to the present day. When a modern scientist needs to name a new idea, process, or object, he tends to avoid existing English words because these already may have several other meanings. Instead he prefers to construct a new English word out of one or more ancient Greek or Latin words. Though ancient Greek has not given us so many English words as Latin, it has been especially preferred as a source of new words in the scientific and technical fields.

Here are twenty-five ancient Greek prefixes and roots that have enriched our language. Each one, as you can see, has produced a separate group of useful English words.

1. PHOBIA: "fear," "dislike," "aversion"

WORD		MEANING
acrophobia	ˌak-rə-ˈfō-bē-ə	fear of being at a great height
agoraphobia	ˌag-ə-rə-ˈfō-bē-ə	fear of open spaces
Anglophobia	ˌaŋ-glə-ˈfō-bē-ə	dislike of England or the English
claustrophobia	ˌklȯ-strə-ˈfō-bē-ə	fear of confined spaces
Germanophobia	jer-ˌman-ə-ˈfō-bē-ə	dislike of Germany or the Germans
hydrophobia	ˌhī-drə-ˈfō-bē-ə	rabies (literally, "fear of water")
monophobia	ˌmä-nō-ˈfō-bē-ə	fear of being alone
phobia	ˈfō-bē-ə	fear; dislike; aversion
photophobia	ˌfōt-ə-ˈfō-bē-ə	morbid aversion to light
xenophobia	ˌzen-ə-ˈfō-bē-ə	aversion to foreigners

The form *phobe* at the end of a word means "one who fears or dislikes." For example:

Russophobe   ˈrə-sə-ˌfōb   one who dislikes Russia or the Russians

Also: **Francophobe, Anglophobe, Germanophobe,** etc.

EXERCISE 1. In each blank insert the most appropriate word from group 1, *phobia.*

1. You wouldn't expect a professional mountain climber to have _____.

2. As we grow up, we overcome our childhood _____ of the dark.

3. Passage of the Chinese Exclusion Act of 1882 proves that some degree of _____ existed in our nation at that time.

4. Youngsters who suffer from _____ do not make a habit of hiding in closets.

5. After many decades of _____, the French joined the West Germans in close economic ties following World War II.

2. PHIL (PHILO): "loving," "fond of"

philanthropist	fə-'lan-thrə-pəst	lover of mankind
philanthropy	fə-'lan-thrə-pē	love of mankind
philately	fə-'lat-ᵊl-ē	collection and study of stamps
philharmonic	ˌfil-ər-'män-ik	pertaining to a musical organization, such as a symphony orchestra (originally, "loving music")
philhellenism	fil-'hel-ə-ˌniz-əm	support of Greece or the Greeks
philogyny	fə-'läj-ə-nē	love of women
philology	fə-'läl-ə-jē	study (love) of language
philosopher	fə-'läs-ə-fə(r)	lover of wisdom

The form *phile* at the end of a word means "one who loves or supports." For example:

Anglophile	'aŋ-glə-ˌfīl	supporter of England or the English
bibliophile	'bib-lē-ə-ˌfīl	lover of books
Francophile	'fraŋ-kə-ˌfīl	supporter of France or the French

EXERCISE 2. In each blank insert the most appropriate word from group 2, *phil (philo).*

1. Socrates, the great Athenian _____, devoted his life to seeking truth and exposing error.

2. The _____ was proud of his fine collection of beautifully bound volumes.

3. If _____ is going to be your hobby, you will have to get a stamp album.

4. A(an) _____ was known as a Tory at the time of the American Revolution.

5. In his will the _____ bequeathed more than a million dollars to charity.

3. MIS: "hate" (MIS means the opposite of PHIL.)

misanthrope	'mis-ᵊn-ˌthrōp	hater of mankind
misanthropy	mis-'an-thrə-pē	hatred of mankind
misogamy	mə-'säg-ə-mē	hatred of marriage
misogyny	mə-'säj-ə-nē	hatred of women
misology	mə-'säl-ə-jē	hatred of argument or discussion
misoneism	ˌmis-ə-'nē-ˌiz-əm	hatred of anything new

EXERCISE 3. In each blank insert the most appropriate word from group 3, *mis.*

1. The proprietor's policy of hiring no women results not from _____ but from his conviction that men can do the work better.

2. When Gulliver returned from his travels, he could not endure the sight of fellow humans; he had become a _____.

3. Surprisingly, the first of the group to marry was the one who had been the loudest advocate of

   -------------------------------.

4. Isabel's --------------------- makes it unlikely that she will join the Debate and Discussion Club.

5. The old folks oppose the proposed innovations not because of --------------------, but for very understandable reasons.

4. DYS: "bad," "ill," "difficult"

dysentery	'dis-ᵊn-ˌter-ē	inflammation of the large intestine
dyspepsia	dis-'pep-shə	difficult digestion; indigestion
ant. **eupepsia**	yu̇-'pep-shə	good digestion
dysphagia	dis-'fā-jə	difficulty in swallowing
dysphasia	dis-'fā-zhə	speech difficulty resulting from brain disease
dystrophy	'dis-trə-fē	faulty nutrition

EXERCISE 4. In each blank insert the most appropriate word from group 4, *dys.*

1. To aid digestion, eat slowly; rapid eating may cause ---------------------.

2. Those who ate the contaminated food later became ill with ---------------------.

3. Injury to the brain may result in ----------------------, a complicated speech disorder.

4. Muscular ---------------------- is a disease in which the muscles waste away.

5. When your throat is badly inflamed, you may experience some ----------------------- in eating.

5. EU: "good," "well," "advantageous" (EU means the opposite of DYS.)

eugenics	yu̇-'jen-iks	science dealing with improving the hereditary qualities of the human race
eulogize	'yü-lə-ˌjīz	write or speak in praise of someone
eupepsia	yu̇-'pep-shə	good digestion
ant. **dyspepsia**	dis-'pep-shə	difficult digestion; indigestion
euphemism	'yü-fə-ˌmiz-əm	substitution of a "good" expression for an unpleasant one. Example: *passed away* for *died.*
euphonious	yu̇-'fō-nē-əs	pleasing in sound
ant. **cacophonous**	ka-'käf-ə-nəs	harsh-sounding
euphoria	yu̇-'fȯr-ē-ə	sense of well-being
euthanasia	ˌyü-thə-'nā-zhə	illegal practice of painlessly putting to death a person suffering from an incurable, painfully distressing disease (literally, "advantageous death")
euthenics	yu̇-'then-iks	science dealing with improving living conditions

EXERCISE 5. In each blank insert the most appropriate word from group 5, *eu.*

1. The audience liked the organist's ---------------------- melodies.

2. Before presenting the prize, it is customary for the principal to ---------------------- the recipient.

3. The employee formerly called a "janitor" is now commonly known by a -------------------- such as "superintendent" or "custodian."

4. In the eyes of the law, anyone who commits ----------------------, regardless of the circumstances, is a murderer.

5. Having recovered from a siege of pneumonia, he soon regained his usual --------------------.

6. MACRO: "large," "long"
7. MICRO: "small"

MACRO

macrocosm	'mak-rə-ˌkäz-əm	great world; universe
ant. **microcosm**		little world
macron	'māk-ˌrän	horizontal mark indicating that the vowel over which it is placed is long
macroscopic	ˌmak-rə-'skäp-ik	large enough to be visible to the naked eye
ant. **microscopic**		invisible to the naked eye

MICRO

microbe	'mī-ˌkrōb	very minute organism; a microorganism
microbicide	mī-'krō-bə-ˌsīd	agent that destroys microbes
microcosm	'mī-krə-ˌkäz-əm	little world
ant. **macrocosm**		great world; universe
microdont	'mī-krə-ˌdänt	having small teeth
microfilm	'mī-krə-ˌfilm	film of very small size
micrometer	mī-'kräm-ət-ə(r)	instrument for measuring very short distances
microscopic	ˌmī-krə-'skäp-ik	invisible to the naked eye
ant. **macroscopic**		large enough to be visible to the naked eye
microwave	'mī-krə-wāv	very short electromagnetic wave

EXERCISE 6. In each blank insert the most appropriate word from groups 6 and 7, *macro* and *micro.*

1. Documents can be recorded in a minimum of space if photographed on --------------------.

2. Space exploration has made us more aware of the vastness of the ----------------------.

3. A ---------------------- can be used to measure distances as minute as one ten-thousandth of an inch.

4. An ant is visible to the naked eye, but an ameba is ----------------------.

5. By means of a ----------------------, the dictionary informs us that the ē in ēra is a long vowel.

8. A (AN): "not," "without"

amoral	ā-'mȯr-əl	without sense of moral responsibility
amorphous	ə-'mȯr-fəs	without (having no) definite form or shape
anemia	ə-'nē-mē-ə	lack of a normal number of red blood cells
anesthesia	ˌan-əs-'thē-zhə	loss of feeling or sensation resulting from ether, chloroform, novocaine, etc.
anhydrous	an-'hī-drəs	destitute of (without) water
anomaly	ˌə-'näm-ə-lē	deviation from the common rule
anonymous	ə-'nän-ə-məs	nameless; of unknown or unnamed origin
anoxia	a-'näk-sē-ə	deprivation of (state of being without) oxygen
aseptic	ā-'sep-tik	free from disease-causing microorganisms
atheism	'ā-thē-ˌiz-əm	godlessness
atrophy	'a-trə-fē	lack of growth from disuse or want of nourishment
ant. hypertrophy	hī-'pər-trə-fē	enlargement of a part or organ, as from excessive use
atypical	ā-'tip-i-kəl	unlike the typical

EXERCISE 7. In each blank insert the most appropriate word from group 8, *a (an)*.

1. The _____ donor of the large contribution stipulated that under no circumstances was his name to be disclosed.

2. In the tropics a snowstorm would be a(an) _____.

3. The administration of _____ prevents the patient from feeling pain during and immediately after an operation.

4. Richard is a(an) _____ youngster in one respect: he doesn't care for ice cream.

5. In _____ surgery, rigid precautions are taken to exclude disease-causing microorganisms.

9. MONO (MON): "one," "single," "alone"
10. POLY: "many"

monarchy	'män-ər-kē	rule by a single person
polyarchy	'pä-lē-ˌär-kē	rule by many
monochromatic	ˌmän-ə-krō-'mat-ik	of one color
polychromatic	ˌpäl-i-krō-'mat-ik	showing a variety of colors
monogamy	mə-'näg-ə-mē	marriage with but one mate at a time
polygamy	pə-'lig-ə-mē	marriage to several mates at the same time
monomorphic	ˌmän-ō-'mȯr-fik	having but a single form
polymorphic	ˌpäl-i-'mȯr-fik	having various forms
monosyllabic	ˌmän-ə-sə-'lab-ik	having but one syllable
polysyllabic	ˌpäl-i-sə-'lab-ik	having more than three syllables
monotheism	'män-ə-thē-ˌiz-əm	belief that there is but one God
polytheism	'päl-i-thē-ˌiz-əm	belief that there is a plurality of gods

monocle	'män-i-kəl	eyeglass for one eye
monogram	'män-ə-ˌgram	two or more letters interwoven to represent a name
monograph	'män-ə-ˌgraf	written account of a single thing or class of things
monolith	'män-ᵊl-ˌith	single stone of large size
monolog(ue)	'män-ᵊl-ˌȯg	long speech by one person in a group
monomania	ˌmän-ə-'mā-nē-ə	derangement of mind on one subject only
monotonous	mə-'nät-ᵊn-əs	continuing in an unchanging tone; wearying

POLY

polyglot	'päl-i-ˌglät	speaking several languages
polygon	'päl-i-ˌgän	closed plane figure having, literally, "many angles" (and, therefore, many sides)
polyphonic	ˌpäl-i-'fän-ik	having many sounds or voices
ant. homophonic	'häm-ə-'fän-ik	having the same sound
polytechnic	ˌpäl-i-'tek-nik	dealing with many arts or sciences

EXERCISE 8. In each blank insert the most appropriate word from groups 9 and 10, *mono* and *poly*.

1. So intense was Ahab's desire for revenge on Moby Dick, the white whale, that it amounted to a _____.

2. Books for beginning readers should contain relatively few _____ words.

3. It is clear that the Romans practiced _____, for they worshiped many gods.

4. For Father's Day I gave Dad some handkerchiefs embroidered with his _____.

5. A discussion in which Janet takes part is usually a _____; she doesn't give anyone else a chance to speak.

6. Our _____ neighbor speaks French, German, Russian, and English.

7. The young chemist's _____ on garden insecticides is being widely read.

8. A _____ institute offers instruction in many applied sciences and technical arts.

9. Finding the work _____ after eight years on the same job, George longed for a change.

10. The 555-foot Washington Monument dominates the skyline of our nation's capital like a huge _____.

EXERCISE 9. In the space before each Greek prefix or root in column I, write the *letter* of its correct meaning in column II.

COLUMN I	COLUMN II
------ 1. PHOBIA	(A) bad; ill; difficult
------ 2. MACRO	(B) small
------ 3. PHIL (PHILO)	(C) not; without
------ 4. MONO (MON)	(D) one; single; alone
------ 5. A (AN)	(E) fear; dislike; aversion
------ 6. DYS	(F) one who loves or supports
------ 7. POLY	(G) many
------ 8. PHOBE	(H) loving; fond of
------ 9. MIS	(I) large; long
------ 10. MICRO	(J) good; well; advantageous
------ 11. EU	(K) hate
------ 12. PHILE	(L) one who fears or dislikes

EXERCISE 10. In the blank space, write the word that means the OPPOSITE of the word defined. (The first answer has been filled in as an example.)

DEFINITION	WORD	OPPOSITE
1. belief in God	theism	atheism
2. supporter of Russia	Russophile	------------------------
3. conforming to a type	typical	------------------------
4. good digestion	eupepsia	------------------------
5. one who dislikes England	Anglophobe	------------------------
6. lover of mankind	philanthropist	------------------------
7. believing there is but one God	monotheistic	------------------------
8. harsh in sound	cacophonous	------------------------
9. showing a variety of colors	polychromatic	------------------------
10. infected	septic	------------------------
11. one who dislikes France	Francophobe	------------------------
12. married to several mates at the same time	polygamous	------------------------
13. invisible to the naked eye	microscopic	------------------------
14. enlargement, as from excessive use	hypertrophy	------------------------

15. rule by many	polyarchy	----------------------------------
16. supporter of Germany	Germanophile	----------------------------------
17. hatred of women	misogyny	----------------------------------
18. having but one syllable	monosyllabic	----------------------------------
19. the great world; universe	macrocosm	----------------------------------
20. having various forms	polymorphic	----------------------------------

EXERCISE 11. Fill each blank with the most appropriate word selected from the vocabulary list below.

VOCABULARY LIST

euphemistic	euphoria	dysentery
monogram	dysphagia	acrophobia
euthanasia	anesthesia	dystrophy
misanthropy	anomalous	philatelist
anonymous	monograph	xenophobia

1. The practice of ---------------------------- is illegal in every civilized society.

2. A two-headed horse would be a(an) ---------------------------- sight.

3. Some isolationists, since they dislike foreigners, exhibit a profound ----------------------------.

4. Though the letter was ----------------------------, I was able to discover who had written it.

5. The term "mortician" is a(an) ---------------------------- term for "undertaker."

6. As a result of drinking contaminated water, he contracted ----------------------------, an inflammation of the large intestine.

7. A(an) ---------------------------- specializes in collecting stamps.

8. Since my companion had a dread of height, his ---------------------------- became more acute as we approached the summit.

9. So effective was the local ---------------------------- that I scarcely felt any pain during the minor surgery.

10. Our biology professor, a skilled writer, has completed a -------------------- on earthworms.

EXERCISE 12. Write the *letter* of the word that means the SAME as or the OPPOSITE of the italicized word.

------ 1. *claustrophobia* (A) acrophobia (C) philanthropy (E) xenophobia
(B) rabies (D) agoraphobia

------ 2. *monotonous* (A) philharmonic (C) polyglot (E) amorphous
(B) interesting (D) polysyllabic

------ 3. *anhydrous* (A) waterless (C) dyspeptic (E) anemic
(B) hydrophobic (D) gaseous

------ 4. *polytheism* (A) atheism (C) disbelief (E) theism
(B) monotheism (D) godlessness

------ 5. *euphonious* (A) polyphonic (C) cacophonous (E) euphemistic
(B) misanthropic (D) homophonic

EXERCISE 13. Write the *letter* of the word that best completes the analogy.

1. *Anemia* is to *red blood cells* as *anoxia* is to ------.

    (A) corpuscles   (C) oxygen   (E) surgery
    (B) disease   (D) tissue

2. *Euthenics* is to *environment* as *eugenics* is to ------.

    (A) surroundings   (C) nutrition   (E) education
    (B) heredity   (D) health

3. *Dysphagia* is to *swallowing* as *dysphasia* is to ------.

    (A) digestion   (C) sight   (E) tasting
    (B) hearing   (D) speech

4. *Misanthropy* is to *mankind* as *misogamy* is to ------.

    (A) women   (C) marriage   (E) foreigners
    (B) novelty   (D) argument

5. *Polychromatic* is to *colors* as *polytechnic* is to ------.

    (A) arts   (C) forms   (E) angles
    (B) sounds   (D) syllables

11. LOGY: "science," "study," "account of"

WORD		MEANING
anthropology	͵an-thrə-'päl-ə-jē	science dealing with the origin, races, customs, and beliefs of man
bacteriology	bak-͵tir-ē-'äl-ə-jē	science dealing with the study of bacteria
biology	bī-'äl-ə-jē	science dealing with the study of living organisms
cardiology	͵kärd-ē-'äl-ə-jē	science dealing with the action and diseases of the heart
criminology	͵krim-ə-'näl-ə-jē	scientific study of crimes and criminals
dermatology	͵dər-mə-'täl-ə-jē	science dealing with the skin and its diseases
ecology	i-'käl-ə-jē	science dealing with the relation of living things to their environment and to each other
ethnology	eth-'näl-ə-jē	science dealing with the races of mankind, their origin, distribution, culture, etc.
genealogy	͵jē-nē-'äl-ə-jē	account of the descent of a person or family from an ancestor
geology	jē-'äl-ə-jē	science dealing with the earth's history as recorded in rocks
meteorology	͵mēt-ē-ə-'räl-ə-jē	science dealing with the atmosphere and weather
morphology	mȯr-'fäl-ə-jē	scientific study of the forms and structures of plants and animals
mythology	mith-'äl-ə-jē	account or study of myths
necrology	nə-'kräl-ə-jē	register of persons who have died
neurology	n(y)u̇-'räl-ə-jē	scientific study of the nervous system and its diseases
paleontology	͵pā-lē-än-'täl-ə-jē	science dealing with life in the remote past as recorded in fossils
pathology	pə-'thäl-ə-jē	science dealing with the nature and causes of disease
petrology	pə-'träl-ə-jē	scientific study of rocks
physiology	͵fiz-ē-'äl-ə-jē	science dealing with the functions of living things or their organs
psychology	sī-'käl-ə-jē	science of the mind
sociology	͵sō-sē-'äl-ə-jē	study of the evolution, development, and functioning of human society
technology	tek-'näl-ə-jē	industrial science
theology	thē-'äl-ə-jē	study of religion and religious ideas

EXERCISE 14. In each blank insert the most appropriate word from group 11, *logy*.

1. Both ethnology and _____ deal with the origin and races of mankind.

2. The tale of Pyramus and Thisbe is one of the most appealing in Greek _____.

3. Advances in _____ have enabled industries to manufacture products at lower costs.

4. Sherlock Holmes is a fictional character who excels in _____, bringing numerous felons to justice.

5. Patients suffering from skin disorders are often referred to a specialist in _____.

12. BIO: "life"

abiogenesis *ant.* **biogenesis**	ˌā-ˌbī-ō-ˈjen-ə-səs	spontaneous generation
amphibious	am-ˈfib-ē-əs	able to live both on land and in water
antibiotic	ˌant-i-bī-ˈät-ik	antibacterial substance produced by a living organism
autobiography	ˌȯt-ə-bī-ˈäg-rə-fē	story of a person's life written by the person himself
biochemistry	ˌbī-ō-ˈkem-ə-strē	chemistry dealing with chemical compounds and processes in living plants and animals
biogenesis *ant.* **abiogenesis**	ˌbī-ō-ˈjen-ə-səs	development of life from preexisting life
biography	bī-ˈäg-rə-fē	story of a person's life written by another person
biology	bī-ˈäl-ə-jē	science dealing with the study of living organisms
biometry	bī-ˈäm-ə-trē	calculation of the probable duration of human life
biopsy	ˈbī-ˌäp-sē	diagnostic examination of a piece of tissue from the living body
biota	bī-ˈōt-ə	the living plants (flora) and living animals (fauna) of a region
microbe	ˈmī-ˌkrōb	very minute living organism
symbiosis	ˌsim-bī-ˈō-səs	the living together in mutually helpful association of two dissimilar organisms

EXERCISE 15. In each blank insert the most appropriate word from group 12, *bio.*

1. Fish can live only in water, but frogs are _____.

2. One _____ widely used to arrest the growth of harmful bacteria is penicillin.

3. In his _____ AN AMERICAN DOCTOR'S ODYSSEY, Victor Heiser tells how he survived the Johnstown flood.

4. An example of _____ is provided by the fungus that lives in a mutually beneficial partnership with the roots of an oak tree.

5. A(an) _____ is a microscopic living organism.

13. TOMY (TOM): "cutting," "operation of incision"

anatomy	ə-ˈnat-ə-mē	1. dissection of plants or animals for the purpose of studying their structure 2. structure of a plant or animal
appendectomy	ˌap-ən-ˈdek-tə-mē	surgical removal of the appendix
atom	ˈat-əm	smallest particle of an element (literally, "not cut," "indivisible")
atomizer	ˈat-ə-ˌmī-zə(r)	instrument for reducing to a fine spray
dichotomy	dī-ˈkät-ə-mē	cutting or division into two; division
lobotomy	lō-ˈbät-ə-mē	brain surgery
phlebotomy	fli-ˈbät-ə-mē	opening of a vein to diminish the blood supply
tonsillectomy	ˌtän-sə-ˈlek-tə-mē	surgical removal of the tonsils

EXERCISE 16. In each blank insert the most appropriate word from group 13, *tomy (tom)*.

1. The sharp _____ between your promises and your deeds suggests that you are not reliable.

2. A(an) _____ is a comparatively simple surgical operation that is more common in youth than an appendectomy.

3. In former times _____ (*bleeding*) was used indiscriminately as a treatment for practically all illnesses.

4. You will learn about the structure of the skeleton, the muscles, the heart, and other parts of the body when you study human _____.

5. Only in certain cases of extremely serious mental illness is a(an) _____ performed.

14. POD: "foot"

antipodes	an-'tip-ə-ˌdēz	parts of the globe (or their inhabitants) diametrically opposite (literally, "with the feet opposite")
arthropod	'är-thrə-ˌpäd	any invertebrate (animal having no backbone) with jointed legs. Example: insects.
chiropodist	kə-'räp-əd-əst	one who treats ailments of the human foot
dipody	'dip-əd-ē	verse (line of poetry) consisting of two feet; a dimeter
monopode	'mä-nō-ˌpōd	one-footed creature
podiatrist	pə-'dī-ə-trəst	chiropodist
podium	'pōd-ē-əm	1. dais 2. low wall serving as a foundation
tripod	'trī-ˌpäd	utensil, stool, or caldron having three legs
unipod	'yü-nə-ˌpäd	one-legged support

EXERCISE 17. In each blank insert the most appropriate word from group 14, *pod*.

1. One who treats ailments of the feet is known as a chiropodist or a(an) _____.

2. Englishmen often call Australia and New Zealand the _____, since these countries are almost diametrically opposite England on the globe.

3. As the guest conductor stepped onto the _____, the audience burst into applause.

4. A crab is a(an) _____; so, too, are lobsters, bees, flies, spiders, and other invertebrates with segmented legs.

5. Having only three legs, a(an) _____ is less stable than a four-legged support.

15. HOMO: "one and the same," "like"
16. HETERO: "different"

homochromatic	ˌhō-mō-krə-'mat-ik	having the same color
heterochromatic	ˌhet-ə-rō-krə-'mat-ik	having different colors
homogeneous	ˌhō-mə-'jē-nē-əs	of the same kind; similar
heterogeneous	ˌhet-ə-rə-'jē-nē-əs	differing in kind; dissimilar
homology	hō-'mäl-ə-jē	fundamental similarity of structure
heterology	ˌhet-ə-'räl-ə-jē	lack of correspondence between parts
homomorphic	ˌhō-mə-'mȯr-fik	exhibiting similarity of form
heteromorphic	ˌhet-ə-rō-'mȯr-fik	exhibiting diversity of form
homonym	'häm-ə-ˌnim	word that sounds like another but differs in meaning. Examples: *principal* and *principle*.
heteronym	'het-ə-rə-ˌnim	word spelled like another, but differing in sound and meaning. Examples: *bass* (the tone, pronounced "base") and *bass* (the fish, rhyming with "pass").

HOMO

homocentric	hō-mō-'sen-trik	having the same center
homophonic	ˌhäm-ə-'fän-ik	having the same sound
ant. **polyphonic**	ˌpäl-i-'fän-ik	having many sounds or voices

HETERO

heteroclite	'het-ə-rə-ˌklīt	1. deviating from the common rule 2. person or thing deviating from the common rule
heterodox	'het-ə-rə-ˌdäks	contrary to some acknowledged standard
ant. **orthodox**	'ȯr-thə-ˌdäks	conforming to an acknowledged standard

EXERCISE 18. In each blank insert the most appropriate word from groups 15 and 16, *homo* and *hetero*.

1. The butterfly is _____; it goes through four stages in its life cycle, and in each of these it has a different form.

2. An archery target usually consists of several _____ circles.

3. People of many races and religions can be found in the _____ population of large American cities.

4. The words *write* and *right* are _____s.

5. The foreleg of a horse and the wing of a bird exhibit _____, for they have a fundamental similarity of structure.

6. To escape persecution for his _____ views, Roger Williams fled from Massachusetts Bay Colony and founded the colony of Rhode Island.

7. *Lower* (which means "inferior") and *lower* (which means "look sullen" and rhymes with "our") are a pair of _____s.

8. Stained-glass windows are _____, since they are composed of glass sections of many colors.

9. The kindergarten children, though fairly _____ in age, were quite heterogeneous in ability.

10. One would not expect heteroclite opinions from a(an) _____ person.

17. HYPER: "over," "above," "beyond the ordinary"
18. HYPO: "under," "beneath," "less than the ordinary"

hyperacidity	ˌhī-pər-ə-ˈsid-ət-ē	excessive acidity
hypoacidity	ˌhī-pō-ə-ˈsid-ət-ē	weak acidity
hyperactive	ˌhī-pə-ˈrak-tiv	overactive
hypoactive	ˌhī-pō-ˈak-tiv	underactive
hypertension	ˌhī-pər-ˈten-shən	abnormally high blood pressure
hypotension	ˌhī-pō-ˈten-shən	low blood pressure
hyperthyroid	ˌhī-pər-ˈthī-ˌroid	marked by excessive activity of the thyroid gland
hypothyroid	ˌhī-pō-ˈthī-ˌroid	marked by deficient activity of the thyroid gland

HYPER

hyperbole	hī-ˈpər-bə-lē	extravagant exaggeration of statement
hypercritical	ˌhī-pər-ˈkrit-i-kəl	overcritical
hyperemia	ˌhī-pə-ˈrē-mē-ə	superabundance of blood
hyperopia	ˌhī-pə-ˈrō-pē-ə	farsightedness
ant. myopia	mī-ˈō-pē-ə	nearsightedness
hypersensitive	ˌhī-pər-ˈsen-sət-iv	excessively sensitive; supersensitive
hypertrophy	hī-ˈpər-trə-fē	enlargement of a part or organ, as from excessive use
ant. atrophy	ˈa-trə-fē	lack of growth from want of nourishment or from disease

HYPO

hypodermic	ˌhī-pə-ˈdər-mik	injected under the skin
hypothesis	hī-ˈpäth-ə-səs	theory or supposition assumed as a basis for reasoning ("something placed under")
hypothetical	ˌhī-pə-ˈthet-i-kəl	assumed without proof for the purpose of reasoning; conjectural

EXERCISE 19. In each blank insert the most appropriate word from groups 17 and 18, *hyper* and *hypo.*

1. Try not to hurt Ann's feelings when you criticize her work, as she is _____.

2. In _____, the blood pressure is lower than normal.

3. The student who judged the composition was _____; he exaggerated minor faults and gave no credit at all for the author's style and humor.

4. Nobody finished the lemonade because of its _____. Evidently, too much lemon juice had been used.

5. The following statement is an example of _____: "I've told you a *million* times to wear your rubbers when it rains."

6. A(an) _____ syringe and needle are used to administer injections under the skin.

7. Billy is a(an) _____ youngster; he won't sit still for a minute.

8. If your _____ is disproved by facts, you should abandon it.

9. In _____, the blood pressure is abnormally high.

10. Excessive activity of the thyroid gland is described as a(an) _____ condition.

19. ENDO: "within"
20. EXO: "out of," "outside"

endocrine	'en-də-krən	secreting internally
exocrine	'ek-sə-krən	secreting externally
endogamy	en-'däg-ə-mē	marriage within the tribe, caste, or social group
exogamy	ek-'säg-ə-mē	marriage outside the tribe, caste, or social group
endogenous	en-'däj-ə-nəs	produced from within; due to internal causes
exogenous	ek-'säj-ə-nəs	produced from without; due to external causes
endoskeleton	ˌen-dō-'skel-ət-°n	internal skeleton or supporting framework in an animal
exoskeleton	ˌek-sō-'skel-ət-°n	hard protective structure developed outside the body, as the shell of a lobster
endosmosis	ˌen-ˌdäs-'mō-səs	osmosis inward
exosmosis	ˌek-ˌsäs-'mō-səs	osmosis outward

ENDO

endocarditis	ˌen-dō-kär-'dīt-əs	inflammation of the lining of the heart
endoderm	'en-də-ˌdərm	membranelike tissue lining the digestive tract
endoparasite	ˌen-dō-'par-ə-ˌsīt	parasite living in the internal organs of an animal
ant. ectoparasite	ˌek-tō-'par-ə-ˌsīt	parasite living on the exterior of an animal
endophyte	'en-də-ˌfīt	plant growing within another plant

EXO

exoteric	ˌek-sə-'ter-ik	external; exterior; readily understandable
ant. esoteric	ˌes-ə-'ter-ik	inner; private; difficult to understand
exotic	eg-'zät-ik	1. introduced from a foreign country 2. excitingly strange

EXERCISE 20. In each blank insert the most appropriate word from groups 19 and 20, *endo* and *exo*.

1. Algae that live within other plants are known as _____s.

2. Foreign visitors can often be identified by their _____ dress.

3. _____ glands discharge their secretions externally through ducts or tubes.

4. _____ glands, having no ducts or tubes, secrete internally.

5. Some primitive tribes observe _____, forbidding marriage outside the tribe.

6. The body louse is a most annoying _____, as it moves freely over the body of its host.

7. The lobster has a thick protective outside shell known as an _____.

8. Unlike the lobster, man has an inside skeleton called an _____.

9. Refusing to admit that the rebellion was _____, the dictator blamed "foreign agitators."

10. Once established in the intestines of its host, an _____ can lead a life of comparative ease.

21. ARCHY: "rule"

anarchy	'an-ər-kē	total absence of rule or government; confusion; disorder
autarchy	'ȯ-ˌtär-kē	rule by an absolute sovereign
hierarchy	'hī-ə-ˌrär-kē	body of rulers or officials grouped in ranks, each being subordinate to the rank above it
matriarchy	'mā-trē-ˌär-kē	form of social organization in which the mother rules the family or tribe, descent being traced through the mother
monarchy	'män-ər-kē	state ruled over by a single person, as a king or queen
oligarchy	'äl-ə-ˌgär-kē	form of government in which a few people have the power
patriarchy	'pā-trē-ˌär-kē	form of social organization in which the father rules the family or tribe, descent being traced through the father

EXERCISE 21. In each blank insert the most appropriate word from group 21, *archy.*

1. In the naval _____, a rear admiral ranks below a vice admiral.

2. Many a supposedly "democratic" organization is controlled by a(an) _____ of three or four influential members.

3. In a constitutional _____, the power of the king is usually limited by a constitution and a legislature.

4. A family in which the mother alone makes all the final decisions could be called a(an) _____.

5. Those who declare that the best form of government is no government at all are advocating _____.

22. GEO: "earth," "ground"

geocentric	ˌjē-ō-'sen-trik	measured from the earth's center
geodetic	ˌjē-ə-'det-ik	pertaining to *geodesy* (mathematics dealing with the earth's shape and dimensions)
geography	jē-'äg-rə-fē	study of the earth's surface, climate, continents, people, products, etc.
geometry	jē-'äm-ə-trē	mathematics dealing with lines, angles, surfaces, and solids (literally, "measurement of land")

geomorphic	ˌjē-ə-'mȯr-fik	pertaining to the shape of the earth or the form of its surface
geophysics	ˌjē-ə-'fiz-iks	science treating of the forces that modify the earth
geopolitics	ˌjē-ō-'päl-ə-ˌtiks	study of government and its policies as affected by physical geography
geoponics	ˌjē-ə-'pän-iks	art or science of agriculture (literally, "working of the earth")
georgic	'jȯr-jik	1. agricultural 2. poem on husbandry (farming)
geotropism	jē-'ä-trə-ˌpiz-əm	response to earth's gravity, as the growing of roots downward in the ground

The form *gee* is used at the end of a word. For example:

| apogee | 'ap-ə-jē | farthest point from the earth in the orbit of a satellite |
| perigee | 'per-ə-jē | nearest point to the earth in the orbit of a satellite |

EXERCISE 22. In each blank insert the most appropriate word from group 22, *geo*.

1. At its apogee the moon is nearly 252,000 miles from the earth; at its _____ it is less than 226,000 miles away.

2. Heliotropism attracts leaves to sunlight; _____ draws roots downward in the earth.

3. To make precise earth measurements, _____ engineers use sensitive instruments.

4. Some earthquakes have little effect on the form of the earth's surface, but others result in noticeable _____ changes.

5. The atmosphere, the sun, and other forces that modify the earth are dealt with in the science of _____.

23. PATH (PATHO, PATHY): (1) "feeling," "suffering"; (2) "disease"

FEELING, SUFFERING

antipathy *ant.* sympathy	an-'tip-ə-thē	aversion ("feeling against"); dislike
apathy	'ap-ə-thē	lack of feeling, emotion, interest, or excitement; indifference
empathy	'em-pə-thē	the complete understanding of another's feelings, motives, etc.
pathetic	pə-'thet-ik	arousing pity
pathos	'pā-thäs	quality in speech, writing, music, events, etc., that arouses a feeling of pity or sadness
sympathy *ant.* antipathy	'sim-pə-thē	a sharing of ("feeling with") another's trouble; compassion
telepathy	tə-'lep-ə-thē	transference of the thoughts and feelings of one person to another by no apparent means of communication

DISEASE

| homeopathy | ˌhō-mē-'äp-ə-thē | system of medical practice that treats disease by administering minute doses of a remedy which, if given to healthy persons, would produce symptoms of the disease treated |

osteopath	'äs-tē-ə-ˌpath	practitioner of *osteopathy* (treatment of diseases by manipulation of bones, muscles, nerves, etc.)
pathogenic	ˌpath-ə-'jen-ik	causing disease
pathological	ˌpath-ə-'läj-i-kəl	due to disease
psychopathic	ˌsī-kə-'path-ik	1. pertaining to mental disease 2. insane

EXERCISE 23. In each blank insert the most appropriate word from group 23, *path (patho, pathy)*.

1. Among the diseases caused by _____ bacteria are pneumonia and scarlet fever.

2. Sometimes, as if by _____, one may know the thoughts of an absent friend or relative.

3. The _____ expression on the youngster's face made everyone feel sorry for him.

4. Such intense _____ resulted from their quarrel that the sisters haven't spoken to each other for years.

5. The reunion of the rescued miners with their families was full of _____.

24. MORPH: "form"

amorphous	ə-'mȯr-fəs	without definite form; shapeless
anthropomorphic	ˌan-thrə-pə-'mȯr-fik	attributing human form or characteristics to beings not human, especially gods
dimorphous	dī-'mȯr-fəs	occurring under two distinct forms
endomorphic	ˌen-də-'mȯr-fik	occurring within; internal
heteromorphic	'het-ə-rō-'mȯr-fik	exhibiting diversity of form
metamorphosis	'met-ə-'mȯr-fə-səs	change of form
monomorphic	ˌmän-ō-'mȯr-fik	having but a single form
morphology	mȯr-'fäl-ə-jē	branch of biology dealing with the form and structure of animals and plants

EXERCISE 24. In each blank insert the most appropriate word from group 24, *morph*.

1. As the fog slowly lifted, _____ objects began to assume definite shapes.

2. When you study cell _____, you will learn about the nucleus, the cell membrane, and other features of cell structure.

3. The drastic _____ from slum area to attractive residential neighborhood was accomplished in less than three years.

4. Individual members of a(an) _____ species are identical or similar in form.

5. The ancient Greeks had a(an) _____ conception of deity; they gave their gods and goddesses the characteristics of men and women.

25. PERI: "around," "about," "near," "enclosing"

pericardium	ˌper-ə-ˈkärd-ē-əm	membranous sac enclosing the heart
perigee	ˈper-ə-jē	nearest point to the earth in the orbit of a satellite
ant. **apogee**	ˈap-ə-jē	farthest point from the earth in the orbit of a satellite
perihelion	ˌper-ə-ˈhēl-yən	nearest point to the sun in the orbit of a planet or comet
ant. **aphelion**	a-ˈfēl-yən	farthest point from the sun in the orbit of a planet or comet
perimeter	pə-ˈrim-ət-ə(r)	the whole outer boundary or measurement of a surface or figure
periphery	pə-ˈrif-ə-rē	outside boundary
periphrastic	ˌper-ə-ˈfras-tik	expressed in a roundabout way
periscope	ˈper-ə-ˌskōp	instrument permitting those in a submarine a view ("look around") of the surface
peristalsis	ˌper-ə-ˈstȯl-səs	wavelike contraction of the intestines which propels contents onward
peristyle	ˈper-ə-ˌstīl	1. row of columns around a building or court 2. the space so enclosed
peritonitis	ˌper-ət-°n-ˈīt-əs	inflammation of the *peritoneum* (membrane lining the abdominal cavity and covering the organs)

EXERCISE 25. In each blank insert the most appropriate word from group 25, *peri.*

1. The _____ of a rectangle is twice its width plus twice its length.

2. At its aphelion, the earth is 94,560,000 miles from the sun; at its _____, it is 91,448,000 miles away.

3. The sections of an orange are narrowest at its center and widest at its _____, or rind.

4. By a series of wavelike contractions, known as _____, food is moved from the mouth through the organs of digestion.

5. Before changing its position, the cautious turtle raised its head like a(an) _____ to survey surrounding conditions.

EXERCISE 26. In the space before each Greek prefix or root in column I, write the *letter* of its correct meaning in column II.

COLUMN I	COLUMN II
------ 1. POD	(A) different
------ 2. EXO	(B) life
------ 3. HETERO	(C) under; beneath; less than ordinary
------ 4. GEO	(D) one and the same; like
------ 5. LOGY	(E) rule
------ 6. HYPO	(F) around; about; near; enclosing
------ 7. BIO	(G) cutting; operation of incision
------ 8. MORPH	(H) feeling; suffering; disease
------ 9. PATH (PATHO, PATHY)	(I) earth; ground
------ 10. ARCHY	(J) within
------ 11. PERI	(K) foot
------ 12. TOMY (TOM)	(L) form
------ 13. HYPER	(M) out of; outside
------ 14. ENDO	(N) over; above; beyond the ordinary
------ 15. HOMO	(O) science; study; account of

EXERCISE 27. In the blank space, write the word that means the OPPOSITE of the word defined.

DEFINITION	WORD	OPPOSITE
1. differing in kind	heterogeneous	---------------------------
2. conforming to an acknowledged standard	orthodox	---------------------------
3. lack of growth from want of nourishment	atrophy	---------------------------
4. a feeling of accord	sympathy	---------------------------
5. having many sounds	polyphonic	---------------------------
6. difficult to understand	esoteric	---------------------------
7. fundamental similarity in structure	homology	---------------------------
8. parasite living on the exterior of an animal	ectoparasite	---------------------------
9. low blood pressure	hypotension	---------------------------
10. nearsightedness	myopia	---------------------------
11. excessive acidity	hyperacidity	---------------------------
12. osmosis outward	exosmosis	---------------------------

13. secreting internally   endocrine   ---------------------------

14. underactive   hypoactive   ---------------------------

15. nearest point to the earth in the orbit of a satellite   perigee   ---------------------------

16. development of life from preexisting life   biogenesis   ---------------------------

17. due to external causes   exogenous   ---------------------------

18. nearest point to the sun in the orbit of a planet   perihelion   ---------------------------

19. exhibiting diversity of form   heteromorphic   ---------------------------

20. marriage outside the tribe, caste, or social group   exogamy   ---------------------------

EXERCISE 28. In each sentence fill in the missing letters of the incomplete word. Each dash stands for one missing letter.

1. Only 9% of the registered voters actually voted in the last primary. How can we explain such a _ _ _ _ _ (*lack of interest*)?

2. The p _ _ _ _ _ _ _ _ (*outer boundary*) of a seven-inch square measures twenty-eight inches.

3. Some TV weather programs have enlarged our m _ _ _ _ _ _ _ _ _ _ _ (*dealing with the atmosphere*) knowledge.

4. Occasionally we prefer e _ _ _ _ _ (*introduced from a foreign country*) dishes to American cookery.

5. Further progress in t _ _ _ _ _ _ _ _ _ _ (*industrial science*) may ultimately bring about a shorter workweek.

6. It is very easy to hurt the feelings of a h _ _ _ _ _ _ _ _ _ _ _ _ _ (*excessively sensitive*) person.

7. Between the toppling of the dictatorship and the setting up of the republic, there was a five-day period of violent a _ _ _ _ _ _ (*total absence of government*).

8. Some of the lecturer's remarks were so e _ _ _ _ _ _ _ (*difficult to understand*) that only advanced scholars could fully comprehend them.

9. While it is noon here, it is midnight in the a _ _ _ _ _ _ _ _ (*diametrically opposite parts of the globe*).

10. By means of a b _ _ _ _ _ (*diagnostic examination of a piece of tissue from the living body*), a surgeon can usually tell whether a growth is benign or malignant.

EXERCISE 29. In the space provided, write the *letter* of the word or expression that has most nearly the SAME MEANING as the italicized word.

------ 1. *Hypercritical* reviewer   (A) uncritical   (C) esoteric
                                 (B) hypersensitive   (D) overcritical

------ 2. Complete *metamorphosis*   (A) change   (C) process
                                 (B) course   (D) misunderstanding

_____ 3. Eminent *podiatrist* (A) criminologist (C) foot specialist
                                (B) world traveler (D) osteopath

_____ 4. Trace one's *genealogy* (A) career   (C) downfall
                                   (B) descent (D) personality

_____ 5. *Hypothetical* statement (A) conjectural   (C) unbiased
                                    (B) introductory (D) incontrovertible

_____ 6. *Anatomical* defect (A) minor   (C) structural
                              (B) irremediable (D) inherited

_____ 7. *Homogeneous* in size (A) different (C) heteromorphic
                                (B) perfect   (D) similar

_____ 8. *Psychopathic* behavior (A) pathetic   (C) mentally disturbed
                                  (B) indifferent (D) unsympathetic

_____ 9. Powerful *oligarchy* (A) conservatives (C) hierarchy
                               (B) ruling few   (D) rank and file

_____ 10. *Amorphous* ideas (A) organized (C) exaggerated
                             (B) original   (D) shapeless

EXERCISE 30. Write the *letter* of the word that best completes the analogy.

1. *Environment* is to *ecology* as *skin* is to _____.

    (A) osteopathy (C) peritonitis (E) endoderm
    (B) dermatology (D) neurology

2. *Lobotomy* is to *brain* as *phlebotomy* is to _____.

    (A) throat (C) foot (E) muscle
    (B) nerve   (D) vein

3. *Government* is to *anarchy* as *sympathy* is to _____.

    (A) pathos   (C) apathy (E) telepathy
    (B) compassion   (D) empathy

4. *Pathology* is to *disease* as *morphology* is to _____.

    (A) structure (C) descent (E) race
    (B) function   (D) health

5. *Animal* is to *tapeworm* as *plant* is to _____.

    (A) earthworm (C) microbe   (E) endophyte
    (B) biota   (D) ectoparasite

CHAPTER IV

WORDS DERIVED FROM LATIN

English began incorporating Latin words into its vocabulary nearly two thousand years ago and is still doing so today.

This process started when the Latin-speaking Romans occupied Britain, approximately 75-410 A.D. It resumed less than two centuries later when, in 597, the Roman monk St. Augustine brought Christianity to the Anglo-Saxons, and with it the Holy Scriptures in Latin.

But Latin had no major impact on English until 1066, when the Normans conquered England. The Normans spoke French, a *Romance* language, i.e., a language developed from the language of the *Romans*. French, which is 85 percent descended from Latin, was England's official language for two hundred years after the Norman Conquest. The language of the Normans gradually blended with the Anglo-Saxon spoken by the common people to form English. In the process, a considerable number of Latin words were incorporated into English indirectly, by way of French.

Later, a considerable number of other words came into English directly from Latin itself. From the Renaissance, in the sixteenth century, to the present day, as English-speaking authors and scientists have needed new words to express new ideas, they have been able to form them from Latin (or Greek).

It is no wonder, then, that more than 50 percent of the vocabulary of English is directly or indirectly derived from Latin.

To boost your word power, study the common Latin prefixes and roots presented in this chapter. Each of them, as the following pages will show, can help you learn a hoard of useful English words.

LATIN PREFIXES—I

PREFIX	MEANING	SAMPLE WORDS
1. **a, ab**	away, from	*a*vert (turn *away*), *ab*duct (lead *from*)
2. **ad**	to	*ad*mit (grant entrance *to*)
3. **ante**	before	*ante*room (a room *before* another)
4. **bi**	two	*bi*cycle (a vehicle having *two* wheels)
5. **circum**	around	*circum*navigate (sail *around*)
6. **con (col, com, cor)**	together, with	*con*spire (plot *together* or *with*), *col*loquy (a talking *together;* conference), *com*pose (put *together*), *cor*respond (agree *with;* communicate *with* by exchange of letters)
7. **contra**	against	*contra*dict (speak *against;* deny)
8. **de**	from, down	*de*duction (a conclusion drawn *from* reasoning), *de*mote (move *down* in rank)
9. **dis**	apart, away	*dis*rupt (break *apart*), *dis*miss (send *away*)
10. **e, ex**	out	*e*mit (send *out;* utter), *ex*pel (drive *out*)
11. **extra**	beyond	*extra*ordinary (*beyond* the ordinary)
12. **in (il, im, ir)**	not	*in*significant (*not* significant), *il*legal (*not* legal), *im*moral (*not* moral), *ir*regular (*not* regular)

PREFIX	MEANING	SAMPLE WORDS
13. **in (il, im, ir)**	in, into, on	*in*ject (throw or force *in*), *il*luminate (direct light *on;* light up), *im*port (bring *into* one country from another), *ir*rigate (pour water *on*)
14. **inter**	between	*inter*rupt (break *between;* stop)
15. **intra**	within	*intra*mural (*within* the walls; inside)

EXERCISES

EXERCISE 1. In the space before each Latin prefix in column I, write the *letter* of its correct meaning in column II.

	COLUMN I	COLUMN II
------	**1.** contra	(A) within
------	**2.** ante	(B) between
------	**3.** de	(C) in; into; on
------	**4.** extra	(D) from; down
------	**5.** a, ab	(E) out
------	**6.** in (il, im, ir)	(F) against
------	**7.** bi	(G) around
------	**8.** intra	(H) beyond
------	**9.** dis	(I) apart; away
------	**10.** e, ex	(J) to
------	**11.** ad	(K) together
------	**12.** inter	(L) before
------	**13.** circum	(M) two
------	**14.** con (col, com, cor)	(N) away; from

EXERCISE 2. Fill in the prefix in column I and the new word in column III. (The answer to question 1 has been inserted as an example.)

	COLUMN I		COLUMN II		COLUMN III
1.	in / *not*	+	tangible / *able to be touched*	=	intangible / *not able to be touched*
2.	------ / *against*	+	vene / *come; go*	=	------ / *go against or contrary to*
3.	------ / *out*	+	hale / *breathe*	=	------ / *breathe out*
4.	------ / *down*	+	mote / *move*	=	------ / *reduce to lower rank*

5. _____ + here = _____
    to   *stick*   *stick to*

6. _____ + gregate = _____
    together   *gather*   *gather together; assemble*

7. _____ + normal = _____
    from   *deviating from the normal*

8. _____ + scribe = _____
    around   *write; draw*   *write or draw a line around; encircle; limit*

9. _____ + cede = _____
    between   *go*   *go between arguing parties; mediate*

10. _____ + sect = _____
    two   *cut*   *cut into two parts*

11. _____ + mural = _____
    beyond   *pertaining to a wall*   *occurring beyond the walls*

12. _____ + diluvian = _____
    before   *pertaining to a flood*   *belonging to the period before the Biblical Flood; therefore, very old*

13. _____ + venous = _____
    within   *pertaining to a vein*   *within a vein*

14. _____ + pel = _____
    apart   *drive*   *drive apart; scatter*

15. _____ + fuse = _____
    in   *pour*   *pour in; fill; instill*

16. _____ + scend = _____
    down   *climb*   *climb down*

17. _____ + sensory = _____
    beyond   *pertaining to the senses*   *beyond the scope of the senses*

18. _____ + sect = _____
    apart   *cut*   *cut apart*

19. _____ + solve = _____
    from   *loose*   *loose from; release from*

20. _____ + pute = _____
    apart   *think*   *think apart (differently from others); argue*

PREFIX	MEANING	SAMPLE WORDS
16. **ob**	against	*ob*loquy (a talking *against;* censure)
17. **per**	through, thoroughly	*per*ennial (lasting *through* the years; enduring), *per*vert (*thoroughly* turn from the right way; corrupt)
18. **post**	after	*post*war (*after* the war)
19. **pre**	before	*pre*monition (a warning *before;* forewarning)
20. **preter**	beyond	*preter*human (*beyond* what is human)
21. **pro**	forward	*pro*gressive (moving *forward*)
22. **re**	again, back	*re*vive (make alive *again*), *re*tort (hurl *back;* reply sharply)
23. **retro**	backward	*retro*gression (act of moving *backward*)
24. **se**	apart	*se*cede (move *apart;* withdraw)
25. **semi**	half	*semi*circle (*half* of a circle)
26. **sub**	under	*sub*merge (put *under* or plunge into water)
27. **super**	above	*super*natural (*above* what is natural; miraculous)
28. **trans**	across, through	*trans*continental (extending *across* a continent), *trans*mit (send *through*)
29. **ultra**	beyond, exceedingly	*ultra*conservative (*exceedingly* conservative)
30. **vice**	in place of	*vice*-president (officer acting *in place of* the president)

EXERCISES

EXERCISE 3. In the space before each Latin prefix in column I, write the *letter* of its correct meaning in column II.

COLUMN I		COLUMN II
------	**1.** semi	(A) against
------	**2.** ob	(B) beyond; exceedingly
------	**3.** sub	(C) again; back
------	**4.** trans	(D) before
------	**5.** vice	(E) after
------	**6.** ultra	(F) half
------	**7.** super	(G) apart
------	**8.** re	(H) under
------	**9.** pro	(I) in place of
------	**10.** post	(J) above
------	**11.** se	(K) forward
------	**12.** pre	(L) across; through

EXERCISE 4. Fill in the prefix in column I and the new word in column III.

COLUMN I	COLUMN II	COLUMN III
1. _____ *in place of*	+ chairman	= _____ *person acting in place of a chairman*
2. _____ *half*	+ annual	= _____ *occurring every half year*
3. _____ *under*	+ vert *turn*	= _____ *turn under; undermine*
4. _____ *apart*	+ clude *shut*	= _____ *shut or keep apart; isolate*
5. _____ *above*	+ sede *sit*	= _____ *sit above; take the place of; replace*
6. _____ *forward*	+ mote *move*	= _____ *move forward; raise in rank*
7. _____ *against*	+ durate *hardened*	= _____ *hardened against; unyielding; stubborn*
8. _____ *through*	+ ient *going*	= _____ *going through (not staying); short-lived*
9. _____ *against*	+ struct *pile up*	= _____ *pile up (an obstacle) against; hinder*
10. _____ *back*	+ calcitrant *kicking*	= _____ *kicking back; rebellious*
11. _____ *after*	+ pone *put*	= _____ *put after; defer; delay*
12. _____ *exceedingly*	+ nationalistic	= _____ *exceedingly nationalistic*
13. _____ *before*	+ requisite *required*	= _____ *required before; necessary as a preliminary*
14. _____ *backward*	+ active	= _____ *acting backward; effective in a prior time*
15. _____ *through*	+ meate *pass*	= _____ *pass through*
16. _____ *again*	+ sume *take*	= _____ *take up or begin again*
17. _____ *thoroughly*	+ turb *disturb*	= _____ *disturb thoroughly; agitate*

18.	----------	+ natural		=	-------------------------------------
	beyond				*beyond what is natural*
19.	----------	+ gregate		=	-------------------------------------
	apart	*gather*			*set apart; gather into separate groups*
20.	----------	+ marine		=	-------------------------------------
	under	*pertaining to the sea*			*used or existing under the sea's surface*

REVIEW

EXERCISE 5. Using your knowledge of Latin prefixes and the hints given below, insert the basic meanings of these fifty English words. (The answer to question 1 has been inserted as an example.)

HINT: **-port** means "carry"

WORD	MEANING		
1. report	carry back	4. deport	-------------------------
2. import	-------------------------	5. export	-------------------------
3. transport	-------------------------		

HINT: **-ject** means "throw"

6. interject	-------------------------	9. project	-------------------------
7. eject	-------------------------	10. inject	-------------------------
8. object	-------------------------		

HINT: **-scribe** means "write"

11. superscribe	-------------------------	14. inscribe	-------------------------
12. transcribe	-------------------------	15. subscribe	-------------------------
13. prescribe	-------------------------		

HINT: **-pel** means "drive"

16. dispel	-------------------------	19. impel	-------------------------
17. propel	-------------------------	20. repel	-------------------------
18. expel	-------------------------		

HINT: **-voke** means "call"

21. evoke	-------------------------	24. revoke	-------------------------
22. convoke	-------------------------	25. invoke	-------------------------
23. provoke	-------------------------		

HINT: **-mit** means "send"

26. permit   -----------------------   29. emit   -----------------------
27. admit   -----------------------   30. remit   -----------------------
28. transmit   -----------------------

HINT: **-tract** means "drag," "draw"

31. protract   -----------------------   34. retract   -----------------------
32. subtract   -----------------------   35. detract   -----------------------
33. distract   -----------------------

HINT: **-duce** means "lead," "draw"

36. seduce   -----------------------   39. deduce   -----------------------
37. induce   -----------------------   40. reduce   -----------------------
38. produce   -----------------------

HINT: **-cede** or **-ceed** means "go"

41. intercede   -----------------------   44. exceed   -----------------------
42. proceed   -----------------------   45. recede   -----------------------
43. secede   -----------------------

HINT: **-fer** means "carry," "bring," "bear"

46. transfer   -----------------------   49. infer   -----------------------
47. prefer   -----------------------   50. defer   -----------------------
48. refer   -----------------------

LATIN ROOTS

1. RUPT: "break," "burst"

WORD		MEANING
abrupt	ə-'brəpt	1. broken off 2. sudden
corrupt	kə-'rəpt	1. changed from good to bad; vicious 2. change from good to bad; debase; pervert; falsify
disrupt	dis-'rəpt	break apart
erupt	i-'rəpt	burst or break out
incorruptible	ˌin-kə-'rəp-tə-bəl	inflexibly honest; incapable of being corrupted or bribed
interrupt	ˌint-ə-'rəpt	break into or between; hinder; stop
rupture	'rəp-chə(r)	1. break; breaking 2. hostility

EXERCISE 6. In each blank insert the most appropriate word from group 1, *rupt*.

1. The simmering antipathy between the rival groups may _____ into open combat.

2. The star's _____ withdrawal from the cast took the producer by surprise.

3. Both sides had faith in the judge's honesty, for he was known to be _____.

4. Many homes were flooded as a result of a(an) _____ in a water main.

5. Please don't _____ me when I am speaking on the telephone.

2. CIDE: "killing," "killer"

fratricide	'fra-trə-ˌsīd	act of killing (or killer of) one's own brother
genocide	'jen-ə-ˌsīd	deliberate extermination of a racial or cultural group
germicide	'jər-mə-ˌsīd	substance that kills germs
homicide	'häm-ə-ˌsīd	killing of one human by another
infanticide	in-'fant-ə-ˌsīd	act of killing (or killer of) an infant
insecticide	in-'sek-tə-ˌsīd	preparation for killing insects
matricide	'ma-trə-ˌsīd	act of killing (or killer of) one's own mother
patricide	'pa-trə-ˌsīd	act of killing (or killer of) one's own father
pesticide	'pes-tə-ˌsīd	substance that kills rats, insects, bacteria, etc.
regicide	'rej-ə-ˌsīd	act of killing (or killer of) a king
sororicide	sə-'ror-ə-ˌsīd	act of killing (or killer of) one's own sister
suicide	'sü-ə-ˌsīd	act of killing (or killer of) one's self
tyrannicide	tə-'ran-ə-ˌsīd	act of killing (or killer of) a tyrant

EXERCISE 7. In each blank insert the most appropriate word from group 2, *cide*.

1. Friends of the victim doubted that he had taken his own life, for they could think of no reason for his committing _____.

2. The assailant was told that he would be charged with _____ if his victim were to die.

3. To prevent the extermination of minorities, the United Nations voted in 1948 to outlaw ----------------------.

4. Claudius, in Shakespeare's HAMLET, is guilty of ----------------------, for he has slain his brother.

5. The attempt at ---------------------- failed when the king's would-be assassins were arrested outside the palace.

3. STRING (STRICT): "bind," "draw tight"

astringent	ə-'strin-jənt	1. drawing (the tissues) tightly together 2. stern; austere 3. substance that shrinks tissues and checks flow of blood by contracting blood vessels.
boa constrictor	'bō-ə kən-'strik-tə(r)	snake that "constricts" or crushes its prey in its coils
constrict	kən-'strikt	draw together; bind
restrict	ri-'strikt	keep within limits; confine
stricture	'strik-chə(r)	an adverse criticism; censure
stringent	'strin-jənt	strict (literally, "binding tight"); rigid; severe
unrestricted	ˌən-ri-'strik-təd	1. not confined within bounds; free 2. open to all

EXERCISE 8. In each blank insert the most appropriate word from group 3, *string (strict).*

1. All residents enjoy ---------------------- use of the pool, except children under 16, who must leave at 5 P.M.

2. Unless you ---------------------- your remarks to the topic on the floor, the chairman will rule you "out of order."

3. Shavers use a styptic pencil or some other ---------------------- to check the bleeding of minor cuts.

4. Jean Valjean's sentence of five years at hard labor for stealing a loaf of bread seems an unusually ---------------------- punishment.

5. If you interpret a minor criticism as a major ----------------------, you are being hypersensitive.

4. VOR: "eat greedily"

carnivorous	kär-'niv-ə-rəs	flesh-eating
devour	di-'vaů-ə(r)	1. eat greedily or ravenously 2. seize upon and destroy
herbivorous	ˌər-'biv-ə-rəs	dependent on plants as food
insectivorous	ˌin-ˌsek-'tiv-ə-rəs	dependent on insects as food
omnivorous	äm-'niv-ə-rəs	1. eating everything 2. fond of all kinds, as an *omnivorous* reader
voracious	vȯ-'rā-shəs	1. greedy in eating 2. insatiable, as a *voracious* reader

EXERCISE 9. In each blank insert the most appropriate word from group 4, *vor.*

1. Spiders are _____; their principal food is insects.

2. Have you ever watched a ravenous eater _____ a sandwich in two or three gulps?

3. The diet of the _____ lion includes the zebra, antelope, buffalo, and ostrich.

4. Since man's foods are obtained from both plants and animals, he may be described as a(an) _____ organism.

5. The rabbit is _____, eating grass, vegetables, and even the bark of trees.

5. VIV: "live," "alive"

convivial	kən-'viv-ē-əl	fond of eating and drinking with friends; jovial; hospitable
revive	ri-'vīv	bring back to life; restore
survive	sər-'vīv	outlive; remain alive after
vivid	'viv-əd	1. full of life 2. sharp and clear; graphic
vivify	'viv-ə-ˌfī	enliven; make vivid
vivisection	ˌviv-ə-'sek-shən	operation on a living animal for scientific investigation

EXERCISE 10. In each blank insert the most appropriate word from group 5, *viv.*

1. A business must eliminate waste if it is to _____ in a competitive market.

2. When fashion designers can offer no new styles, they usually _____ old ones.

3. By proper use of verbs and adjectives, you can turn a dull description into a _____ one.

4. David Copperfield found a warm welcome in the _____ Peggotty family.

5. A few inexpensive art reproductions, cleverly arranged, can _____ an otherwise drab wall.

6. TORT (TORS): "twist"

contortionist	kən-'tȯr-shə-nəst	person who can twist his body into odd postures
distort	dis-'tȯrt	1. twist out of shape; contort 2. falsify
extort	ek-'stȯrt	wrest (money, promises, etc.) from a person by force (literally, "twist out")
retort	ri-'tȯrt	reply quickly or sharply in kind ("twist back")
torsion	'tȯr-shən	act of twisting; twisting of a body by two equal and opposite forces
tortuous	'tȯrch-ə-wəs	1. full of twists or curves; winding, as a *tortuous* road 2. tricky; crooked
torture	'tȯr-chə(r)	1. wrench; twist 2. inflict severe pain upon

EXERCISE 11. In each blank insert the most appropriate word from group 6, *tort (tors)*.

1. The captured officer knew that the enemy would use clever means to _____ military secrets from him.

2. It is very easy to _____ an author's ideas if you quote them out of context.

3. When I ask my brothers to help with the chores, they usually _____ that they have no time.

4. The _____ amazed us by his ability to throw his body into extraordinary postures.

5. Near its mouth, the Mississippi winds among numerous swamps in a(an) _____ course to the Gulf of Mexico.

7. VICT (VINC): "conquer," "show conclusively"

convict	kən-'vikt 'kän-ˌvikt	1. prove guilty; show conclusively to be guilty 2. person serving a prison sentence
convince	kən-'vins	persuade or show conclusively by argument or proof
evict	ē-'vikt	1. expel by legal process, as to *evict* a tenant 2. oust
evince	ē-'vins	show clearly; disclose
invincible	in-'vin-sə-bəl	incapable of being conquered
vanquish	'vaŋ-kwish	overcome in battle; conquer
victor	'vik-tə(r)	winner; conqueror

EXERCISE 12. In each blank insert the most appropriate word from group 7, *vict (vinc)*.

1. Stadium police are empowered to _____ any spectator who creates a disturbance.

2. After the match, the _____ shook hands with the loser.

3. Students who _____ a talent for writing should be encouraged to contribute to school publications.

4. It is difficult to _____ a biased person that he is wrong, no matter how much evidence you may present.

5. For the past two seasons our swimming team has been _____, having been neither beaten nor tied.

8. FRACT (FRAG): "break"

fraction	'frak-shən	one or more of the equal parts of a whole; fragment
fractious	'frak-shəs	apt to break out into a passion; cross; irritable
fracture	'frak-chə(r)	1. break or crack 2. breaking of a bone
fragile	'fraj-əl	easily broken; frail; delicate
fragment	'frag-mənt	part broken off
infraction	in-'frak-shən	act of breaking; breach; violation, as an *infraction* of a law

| refract | ri-'frakt | bend (literally, "break back") a ray of light, heat, sound, etc., from a straight course |
| refractory | ri-'frak-tə-rē | resisting; intractable; hard to manage, as a *refractory* mule |

EXERCISE 13. In each blank insert the most appropriate word from group 8, *fract (frag).*

1. Glassware and other _____ materials require special packaging to prevent breakage.

2. Though the motorist protested that he had committed no _____, he was charged with failure to stop at a "full stop" sign.

3. X-ray diagnosis disclosed that the child had sustained no _____ in his fall.

4. If I could find the one missing _____, I would be able to restore the broken vase.

5. The teacher said that I should have reduced the _____ $\frac{3}{12}$ to $\frac{1}{4}$.

9. OMNI: "all," "every," "everywhere"

omnibus	'äm-ni-bəs	1. covering many things at once, as an *omnibus* bill
		2. bus
		3. book containing a variety of works by one author, as a Terhune *omnibus*
omnifarious	‚äm-nə-'far-ē-əs	of all varieties, forms, or kinds
omnific	äm-'nif-ik	all-creating
omnipotent	äm-'nip-ət-ənt	unlimited in power; almighty
omnipresent	‚äm-ni-'prez-ᵊnt	present everywhere at the same time
omniscient	äm-'nish-ənt	knowing everything
omnivorous	äm-'niv-ə-rəs	1. eating everything
		2. fond of all kinds, as an *omnivorous* reader

EXERCISE 14. In each blank insert the most appropriate word from group 9, *omni.*

1. I cannot answer all questions, since I am not _____.

2. With his magic lamp, Aladdin was _____, for no feat was beyond his power.

3. Because of its _____ uses, a boy scout knife is indispensable equipment for a camping trip.

4. Having received several desirable invitations for the same evening, I regretted that I could not be

_____.

5. To the ancient Egyptians, the sun god Re was _____, having created all that exists or will exist.

10. FLECT (FLEX): "bend"

deflect	di-'flekt	turn ("bend") aside
flex	'fleks	bend, as to *flex* a limb
flexible	'flek-sə-bəl	pliable ("capable of being bent"); not rigid; tractable
flexor	'flek-sə(r)	muscle that serves to bend a limb

genuflect	ˈjen-yə-ˌflekt	bend the knee; touch the right knee to the ground, as in worship
inflexibility	in-ˌflek-sə-ˈbil-ət-ē	rigidity; firmness
reflect	ri'flekt	1. throw ("bend") back light, heat, sound, etc. 2. think
reflex	ˈrē-ˌfleks	involuntary response ("bending back") to a stimulus; for example, sneezing is a *reflex*

EXERCISE 15. In each blank insert the most appropriate word from group 10, *flect (flex)*.

1. The secretion of tears, as when a cinder enters the eye, is a (an) ----------------------, since it is beyond our control.

2. Copper tubing is easy to shape but much less ---------------------- than rubber hose.

3. Unable to catch the line drive, I managed to ---------------------- the ball toward the infield, holding the batter to a single.

4. Obedient subjects were expected to ---------------------- when admitted to the presence of an absolute monarch.

5. Only in one respect does our teacher show ----------------------: he will mark you late if you are out of your seat when the bell rings, regardless of the circumstances.

11. TEN (TIN, TENT): "hold," "keep"

detention	di-ˈten-shən	act of keeping back or detaining
impertinent	im-ˈpərt-ᵊn-ənt	1. not pertinent; inappropriate 2. rude
pertinacious	ˌpərt-ᵊn-ˈā-shəs	adhering firmly to a purpose or opinion; very persistent
pertinent	ˈpərt-ᵊn-ənt	having to do with ("holding to") the matter in hand
retentive	ri-ˈtent-iv	tenacious; able to retain or remember
retinue	ˈret-ᵊn-ˌyü	group of followers accompanying a distinguished person
tenacity	tə-ˈnas-ət-ē	firmness in holding fast; persistence
tenancy	ˈten-ən-sē	period of a tenant's temporary holding of real estate
tenure	ˈten-yə(r)	period for which an office or position is held, as: "U.S. Supreme Court Justices enjoy life *tenure*."
untenable	ˌən-ˈten-ə-bəl	incapable of being held or defended

EXERCISE 16. In each blank insert the most appropriate word from group 11, *ten (tin, tent)*.

1. The ---------------------- of a member of the House of Representatives is only two years.

2. Retreating from their ---------------------- coastal positions, the rebels sought a more defensible foothold in the hills.

3. Since we are talking about the coming Thanksgiving Day dance, I fail to see how your question about the French test can possibly be ----------------------.

4. Though she can't recall names, Sylvia has a (an) ---------------------- memory for faces.

5. The basketball star was accompanied by a (an) ---------------------- of admirers.

12. MON (MONIT): "warn"

admonish	ad-'măn-ish	warn of a fault; reprove
admonition	ˌad-mə-'nish-ən	gentle reproof; counseling against a fault or error
admonitory	ad-'măn-ə-ˌtȯr-ē	conveying a gentle reproof
monitor	'măn-ət-ə(r)	one who admonishes
monument	'măn-yə-mənt	a means of reminding us of a person or event; for example, a statue or a tomb
premonition	ˌprē-mə-'nish-ən	forewarning
premonitory	prē-'măn-ə-ˌtȯr-ē	conveying a forewarning

EXERCISE 17. In each blank insert the most appropriate word from group 12, *mon (monit)*.

1. Had I heeded Bob's _____ to review my class notes, I would have done much better on the test.

2. I must _____ you that you will be unable to vote if you fail to register.

3. Some people think that an early autumn snowstorm is a (an) _____ of a severe winter, but you really can't tell in advance.

4. A (an) _____ was erected in the village square in memory of the local men who fell in World War II.

5. The approach of the storm was signaled by a low, _____ rumbling from the distant hills.

13. MAND (MANDAT): "order," "command," "commit"

countermand	'kau̇nt-ər-ˌmand	issue a contrary order
mandate	'man-ˌdāt	1. authoritative command 2. territory administered by a trustee (supervisory nation)
mandatory	'man-də-ˌtȯr-ē	obligatory; required by command
remand	ri-'mand	send ("order") back; recommit, as to a prison
writ of mandamus	'rit; man-'dā-məs	written order from a court to enforce the performance of some public duty

EXERCISE 18. In each blank insert the most appropriate word from group 13, *mand (mandat)*.

1. The reelected candidate regarded his huge popular vote as a _____ from the people to continue the policies of his first term in office.

2. When the captain heard of the lieutenant's ill-advised order to retreat to the hills, he hastened to _____ it.

3. Several prominent citizens have applied for a _____ to compel the mayor to publish the budget, as required by law.

4. The coach said that attendance at today's practice session is _____; no one may be excused.

5. Since the prisoner's retrial resulted in a verdict of "guilty," the judge was therefore obliged to _____ him to the state penitentiary.

14. CRED (CREDIT): "believe"

accredit	ə-'kred-ət	1. accept as worthy of belief 2. provide with credentials
credence	'krēd-ᵊns	belief
credentials	kri-'den-shəlz	documents, letters, references, etc., that inspire belief or trust
credit	'kred-ət	belief; faith; trust
credulous	'krej-ə-ləs	too ready to believe; easily deceived
creed	'krēd	summary of principles believed in or adhered to
discredit	dis-'kred-ət	1. cast doubt on; refuse to believe 2. disgrace
incredible	in-'kred-ə-bəl	not believable
incredulity	ˌin-kri-'d(y)ü-lət-ē	disbelief

EXERCISE 19. In each blank insert the most appropriate word from group 14, *cred (credit)*.

1. His unsportsmanlike behavior brought _____ not only upon himself, but also upon his team.

2. On the test I showed _____ negligence by completely overlooking a twenty-point question.

3. After showing his _____ as an F.B.I. agent, he was given a confidential file on the suspect.

4. Gerald is too _____; he will believe anything a salesman may tell him.

5. Mother received the announcement of her winning the door prize with a look of baffled

   _____ .

15. FID: "faith," "trust"

confidant	'kän-fə-ˌdant	(*confidante,* if a woman) one to whom secrets are entrusted
confident	'kän-fəd-ənt	having faith in oneself; self-reliant; sure
confidential	ˌkän-fə-'den-shəl	communicated in trust; secret; private
diffident	'dif-əd-ənt	lacking faith in oneself; timid; shy
fidelity	fə-'del-ət-ē	1. faithfulness to a trust or vow 2. accuracy, as of a recording
fiduciary	fə-'d(y)ü-shē-ˌer-ē	held in trust; confidential
infidel	'in-fəd-ᵊl	one who does not accept a particular faith; an unbeliever
perfidious	pər-'fid-ē-əs	false to a trust; faithless
perfidy	'pər-fəd-ē	violation of a trust; treachery; faithlessness

EXERCISE 20. In each blank insert the most appropriate word from group 15, *fid.*

1. Tom's disclosure of our club's secrets to an outsider is unforgivable _____ .

2. Marie looks upon her cousin Nancy as a (an) _____ with whom she can freely discuss her personal problems.

3. At first, new motorists are usually nervous but, with added driving experience, they become more ----------------------.

4. Our English teacher recommended a particular translation of the ODYSSEY because of its close ---------------------- to the original.

5. Sybil was very ---------------------- as she mounted the platform, even though she knew her speech by heart.

REVIEW

EXERCISE 21. In the space before each Latin root in column I, write the *letter* of its correct meaning in column II.

COLUMN I	COLUMN II
------ 1. CIDE	(A) live; alive
------ 2. VOR	(B) break
------ 3. FLECT (FLEX)	(C) order; command; commit
------ 4. TORT (TORS)	(D) bind; draw tight
------ 5. OMNI	(E) faith; trust
------ 6. VICT (VINC)	(F) warn
------ 7. TEN (TIN, TENT)	(G) killing; killer
------ 8. MAND (MANDAT)	(H) believe
------ 9. FID	(I) conquer; show conclusively
------ 10. FRACT (FRAG, FRANG)	(J) bend
------ 11. VIV	(K) eat greedily
------ 12. MON (MONIT)	(L) twist
------ 13. CRED (CREDIT)	(M) hold; keep
------ 14. STRING (STRICT)	(N) all; every; everywhere

EXERCISE 22. Supply the missing letters of the words defined. Each dash stands for one missing letter.

DEFINITION	WORD
1. break asunder	— — — RUPT
2. germ-killing substance	G — — — — CIDE
3. part broken off	FRAG — — — —
4. faithfulness to a trust	FID — — — — —
5. one who conquers	VICT — —
6. flesh-eating	— — — — VOR — — —
7. issue a contrary order	— — — — — — — MAND
8. forewarning	— — — MONIT — — —
9. muscle that serves to bend a limb	FLEX — —

10. readiness to believe on slight evidence   CRED __ __ __ __ __

11. snake that crushes (constricts) its prey   __ __ __ __ __ __ STRICT __ __

12. bring back to life   __ __ VIV __

13. adhering firmly to a purpose or opinion   __ __ __ TIN __ __ __ __ __ __

14. present everywhere at the same time   OMNI __ __ __ __ __ __

15. throw (bend) back heat, light, sound, etc.   __ __ FLECT

16. greedy in eating   VOR __ __ __ __ __ __

17. breaking of a bone   FRACT __ __ __

18. show conclusively by proof   __ __ __ VINC __

19. killing of a human by another   __ __ __ __ CIDE

20. documents inspiring trust   CRED __ __ __ __ __ __

EXERCISE 23. Write the *letter* of the word (or set of words) which, if inserted in the sentence, would agree most closely with the thought of the sentence.

1. At the afternoon performance the trainer found his favorite elephant refractory, rather than
   _____.

   (A) unmanageable   (C) tractable   (E) resisting
   (B) stubborn   (D) uncooperative

2. Harvey believes he is omniscient, but we are not particularly impressed by his _____.

   (A) power   (C) manners   (E) appearance
   (B) knowledge   (D) personality

3. The promise had been extorted and, like all promises growing out of _____, it was _____.

   (A) ignorance ...... perfidious   (D) compulsion ...... unreliable
   (B) haste ...... untenable   (E) friendship ...... dependable
   (C) rumor ...... false

4. An act of regicide always has a _____ as its victim.

   (A) rebel   (C) president   (E) monarch
   (B) general   (D) prime minister

5. I usually admonish my brother for distorting facts, but Mother seldom _____ him.

   (A) reproves   (C) remands   (E) supports
   (B) encourages   (D) praises

6. An omnibus bill deals with proposed legislation on _____ problems.

   (A) economic   (C) minor   (E) few
   (B) many   (D) transportation

7. The rapid withdrawal of your hand from the flame was a reflex, not a (an) _____ reaction.

   (A) protective   (C) involuntary   (E) voluntary
   (B) dangerous   (D) natural

8. The author read the critics' _____ with incredulity; they were too laudatory to be _____.

   (A) censures ...... heeded   (D) encomiums ...... believed
   (B) strictures ...... ignored   (E) rebukes ...... answered
   (C) admonitions ...... challenged

9. It is advisable to take along plenty of sandwiches because hungry hikers are _____ eaters.

    (A) admonitory   (C) omnifarious   (E) voracious
    (B) abstemious   (D) heterogeneous

10. No one would dare to offer a bribe to an official who has shown himself extraordinarily _____.

    (A) incorruptible   (C) credulous   (E) convivial
    (B) invincible   (D) retentive

EXERCISE 24. Each word or expression in column I has an ANTONYM (opposite) in column II. Insert the *letter* of the correct ANTONYM in the space provided.

	COLUMN I		COLUMN II
_____	1. clear of guilt	(A)	survive
_____	2. victorious	(B)	evince
_____	3. not required	(C)	convict
_____	4. perish	(D)	constrict
_____	5. of one kind	(E)	infidel
_____	6. believer	(F)	omniscient
_____	7. extremely ignorant	(G)	vanquished
_____	8. conceal	(H)	omnifarious
_____	9. loosen	(I)	perfidious
_____	10. true to a trust	(J)	mandatory

EXERCISE 25. Write the *letter* of the word NOT RELATED in meaning to the other words in each group.

1. (A) controllable (B) tractable (C) refractory (D) obedient (E) manageable _____
2. (A) gay (B) convivial (C) festive (D) inhospitable (E) jovial _____
3. (A) inhuman (B) tortuous (C) winding (D) curving (E) bending _____
4. (A) hasty (B) abrupt (C) restricted (D) unexpected (E) sudden _____
5. (A) delicate (B) weak (C) feeble (D) fragile (E) fractious _____
6. (A) trustworthy (B) accredited (C) credible (D) believable (E) incredulous _____
7. (A) disclosed (B) revealed (C) shone (D) evinced (E) displayed _____
8. (A) satiable (B) ravenous (C) voracious (D) devouring (E) greedy _____
9. (A) stringent (B) inflexible (C) pliable (D) rigid (E) firm _____
10. (A) distorted (B) corrupted (C) admonished (D) contorted (E) falsified _____

EXERCISE 26. In the space provided, write the *letter* of the word that has most nearly the SAME MEANING as the italicized word.

_____ **1.** *Fragile* flower

    (A) fragrant   (C) colorful
    (B) broken   (D) frail

_____ **2.** Cling *tenaciously*

    (A) stubbornly   (C) hopefully
    (B) dangerously   (D) timidly

------ **3.** Beyond *credence*　　　　(A) detention　　(C) belief
　　　　　　　　　　　　　　　　　　 (B) doubt　　　　(D) recall

------ **4.** *Omnipotent* ruler　　　　(A) almighty　　 (C) cruel
　　　　　　　　　　　　　　　　　　 (B) wise　　　　 (D) greedy

------ **5.** *Mandatory* increase　　　 (A) deserved　　 (C) temporary
　　　　　　　　　　　　　　　　　　 (B) required　　 (D) substantial

------ **6.** Surprising *impertinence*　 (A) firmness　　 (C) impatience
　　　　　　　　　　　　　　　　　　 (B) unreliability　(D) rudeness

------ **7.** *Breach* of trust　　　　　(A) atmosphere　(C) breaking
　　　　　　　　　　　　　　　　　　 (B) testing　　　(D) abundance

------ **8.** *Unvanquished* foe　　　　 (A) defeated　　 (C) treacherous
　　　　　　　　　　　　　　　　　　 (B) exhausted　 (D) unbeaten

------ **9.** In a *fiduciary* capacity　　 (A) confidential　(C) professional
　　　　　　　　　　　　　　　　　　 (B) special　　 (D) important

------ **10.** Refused to *genuflect*　　　(A) admit　　　 (C) cooperate
　　　　　　　　　　　　　　　　　　 (B) kneel　　　 (D) disclose

EXERCISE 27. Fill each blank with the most appropriate word selected from the vocabulary list below. (Hint: For a clue to the missing word, study the italicized expression.)

VOCABULARY LIST

evict	fratricide	omnivorous
tortuous	mandate	confidential
regicide	fractious	vivisection
tenure	evince	genocide
omnipotent	infraction	extort

1. Every tyrant who considers himself *unlimited in power* will learn sooner or later that he is not

----------------------.

2. To prevent *the deliberate extermination of racial or cultural groups,* the United Nations has

made ---------------------- an international crime.

3. When you send a letter of a *private* nature to an executive, it is advisable to write the word

"------------------------" on the envelope.

4. If a teacher is quick to *oust* one of the unruly pupils as an example to the rest, she may not

have to ----------------------anyone else for the rest of the lesson.

5. Herbert is *apt to break into a passion* if he disagrees with you; his ----------------------
disposition makes him hard to get along with.

6. In some communities, persons opposed to *the performance of research operations on living animals* have joined anti----------------------- leagues.

7. Since you dislike driving on *winding* roads, avoid the Interborough Parkway, which is extremely

----------------------.

8. Cain's *slaying of* his *brother* Abel is regarded as the first instance of ----------------------.

9. *The period for which office is held* is not the same for all Congressmen: members of the Senate serve for six years, but members of the House have a much briefer _____, only two years.

10. Dad has never received a summons for a serious traffic *violation* such as speeding, passing a red light, or a similar _____.

EXERCISE 28. Write the *letter* of the word that best completes the analogy.

1. *Matricide* is to *mother* as *genocide* is to _____.

   (A) uncle   (C) race   (E) general
   (B) country   (D) tyrant

2. *Flesh* is to *carnivorous* as *grass* is to _____.

   (A) omnivorous   (C) vegetarian   (E) agricultural
   (B) insectivorous   (D) herbivorous

3. *Fraction* is to *whole* as *follower* is to _____.

   (A) creed   (C) tenure   (E) torsion
   (B) retinue   (D) fragment

4. *Reservation* is to *cancel* as *directive* is to _____.

   (A) command   (C) flex   (E) countermand
   (B) proclaim   (D) demand

5. *Orphan* is to *guardian* as *mandate* is to _____.

   (A) victor   (C) trustee   (E) commission
   (B) monitor   (D) confidant

16. GRAT: "pleasant," "thank," "favor"

WORD		MEANING
congratulate	kən-'grach-ə-ˌlāt	express pleasure at another's success; felicitate
gracious	'grā-shəs	pleasant; courteous; kindly
grateful	'grāt-fəl	thankful
gratis	'grāt-əs	1. out of kindness or favor 2. free; without recompense
gratitude	'grat-ə-ˌt(y)üd	thankfulness
gratuitous	grə-'t(y)ü-ət-əs	1. given freely; gratis 2. unwarranted, as a *gratuitous* remark
gratuity	grə-'t(y)ü-ət-ē	present of money in return for a favor or service; tip
ingrate	'in-ˌgrāt	ungrateful ("not thankful") person
ingratiate	in-'grā-shē-ˌāt	work (oneself) into another's favor

EXERCISE 29. In each blank insert the most appropriate word from group 16, *grat*.

1. I would consider myself a (an) _____ if I failed to express my gratitude to those who have helped me.

2. Some restaurants charge for a second cup of coffee, but others provide it _____.

3. Dad was so pleased with the service that he left the waiter a generous _____.

4. Shouting out answers without waiting to be called on is no way to _____ yourself with your teacher.

5. The teacher was pleased that the lad who had been so discourteous at the beginning became more _____ as the term progressed.

17. MOR (MORT): "death"

immortality	ˌim-ȯr-'tal-ət-ē	1. eternal life 2. lasting fame
moribund	'mȯr-ə-bənd	dying; near death
mortal	'mȯrt-ᵊl	1. destined to die 2. human 3. causing death; fatal, as a *mortal* blow
mortality	mȯr-'tal-ət-ē	1. death rate 2. mortal nature
mortician	mȯr-'tish-ən	undertaker
mortification	ˌmȯrt-ə-fə-'kā-shən	shame; humiliation; embarrassment
mortuary	'mȯr-chə-ˌwer-ē	morgue

EXERCISE 30. In each blank insert the most appropriate word from group 17, *mor (mort)*.

1. Patrick Henry's _____ rests on a few speeches, especially the one ending "Give me liberty, or give me death!"

2. Infant _____ is relatively high in nations that have few physicians and hospitals.

3. Mr. Olsen did not realize what _____ he caused his daughter when he scolded her in the presence of her classmates.

4. Though the mountain climber's injury is critical, it may not be _____, for he is said to have a chance of recovery.

5. As a result of the reopening of two large factories, the _____ community has received a new lease on life.

18. CORP: "body"

corporal	'kȯr-p(ə-)rəl	bodily, as *corporal* punishment
corps	'kȯ(ə)r	1. organized body of persons 2. branch of the military
corpse	'kȯrps	dead body
corpulent	'kȯr-pyə-lənt	bulky; obese; very fat
corpus	'kȯr-pəs	general collection of writings, laws, etc.
corpuscle	'kȯr-pəs-əl	1. blood cell (literally, a "little body") 2. minute particle
corpus delicti	ˌkȯr-pəs-di-'lik-ˌtī	facts proving a crime has been committed (literally, "body of the crime")
incorporate	in-'kȯr-pə-ˌrāt	combine so as to form one body

EXERCISE 31. In each blank insert the most appropriate word from group 18, *corp*.

1. The executive in charge of administration has a (an) _____ of able assistants.

2. Criminals were flogged or put in the stocks in olden times, but such _____ punishment is rare today.

3. The _____ patient was advised by his physician to get rid of his excess weight.

4. Publishers often _____ two or more works of an author into one volume.

5. Until the _____ is produced, it cannot be established that a crime has been committed.

19. DUC (DUCT): "lead," "conduct," "draw"

aqueduct	'ak-wə-ˌdəkt	artificial channel for conducting water from a distance
conducive	kən-'d(y)ü-siv	tending to lead to; contributive; helpful
deduction	di-'dək-shən	1. taking away; subtraction 2. reasoning from the general to the particular
duct	'dəkt	tube or channel for conducting a liquid, air, etc.
ductile	'dək-tᵊl	1. able to be drawn out or hammered thin (said of a metal) 2. easily led; docile
induce	in-'d(y)üs	lead on; move by persuasion
induction	in-'dək-shən	reasoning from the particular to the general
seduction	si-'dək-shən	act of leading astray into wrongdoing
traduce	trə-'d(y)üs	slander (literally, "lead across" or parade in public by way of disgrace); vilify; calumniate
viaduct	'vī-ə-ˌdəkt	bridge for conducting a road or railroad over a valley, river, etc.

EXERCISE 32. In each blank insert the most appropriate word from group 19, *duc (duct)*.

1. A (an) _____ is an artificial channel for conducting water from a source of supply to a point of distribution.

2. How much of a (an) _____ is made from your weekly salary for taxes?

3. Though John had said that he wouldn't join, I was able to _____ him to become a member.

4. As the train passed over the _____, we had an excellent view of the valley below.

5. Movies that exaggerate the luxury and idleness of American life _____ our good name when shown abroad.

20. SECUT (SEQU): "follow"

consecutive	kən-'sek-yət-iv	following in regular order; successive
consequence	'kän-sə-ˌkwens	1. that which follows logically; result 2. importance, as a person of *consequence*
execute	'ek-sə-ˌkyüt	1. follow through to completion; carry out 2. put to death
inconsequential	in-ˌkän-sə-'kwen-shəl	unimportant
prosecute	'präs-i-ˌkyüt	1. follow to the end or until finished 2. conduct legal proceedings against; sue
sequel	'sē-kwəl	something that follows; continuation; consequence; outcome
sequence	'sē-kwəns	the following of one thing after another; succession; orderly series

EXERCISE 33. In each blank insert the most appropriate word from group 20, *secut (sequ)*.

1. If the person responsible for the damage refuses to pay, I shall _____ him.

2. After a string of seven _____ victories, our team lost to Madison High.

3. The book about the clever detective proved so popular that the author was induced to write a (an) _____.

4. The cards in the card catalog are arranged in strict alphabetical _____.

5. In some communities the shortage of water is a matter of serious _____.

21. CUR (CURR, CURS): "run"

concur	kən-'kə(r)	1. agree; be of the same opinion (literally, "run together") 2. happen together; coincide
concurrent	kən-'kər-ənt	running together; occurring at the same time
current	'kər-ənt	1. running or flowing (said of water or electricity) 2. now in progress; prevailing
curriculum	kə-'rik-yə-ləm	specific course of study in a school or college
cursive	'kər-siv	running or flowing (said of handwriting in which the letters are joined)

cursory	'kərs-ə-rē	running over hastily; superficially done, as a *cursory* glance
discursive	dis-'kər-siv	wandering ("running") from one topic to another; rambling; digressive
incur	in-'kə(r)	1. meet with ("run into") something undesirable 2. bring upon onself
incursion	in-'kər-zhən	1. a rushing into 2. hostile invasion; raid
precursor	pri-'kər-sə(r)	forerunner; predecessor
recur	ri-'kə(r)	happen again (literally, "run again")

EXERCISE 34. In each blank insert the most appropriate word from group 21, *cur (curr, curs)*.

1. If you are habitually late, you will ----------------------- the displeasure of your employer.

2. Our high school has expanded its ----------------------- to include advanced placement courses in English, mathematics, and science.

3. The ----------------- film at the Bijou is a western; the war drama is no longer playing there.

4. A difficult test question requires much more than a(an) ----------------------- reading if it is to be fully understood.

5. Our conversation on the bus was, as usual, -----------------------, ranging from the latest dance step to irregular French verbs.

22. GRESS (GRAD): "step," "walk," "go"

aggressive	ə-'gres-iv	disposed to attack (literally, "step toward"); militant; assertive; pushing
egress	'ē-ˌgres	a going or a way out; an exit
gradation	grā-'dā-shən	1. a change by steps or stages 2. act of grading
grade	'grād	step; stage; degree; rating
gradient	'grād-ē-ənt	1. rate at which a road, railroad track, etc., rises ("steps" up) 2. slope
gradual	'graj-ə-wəl	by steps or degrees; bit by bit
graduate	'graj-ə-ˌwāt	complete all the steps of a course and receive a diploma or degree
graduated	'graj-ə-ˌwāt-əd	arranged in regular steps, stages, or degrees
progressive	prə-'gres-iv	going forward to something better
regressive	ri-'gres-iv	disposed to move ("step") backward; retrogressive
retrograde	're-trə-ˌgrād	1. going backward 2. becoming worse
retrogression	ˌre-trə-'gresh-ən	act of going from a better to a worse state
transgress	trans-'gres	step beyond the limits; go beyond; break a law

EXERCISE 35. In each blank insert the most appropriate word from group 22, *gress (grad)*.

1. Learning to play an instrument is a(an) ----------------------- process; it cannot be achieved overnight.

2. The offender was told he would be suspended if he should _____ again.

3. When the game ended, hordes of spectators jammed the exits, making _____ from the stadium painfully slow.

4. For two pupils, the second test showed _____ rather than progress, since they received lower marks than on the first test.

5. In a string of _____ pearls, the individual pearls are arranged in the order of increasing size on both halves of the string.

23. PED: "foot"

biped	'bī-ˌped	two-footed animal
centipede	'sent-ə-ˌpēd	small wormlike animal with many pairs of (literally, "a hundred") legs
expedite	'ek-spə-ˌdīt	1. facilitate (literally, "free one caught by the foot") 2. accelerate or speed up
impede	im-'pēd	hinder (literally, "entangle the feet"); obstruct
impediment	im-'ped-ə-mənt	1. hindrance; obstacle (literally, "something entangling the feet") 2. defect
pedal	'ped-əl	lever acted on by the foot
pedestal	'ped-əst-əl	1. support or foot of a column or statue 2. foundation
pedestrian	pə-'des-trē-ən	1. foot traveler 2. commonplace or dull, as a *pedestrian* performance
velocipede	və-'läs-ə-ˌpēd	1. child's tricycle (literally, "swift foot") 2. early form of bicycle

EXERCISE 36. In each blank insert the most appropriate word from group 23, *ped*.

1. A foreman is expected to _____, not impede, production.

2. It is foolhardy for a(an) _____ to cross a busy thoroughfare against the light.

3. For a smooth stop, apply foot pressure to the brake _____ gradually, not abruptly.

4. If you have a speech _____, your speech teacher will help you to overcome it.

5. At the age of 6 Junior abandoned his _____ and learned to ride a bicycle.

24. TACT (TANG): "touch"

contact	'kän-ˌtakt	touching or meeting; association; connection
contiguous	kən-'tig-yə-wəs	touching; in contact; adjoining
contingent	kən-'tin-jənt	1. dependent on something else (literally, "touching together") 2. accidental
intact	in-'takt	untouched or uninjured; kept or left whole
intangible	in-'tan-jə-bəl	not capable of being touched
tact	'takt	sensitive mental perception of what is appropriate on a given occasion (literally, "sense of touch")

tactful	'takt-fəl	having or showing tact
ant. **tactless**		
tactile	'tak-t°l	1. pertaining to the sense of touch
		2. tangible
tangent	'tan-jənt	1. touching
		2. line or surface meeting a curved line or surface at one point, but not intersecting it

EXERCISE 37. In each blank insert the most appropriate word from group 24, *tact (tang)*.

1. To discuss your admission to Arista in the presence of someone who you know has been rejected is _____.

2. The missing sum was found _____; not a penny had been spent.

3. Mr. Turner told me that my passing for the term is _____ on the mark I get in the final examination.

4. A firm's good will with its clients is a most valuable, though _____, asset.

5. If you wish to maintain _____ with your school and classmates after graduation, join the Alumni Association.

25. PREHEND (PREHENS): "seize," "grasp"

apprehend	‚ap-ri-'hend	1. seize or take into custody
		2. understand
apprehensive	‚ap-ri-'hen-siv	1. quick to understand or grasp
		2. fearful of what may come; anxious
comprehensible	‚käm-pri-'hen-sə-bəl	able to be grasped mentally; understandable
comprehensive	‚käm-pri-'hen-siv	including ("seizing") very much; extensive
prehensile	prē-'hen-səl	adapted for seizing, as a *prehensile* claw
reprehensible	‚rep-ri-'hen-sə-bəl	blamable; culpable; censurable

EXERCISE 38. In each blank insert the most appropriate word from group 25, *prehend (prehens)*.

1. Ignorance can be forgiven, but cheating is utterly _____.

2. From the public observatory on the 102nd floor of the Empire State Building, you can get a(an) _____ view of New York City and its environs.

3. A coded message is _____ only to those who know the code.

4. Had you paid attention in class and done your assignments, you would have no reason to be _____ of failure.

5. Law enforcement officials are doing their best to _____ the escaped convict.

26. JECT: "throw"

abject	'ab-‚jekt	sunk to a low condition; deserving contempt
conjecture	kən-'jek-chə(r)	a guess; supposition; inference

dejected	di-'jek-təd	downcast ("thrown down"); discouraged; depressed
eject	ē-'jekt	throw out or expel; evict
inject	in-'jekt	force or introduce (literally, "throw in") a liquid, a remark, etc.
interject	,int-ər-'jekt	throw in between; insert; interpose
projectile	prə-'jek-t°l	1. object (bullet, shell, etc.) designed to be shot forward 2. anything thrown forward
reject	ri-'jekt	refuse to take; discard (literally, "throw back")

EXERCISE 39. In each blank insert the most appropriate word from group 26, *ject*.

1. When he heard that his best friend was moving, my little brother became ------------------.

2. A wise policy in buying shares of stock is to be guided by fact rather than ------------------.

3. The librarian was obliged to --------------------- the student who refused to be quiet.

4. A hypodermic syringe is used to --------------------- a dose of medicine beneath the skin.

5. The mob hurled stones, bricks, bottles, eggs, and anything else that could serve as a(an)

---------------------.

27. VERT (VERS): "turn"

avert	ə-'vərt	1. turn away 2. prevent; avoid
controversy	'kän-trə-,vər-sē	dispute (literally, a "turning against"); debate; quarrel
divert	də-'vərt	1. turn aside 2. amuse; entertain
extrovert	'ek-strə-,vərt	person more interested in what is going on around him than in his own thoughts and feelings
introvert	'in-trə-,vərt	1. person more interested in his own thoughts than in what is going on around him 2. to turn inward
invert	in-'vərt	turn upside down
obverse *ant.* **reverse**	'äb-,vərs	side turned toward the observer; therefore, the front of a coin, medal, etc.
pervert	pər-'vərt 'pər-,vərt	1. turn away from right or truth; give a wrong meaning to 2. person who has turned from what is normal or natural
revert	ri-'vərt	return; go back, as: "A man's estate *reverts* to the state if he has no heirs."
versatile	'vər-sət-°l	able to turn with ease from one thing to another
verse	'vərs	line of poetry (literally, "a turning around." After a fixed number of syllables, the poet has to "turn around" to begin a new line.)

EXERCISE 40. In each blank insert the most appropriate word from group 27, *vert (vers)*.

1. Between Thanksgiving and Christmas most department store employees work overtime, but thereafter they --------------------- to their normal working hours.

2. The words "In God We Trust" appear above Lincoln's image on the ------------- of a cent.

3. The girls in the upstairs family are always quarreling, but the boys seldom have a(an)

------------------------------.

4. The first ------------------------ of Katherine Lee Bates' "America, the Beautiful" is "O beautiful for spacious skies."

5. A(an) ---------------------- musician knows how to play several instruments.

28. MIS (MISS, MIT, MITT): "send"

demise	di-'mīz	death (literally, "sending or putting down")
emissary	'em-ə-ˌser-ē	person sent on a mission
emit	ē-'mit	send out; give off
intermittent	ˌint-ər-'mit-ᵊnt	coming and going at intervals, as an *intermittent* fever (literally, "sending between")
missile	'mis-əl	weapon (spear, bullet, rocket, etc.) propelled (literally, "capable of being sent") to hit a distant object
missive	'mis-iv	written message sent; a letter
remiss	ri-'mis	negligent (literally, "sent back"); careless; lax
remit	ri-'mit	1. send money due 2. forgive, as to have one's sins *remitted*

EXERCISE 41. In each blank insert the most appropriate word from group 28, *mis (miss, mit, mitt)*.

1. This morning's rain was --------------------------, starting and stopping several times.

2. Children at camp are often ---------------------- in their obligation to write home regularly.

3. The President chose a distinguished elder statesman as his ------------------------ to the international conference.

4. If Dad fails to ---------------------- the mortgage payment by the tenth of the month, he has to pay a late fee.

5. My large searchlight can ---------------------- a powerful beam.

29. LOCUT (LOQU): "speak," "talk"

circumlocution	ˌsər-kəm-lō-'kyü-shən	roundabout way of speaking
colloquy	'käl-ə-kwē	a talking together; conference; conversation
elocution	ˌel-ə-'kyü-shən	art of speaking or reading effectively in public
eloquent	'el-ə-kwənt	speaking with force and fluency; movingly expressive
grandiloquent	gran-'dil-ə-kwənt	using lofty or pompous words; bombastic
interlocutor	ˌint-ə(r)-'läk-yət-ə(r)	1. questioner 2. one who participates in a conversation
loquacious	lō-'kwā-shəs	talkative; garrulous
obloquy	'äb-lə-kwē	1. a speaking against; censure 2. public reproach

EXERCISE 42. In each blank insert the most appropriate word from group 29, *locut (loqu)*.

1. "Your services will be terminated if you persist in disregarding our requirement of punctuality"

   is a(an) _____. It would be more direct to say, "You will be dismissed if you come late again."

2. _____ students who carry on noisy conversations in the library prevent others from concentrating.

3. A course in _____ will help you to be an effective public speaker.

4. The referee held a short _____ with the judges before announcing the winner.

5. Witnesses appearing before the investigating committee found that the chairman was the princi-

   pal _____; the other committee members asked very few questions.

30. FER(ous): "bearing," "producing," "yielding"

coniferous	kō-'nif-ə-rəs	bearing cones, as the pine
odoriferous	ˌōd-ə-'rif-ə-rəs	yielding an odor, usually fragrant
pestiferous	pe-'stif-ə-rəs	1. infected with or bearing disease; pestilential 2. evil
somniferous	säm-'nif-ə-rəs	bearing or inducing sleep
vociferous	vō-'sif-ə-rəs	producing a loud outcry; clamorous; noisy

EXERCISE 43. In each blank insert the most appropriate word from group 30, *fer(ous)*.

1. The infant emitted so _____ a protest when placed in the crib that his mother took him up at once.

2. A bunch of _____ lilacs in a vase on the table gave the room an inviting fragrance.

3. Some people who have difficulty falling asleep have found that a glass of warm milk taken before

   retiring has a(an) _____ effect.

4. The settlers were heartbroken to see their fields of corn and wheat devastated by swarms of

   _____ locusts.

5. The seed-bearing part of pines, cedars, firs, and other _____ trees is known as a cone.

REVIEW

EXERCISE 44. Supply the missing letters of the words defined. Each dash stands for one missing letter.

DEFINITION	WORD
1. moved forward to something better	_ _ _ GRESS _ _
2. foot traveler	PED _ _ _ _ _ _
3. combine so as to form one body	_ _ CORP _ _ _ _ _

4. something that follows; continuation   SEQU __ __

5. artificial channel for conducting water   __ __ __ __ DUCT

6. undertaker   MORT __ __ __ __ __

7. gift of money in return for a favor   GRAT __ __ __ __

8. producing a loud outcry   __ __ __ __ FEROUS

9. turning away; avoiding   __ VERT __ __ __

10. pertaining to the sense of touch   TACT __ __ __

11. a speaking against; censure   __ __ LOQU __

12. running or flowing (writing)   CURS __ __ __

13. by steps or degrees   GRAD __ __ __

14. a written message   MISS __ __ __

15. talkative   LOQU __ __ __ __ __

16. throw in between; interpose   __ __ __ __ __ JECT

17. tending to lead to; contributive   __ __ __ DUC __ __ __

18. person sent on a mission   __ MISS __ __ __

19. running together; occurring simultaneously   __ __ __ CURR __ __ __

20. turning easily from one thing to another   VERS __ __ __ __ __

EXERCISE 45. In the space before each Latin root in column I, write the *letter* of its correct meaning in column II.

COLUMN I	COLUMN II
------ 1. MOR (MORT)	(A) body
------ 2. TACT (TANG)	(B) step; walk; go
------ 3. LOCUT (LOQU)	(C) run
------ 4. GRAT	(D) bearing; producing; yielding
------ 5. SECUT (SEQU)	(E) speak; talk
------ 6. CORP	(F) throw
------ 7. CUR (CURR, CURS)	(G) touch
------ 8. PED	(H) pleasant; thank; favor
------ 9. PREHEND (PREHENS)	(I) lead; conduct; draw
------ 10. JECT	(J) death
------ 11. VERT (VERS)	(K) send
------ 12. FER(ous)	(L) turn
------ 13. GRESS (GRAD)	(M) seize; grasp
------ 14. MIS (MISS, MIT, MITT)	(N) foot
------ 15. DUC (DUCT)	(O) follow

EXERCISE 46. In the space before each word or expression in column I, write the *letter* of its correct meaning in column II.

COLUMN I

		COLUMN II
------	1. death rate	(A) invert
------	2. turn upside down	(B) grandiloquent
------	3. felicitate	(C) retrograde
------	4. adapted for seizing	(D) congratulate
------	5. give a wrong meaning to	(E) mortality
------	6. bombastic	(F) pervert
------	7. interpose	(G) ductile
------	8. going backward	(H) corpuscle
------	9. minute particle	(I) interject
------	10. able to be hammered thin	(J) prehensile

EXERCISE 47. Write the word that means the OPPOSITE of the defined word by adding, dropping, or changing a prefix or a suffix. (The first answer has been filled in as an example.)

	DEFINITION	WORD	OPPOSITE
1.	important	consequential	inconsequential
2.	unbelievable	incredible	------------------
3.	having no tact	tactless	------------------
4.	discourteous, rude	ungracious	------------------
5.	disposed to move backward	regressive	------------------
6.	thrown in	injected	------------------
7.	yielding no odor	odorless	------------------
8.	indefensible	untenable	------------------
9.	having faith in oneself	confident	------------------
10.	unrelated to the matter in hand	impertinent	------------------
11.	front of a coin	obverse	------------------
12.	capable of being corrupted	corruptible	------------------
13.	a going ("running") out	excursion	------------------
14.	touchable; objective	tangible	------------------
15.	reasoning from particular to general	induction	------------------
16.	understandable	comprehensible	------------------
17.	trust in the truth of	credit	------------------
18.	faithfulness to a trust	fidelity	------------------
19.	unconquered	unvanquished	------------------
20.	person more interested in his own thoughts than in his surroundings	introvert	------------------

EXERCISE 48. Which of the two terms makes the sentence correct? Write the *letter* of the correct answer in the space provided.

1. The _____ speaker moved the audience deeply in his brief address.

   (A) loquacious   (B) eloquent

2. Andrew is too much of an _____; he doesn't show enough interest in what is going on around him.

   (A) extrovert   (B) introvert

3. The authorities know the identity of the _____ and expect to apprehend him soon.

   (A) transgressor   (B) precursor

4. Larry's diverting account of his experiment _____ the class.

   (A) confused   (B) amused

5. The entire foreign diplomatic _____ was present at the funeral rites for the distinguished leader.

   (A) corpse   (B) corps

6. For all the kindness you have shown us, we are extremely _____.

   (A) grateful   (B) gratuitous

7. Since her motion was adopted by a 5-to-2 vote, it was clear that most of the girls _____.

   (A) incurred   (B) concurred

8. If you had used fewer technical terms in your report on space exploration, it would have been more _____.

   (A) comprehensible   (B) comprehensive

9. The employer explained that salary increases are not automatic but _____ on satisfactory service.

   (A) contiguous   (B) contingent

10. The following is an example of _____: "Swimmers come to the surface within seconds after a dive; when Ken didn't come up immediately, we knew he was in trouble."

   (A) induction   (B) deduction

EXERCISE 49. Write the *letter* of the word NOT RELATED in meaning to the other words in each group.

1. (A) transgression   (B) breach   (C) overstepping   (D) retrogression   _____

2. (A) commonplace   (B) dull   (C) pedestrian   (D) diverting   _____

3. (A) dejection   (B) conjecture   (C) sadness   (D) depression   _____

4. (A) vilify   (B) slander   (C) induce   (D) calumniate   _____

5. (A) deathless   (B) moribund   (C) everlasting   (D) immortal   _____

6. (A) block   (B) impede   (C) obstruct   (D) expedite   _____

7. (A) dependent   (B) conditional   (C) abject   (D) contingent   _____

8. (A) diffidently   (B) aggressively   (C) fearfully   (D) apprehensively   _____

9. (A) perfumed   (B) rank   (C) fragrant   (D) aromatic   _____

10. (A) ancestor   (B) forerunner   (C) precursor   (D) emissary   _____

EXERCISE 50. Fill each blank with the most appropriate word selected from the list below.

VOCABULARY LIST

mortal	inconsequential	incurred
versatile	expedited	reprehensible
diverted	induced	intermittently
ingrate	moribund	gratis
comprehensive	discursive	apprehensive

1. He _____ (*brought upon himself*) the instructor's displeasure by the cursory manner in which he had done his reading assignments.

2. Don't have anything to do with that _____ (*unthankful person*); he never appreciates a favor.

3. Many businesses have _____ (*increased the speed of*) delivery by extensive use of air-mail service.

4. Nelson incurred a(an) _____ (*causing death*) wound in the Battle of Trafalgar.

5. Forgetting to bring my lunch turned out to be _____ (*of no importance*), since I was able to purchase lunch at school.

6. George is the most _____ (*equipped with many aptitudes*) player on our team; he can play any position except first base.

7. Residents may borrow books from the library _____ (*without charge*).

8. Some of the passengers were nervous because Sam, a newly licensed driver, was at the wheel, but I was not _____ (*fearful of what might come*).

9. The strikers were _____ (*moved by persuasion*) to return to their jobs with the promise of a new contract.

10. Mrs. Green realized that she would not finish the lesson on time if she permitted the discussion to become too _____ (*wandering from one topic to another*).

EXERCISE 51. Write the *letter* of the word that best completes the analogy.

1. *River* is to *bridge* as *valley* is to _____.
   - (A) viaduct
   - (B) mountain
   - (C) pontoon
   - (D) projectile
   - (E) road

2. *Olfactory* is to *smell* as *tactile* is to _____.
   - (A) see
   - (B) grasp
   - (C) touch
   - (D) hear
   - (E) taste

3. *Birth* is to *demise* as *preface* is to _____.
   - (A) foreword
   - (B) conclusion
   - (C) footnote
   - (D) introduction
   - (E) outline

4. *Corpse* is to *life* as *ingrate* is to _____.
   - (A) fear
   - (B) ingratitude
   - (C) unkindness
   - (D) dejection
   - (E) gratitude

5. *Plan* is to *execution* as *outline* is to _____.
   - (A) summary
   - (B) organization
   - (C) killing
   - (D) composition
   - (E) topic

CHAPTER V

WORDS FROM CLASSICAL MYTHOLOGY AND HISTORY

This chapter will teach you to use important words taken from classical (ancient Greek and Roman) mythology. The beautiful and profoundly significant myths created by the Greeks and adopted by the Romans have contributed words that an educated person is expected to know. All the words discussed below originate from myths, except the following which are based on historical fact: *Draconian, laconic, Lucullan, philippic, Pyrrhic, solon,* and *thespian.*

WORD LIST

WORD	MEANING	TYPICAL USE
Adonis ə-'dän-əs	very handsome young man (from *Adonis,* a handsome youth loved by Aphrodite, goddess of love)	Peter, who was chosen the handsomest boy in the senior class, is quite an *Adonis.*
aegis 'ē-jəs	1. shield or protection 2. auspices or sponsorship (from *aegis,* the protective shield of Zeus)	An international force under the *aegis* of the United Nations has been dispatched to the troubled area.
amazon 'am-ə-ˌzän	tall, strong, masculine woman (from the *Amazons,* a mythological race of women warriors)	Pioneer women were veritable *amazons,* performing heavy household chores in addition to toiling in the fields beside their menfolk.
ambrosial am-'brō-zhəl	exceptionally pleasing to taste or smell; extremely delicious; excellent (from *ambrosia,* the food of the gods)	The *ambrosial* aroma of the roast whetted our appetites.
atlas 'at-ləs	book of maps (from *Atlas,* a giant who supported the heavens on his shoulders. The figure of Atlas supporting the world was prefaced to early map collections; hence the name *atlas.*)	For reliable information about present national boundaries, consult an up-to-date *atlas.*
auroral ə-'ror-əl	1. pertaining to or resembling the dawn 2. rosy (from *Aurora,* goddess of the dawn)	The darkness waned and a faint *auroral* glow began to appear in the east.
bacchanalian ˌbak-ə-'nāl-yən (or **bacchic**)	jovial or wild with drunkenness (from *Bacchus,* the god of wine)	At 2 A.M. the neighbors called the police to quell the *bacchanalian* revelry in the upstairs apartment.

chimerical
kī-'mer-i-kəl
(or **chimeric**)

fantastic; unreal; impossible; absurd

(from the *Chimera,* a fire-breathing monster with a lion's head, goat's body, and serpent's tail)

At first, Robert Fulton's plans for his steamboat were derided as *chimerical* nonsense.

Draconian
drə-'kō-nē-ən
(or **Draconic**)

cruel; harsh; severe

(from *Draco,* an Athenian lawmaker who drew up a harsh code of laws)

The dictator took *Draconian* measures against those he suspected of plotting a rebellion.

Elysian
i-'lizh-ən

delightful; blissful; heavenly

(from *Elysium,* the mythological paradise where the brave and good live after death)

Students studying for final examinations yearn for the *Elysian* idleness of the summer vacation.

hector
'hek-tə(r)

1. bully; intimidate with threats
2. bluster

(from *Hector,* bravest of the Trojans)

The pickets did not allow themselves to be provoked, despite the unruly crowds that gathered to *hector* them.

Herculean
‚hər-kyə-'lē-ən

1. very difficult
2. having or requiring the strength of *Hercules* (a hero of superhuman strength)

Among the *Herculean* tasks confronting large cities are slum clearance and traffic control.

hermetic
hər-'met-ik

airtight

(from *Hermes,* who, among his other attributes, was god of magic)

Dad had to break the *hermetic* seal to get a pill from the new bottle.

iridescent
‚ir-ə-'des-°nt

having colors like the rainbow

(from *Iris,* goddess of the rainbow)

Children enjoy blowing *iridescent* soap bubbles from pipes.

jovial
'jō-vē-əl

jolly; merry; good-humored

(from *Jove,* or Jupiter. The planet Jupiter was believed to make persons born under its influence cheerful or *jovial.*)

Our *jovial* host entertained us with several amusing anecdotes about his employer.

labyrinthine
lab-ə-'rin-thən

1. full of confusing passageways; intricate
2. complicated, like the *Labyrinth* (a fabled maze in Crete)

Out-of-towners may easily lose their way in New York City's *labyrinthine* subway passages.

laconic
lə-'kän-ik

using words sparingly; terse; concise

(from *Lakonikos,* meaning "Spartan." The Spartans were known for their terseness.)

All I received in response to my request was the *laconic* reply "Wait."

lethargic
li-'thär-jik

unnaturally drowsy; sluggish; dull

(from *Lethe,* river in Hades whose water, if drunk, caused forgetfulness of the past)

For several hours after the operation the patient was *lethargic* because of the anesthetic.

Lucullan lü-'kəl-ən	sumptuous; luxurious (from *Lucullus,* a Roman who gave lavish banquets)	Thanksgiving dinner at Grandmother's is almost a *Lucullan* feast.
martial 'mär-shəl	pertaining to war; warlike (from *Mars,* god of war)	The Helvetians were a *martial* people who tried to conquer southern Gaul.
mentor 'men-₁tȯ(r)	1. wise and trusted adviser 2. athletic coach (from *Mentor,* to whom Odysseus entrusted the education of his son)	The retiring foreman was persuaded to stay on for a month as *mentor* to his successor.
mercurial mər-'kyu̇r-ē-əl (*ant.* **saturnine**)	1. quick; vivacious 2. changeable 3. crafty 4. eloquent (These are characteristics of *Mercury,* the messenger of the gods, who was also god of commerce, magic, and eloquence, as well as the patron of travelers, rogues, and thieves. His name designates a planet as well as a metal.)	The older partner is rather dull and morose, but the younger has a *mercurial* temperament that appeals to customers.
myrmidon 'mər-mə-₁dän	obedient and unquestioning follower (from the *Myrmidons,* a martial tribe who accompanied Achilles to the Trojan War)	The dictator surrounded himself with *myrmidons* who would loyally and pitilessly execute all orders.
nemesis 'nem-ə-səs	1. due punishment for evil deeds 2. one who inflicts such punishment (from *Nemesis,* goddess of vengeance)	Napoleon crushed many opponents, but Wellington proved to be his *nemesis.*
odyssey 'äd-ə-sē	any long series of wanderings or travels (from the *Odyssey,* the poem dealing with Odysseus' ten years of wandering on his way home from the Trojan War)	Your travel agent will gladly plan a year's *odyssey* to places of interest around the world.
paean 'pē-ən	song or hymn of praise, joy, or triumph (A *paean* was a hymn in praise of Apollo, the god of deliverance.)	When the victory was announced, people danced in the streets and sang *paeans* of joy.
palladium pə-'lād-ē-əm	safeguard or protection (from *Palladium,* the statue of Pallas Athena, which was thought to protect the city of Troy)	The little girl habitually fell asleep clutching a battered doll, her *palladium.*

panic
'pan-ik

unreasoning, sudden fright that grips a multitude

(from *Pan,* a god believed to cause fear)

A *panic* ensued when someone in the crowded auditorium yelled "Fire!"

philippic
fə-'lip-ik

bitter denunciation

(from the *Philippics,* orations by Demosthenes denouncing King Philip of Macedon)

In an hour-long *philippic,* the legislator denounced the lobbyists opposing his bill.

plutocratic
ˌplüt-ə-'krat-ik

having great influence because of one's wealth

(from *Plutus,* god of wealth)

A handful of *plutocratic* investors, each owning more than a thousand shares, determined the policies of the corporation.

procrustean
prə-'krəs-tē-ən
(or **Procrustean**)

cruel or inflexible in enforcing conformity

(from *Procrustes,* a robber who made his victims fit the length of his bed, either stretching them or cutting off their legs)

The martinet governed his classroom with *procrustean* discipline, assigning a week's detention to all offenders, no matter what the offense.

protean
'prōt-ē-ən

1. exceedingly variable
2. readily assuming different forms or shapes

(from *Proteus,* a sea god who could readily change his shape to elude capture)

The witness' *protean* tactics under cross-examination gave the impression that he was untrustworthy.

Pyrrhic
ˌpir-ik

ruinous; gained at too great a cost

(from *Pyrrhus,* who suffered enormous losses in a "victory" over the Romans)

Our winning the opening game was a *Pyrrhic* victory, as our leading scorer was injured and put out of action for the balance of the season.

saturnine
'sat-ər-ˌnīn
(*ant.* **mercurial**)

heavy; dull; gloomy; morose

(from *Saturn,* father of Jupiter. Though Saturn's reign was supposedly a golden age, he has become a symbol of heaviness and dullness because the alchemists and astrologers associated his name with the metal lead.)

My former roommate was a *saturnine* scholar who said very little and smiled rarely.

siren
'sī-rən

1. dangerous, attractive woman
2. a woman who sings sweetly
3. apparatus for sounding loud warnings

(from the *Sirens,* creatures half woman and half bird, whose sweet singing lured sailors to destruction on the rocks)

The enemy employed a red-haired *siren* as a spy.

solon 'sō-lən	1. legislator 2. wise man (from *Solon,* noted Athenian law-giver)	Next week the *solons* will return to the capital for the opening of the legislature.
stentorian sten-'tȯr-ē-ən	very loud (from *Stentor,* a legendary herald whose voice was as loud as fifty voices)	Speak softly; you don't need a *stentorian* voice to be heard in this small room.
Stygian 'stij-ē-ən	infernal; dark; gloomy (from *Styx,* a river of the lower world leading into Hades, or Hell)	A power failure at 11:03 P.M. plunged the city into *Stygian* blackness.
tantalize 'tant-ᵊl-ˌīz	1. excite a hope but prevent its fulfillment 2. tease (from *Tantalus,* who was kept hungry and thirsty in the lower world with food and water very near but just beyond his reach)	The considerate hostess removed the strawberry shortcake from the table so as not to *tantalize* her weight-conscious guest.
terpsichorean ˌtərp-sik-ə-'rē-ən	pertaining to dancing (from *Terpsichore,* the muse of dancing)	The reviewers lauded the ballet troupe for its *terpsichorean* artistry.
thespian 'thes-pē-ən (or **Thespian**)	pertaining to the drama or acting (from *Thespis,* reputed father of Greek drama)	If you enjoy acting in plays, join your school's *thespian* club.
titanic tī-'tan-ik	of enormous strength, size, or power (from the *Titans,* lawless, powerful giants defeated by Zeus)	By a *titanic* effort, our football team halted an onrush at our one-yard line.

EXERCISES

EXERCISE 1. If the italicized word is *correctly* used in the sentence, write *C* in the space provided. If *incorrectly* used, write *X.*

------ 1. Our new track *mentor* has had years of coaching experience.

------ 2. I was grateful for my sunglasses as we drove through the desert in the glaring *auroral* light of midday.

------ 3. A *laconic* person habitually uses more words than necessary.

------ 4. The Egyptian pyramids are structures of *titanic* dimensions.

------ 5. A *saturnine* expression on a child's face may be taken as a sign of cheerfulness.

------ 6. The refugee told of his *odyssey* from country to country in search of a new homeland.

------ 7. By imposing *Draconian* fines, the judge acquired a reputation for leniency.

------ 8. The notorious bank robber finally met his *nemesis* in the person of a courageous teller who set off the burglar alarm.

------ **9.** Do not *tantalize* the lad by promising him a reward and then failing to keep that promise.

------ **10.** A practical person does not offer *chimerical* suggestions.

EXERCISE 2. Write the *letter* of the word (or set of words) which, if inserted in the sentence, would agree most closely with the thought of the sentence.

1. Photographs of _____ celebrities decorated the walls of the dance studio.

(A) operatic   (C) thespian   (E) terpsichorean
(B) modern   (D) famous

2. The wrestler's _____ maneuvers made it difficult for his opponent to obtain a hold.

(A) hermetic   (C) titanic   (E) philippic
(B) protean   (D) procrustean

3. In a locker-room speech between halves, the _____ reaffirmed his confidence in his _____.

(A) conductor . . . . . myrmidons   (D) mentor . . . . . . squad
(B) amazon . . . . . . team   (E) conductor . . . . . . mentors
(C) myrmidon . . . . . . adherents

4. Many literatures describe a paradise where the _____ dwell in _____ repose.

(A) heroic . . . . . . Stygian   (D) perfidious . . . . . . ambrosial
(B) unvanquished . . . . . bacchanalian   (E) brave . . . . . . Elysian
(C) sirens . . . . . . abject

5. When people become _____, their ability to reason gives way to fear.

(A) lethargic   (C) panicky   (E) plutocratic
(B) saturnine   (D) Draconian

6. The audience laughed to see the corpulent actor _____ by his puny companion's hectoring.

(A) convinced   (C) tripped   (E) encouraged
(B) betrayed   (D) intimidated

7. The Pyrrhic victory was cause for widespread _____.

(A) dejection   (C) paeans   (E) promotions
(B) optimism   (D) satisfaction

8. Only a person with a _____ voice could have made himself heard above the din of the angry crowd.

(A) Herculean   (C) jovial   (E) titanic
(B) stentorian   (D) laconic

9. Our _____ host always enjoys having friends to share his Lucullan suppers.

(A) cursive   (C) fractious   (E) sanguine
(B) martial   (D) convivial

10. Psychoanalysis can help a patient recall long-forgotten experiences lost in the _____ recesses of his mind.

(A) labyrinthine   (C) iridescent   (E) mercurial
(B) chimerical   (D) auroral

V. WORDS FROM CLASSICAL MYTHOLOGY AND HISTORY   99

EXERCISE 3. In the space provided, write the *letter* of the word or expression that has most nearly the SAME MEANING as the italicized word.

------ 1. *Ambrosial* fare
(A) expensive
(B) cut-rate
(C) railroad
(D) delicious

------ 2. Unemployed *thespians*
(A) musicians
(B) actors
(C) dancers
(D) loafers

------ 3. *Martial* airs
(A) matrimonial
(B) tuneful
(C) military
(D) soothing

------ 4. Impassioned *philippic*
(A) plea
(B) message
(C) praise
(D) denunciation

------ 5. *Plutocratic* associates
(A) loyal and wealthy
(B) jovial
(C) carefree
(D) rich and influential

------ 6. *Draconian* laws
(A) democratic
(B) severe
(C) unpopular
(D) unenforced

------ 7. *Hermetic* compartments
(A) rigid
(B) tiny
(C) airtight
(D) labyrinthine

------ 8. Road *atlas*
(A) highwayman
(B) map collection
(C) network
(D) blind alley

------ 9. Endless *odyssey*
(A) story
(B) wanderings
(C) sufferings
(D) errands

------ 10. A new *Adonis*
(A) lover
(B) movie actor
(C) myrmidon
(D) handsome youth

EXERCISE 4. In each sentence fill in the missing letters of the incomplete word. Each dash stands for one missing letter.

1. I found it difficult to study, since a heavy dinner had made me l__ __ __ __ __ __ __ __.

2. Jean Valjean's H__ __ __ __ __ __ __ __ strength enabled him to lift the heaviest of objects with ease.

3. You may see an i__ __ __ __ __ __ __ __ __ arc, known as a rainbow, when you look at the sky just after a summer shower.

4. A glass jar is airtight if it is h__ __ __ __ __ __ __ally sealed.

5. The band concerts, formerly under private sponsorship, will be given under the a__ __ __ __ __ of our city from now on.

EXERCISE 5. Write the *letter* of the word-pair that best expresses a relationship similar to that existing between the capitalized word-pair.

------ 1. SOLON : LAWS
(A) atlas : maps
(B) ruler : subjects
(C) philosopher : credentials
(D) craftsman : trade
(E) composer : operas

------ **2. SIREN : BEAUTY**
      (A) victim : trap   (D) alarm : confidence
      (B) temptress : prey   (E) worm : fish
      (C) hunter : bait

------ **3. TANTALIZE : SATISFY**
      (A) Elysian : blissful   (D) agree : differ
      (B) encomium : commendation   (E) delay : postpone
      (C) rainbow : iridescent

------ **4. NEMESIS : EVILDOER**
      (A) avenger : victim   (D) justice : misdeed
      (B) retribution : wrongdoer   (E) penalty : evil
      (C) punishment : benefactor

------ **5. AMAZON : STRENGTH**
      (A) comedienne : humor   (D) warrior : civilian
      (B) river : jungle   (E) servant : indifference
      (C) nurse : invalid

------ **6. PALLADIUM : DANGER**
      (A) rumor : panic   (D) experience : skill
      (B) arena : excitement   (E) rain : drought
      (C) investigation : truth

------ **7. MERCURIAL : VIVACITY**
      (A) procrustean : rigidity   (D) saturnine : hilarity
      (B) protean : uniformity   (E) ambrosial : dawn
      (C) ethereal : earth

------ **8. PAEAN : ECSTASY**
      (A) anthem : nation   (D) sadness : joy
      (B) suffering : rejoicing   (E) hymn : congregation
      (C) lament : sorrow

------ **9. THESPIAN : TERPSICHOREAN**
      (A) painting : ballet   (D) drama : dancing
      (B) oratory : music   (E) composing : singing
      (C) acting : sculpture

------ **10. AURORAL : DAY**
      (A) overture : opera   (D) introductory : conclusion
      (B) infantile : human being   (E) tadpole : frog
      (C) preface : book

CHAPTER VI

ANGLO-SAXON VOCABULARY AND ITS ENRICHMENT THROUGH LATIN

About 25 percent of our English vocabulary comes from the language of the Angles and Saxons, Germanic tribes who invaded Britain beginning about the year 450 A.D. Despite the vast numbers of foreign words incorporated into English over the years, particularly from Latin and French, the basic words of English today are of Anglo-Saxon origin. They include the articles (*a, an, the*), the words for numbers, the verb *to be*, prepositions (*at, by, from, in, out, with*, etc.), conjunctions (*and, but, as, when*, etc.), many commonly used verbs (*to go, to fight, to sleep, to eat*, etc.), many commonly used nouns (*father, mother, land, house, water*, etc.), and most pronouns.

This brief chapter deals with (1) Anglo-Saxon elements selected to help you increase your store of words, and (2) Latin enrichment of Anglo-Saxon.

ANGLO-SAXON PREFIXES

1. A-: "on," "in," "at"

aboard	ə-'bȯrd	on a ship, train, bus, etc.
afoul	ə-'faul	in collision
aloof	ə-'lüf	at or from a distance; withdrawn; apart

  Also: **abed, adrift, afield, afloat, aloft**, etc.

2. WITH-: "against," "back"

withdraw	with-'drȯ	draw back; take back
withhold	with-'hōld	hold back
withstand	with-'stand	stand against; resist
notwithstanding	ˌnät-with-'stan-diŋ	despite the fact that (literally, "not standing against")

3. BE- has these meanings:

  (*a*) "all around," "on all sides," "thoroughly"

beset	bi-'set	attack on all sides; surround

  Also: **begrudge, belabor, bemuddle, besiege, besmirch**, etc.

  (*b*) "affect with," "cover with"

begrime	bi-'grīm	cover with grime; make dirty

  Also: **becloud, bedevil, befog, belie, bewitch**, etc.

  (*c*) "cause to be"

belittle	bi-'lit-ᵊl	cause to be little or unimportant; disparage

  Also: **becalm, bedim, bewilder**, etc.

ANGLO-SAXON SUFFIXES

1. -WISE: "way," "manner"

contrariwise   'kän-ˌtrer-ē-ˌwīz   on the contrary
   ant. likewise
nowise   'nō-ˌwīz   in no way; not at all
   Also: **breadthwise, lengthwise, otherwise,** etc.

2. -DOM: "dignity," "office," "realm," "state of being," "those having the character of"

earldom   'ərl-dəm   realm or dignity of an earl
martyrdom   'märt-ərd-əm   state of being a martyr
officialdom   ə-'fish-əl-dəm   those having the authority of officials; officials collectively
   Also: **dukedom, kingdom, serfdom, sheikdom, stardom,** etc.

3. -SOME has these meanings:

(*a*) "having a considerable degree of the thing or quality denoted in the first part of the *-SOME* word"

cumbersome   'kəm-bər-səm   full of encumbrances; burdensome
fulsome   'fûl-səm   offensive because of excessive display or insincerity (literally, "full of fullness")
lissom(e)   'lis-əm   lithesome (literally, "full of a lithe or supple quality"); nimble
mettlesome   'met-ᵊl-səm   full of mettle (courage); spirited
noisome   'noi-səm   offensive to the sense of smell (literally, "full of an annoying quality"); unwholesome
winsome   'win-səm   full of a winning quality (literally, "full of *wynn*," the Anglo-Saxon word for *joy*); cheerful; merry
   Also: **awesome, bothersome, fearsome, frolicsome, gruesome, irksome, lonesome, quarrelsome, toothsome, troublesome,** etc.

(*b*) "group of"

twosome   'tü-səm   group of two
   Also: **threesome, foursome,** etc.

4. -LING has these meanings:

(*a*) "one pertaining to or concerned with whatever is denoted in the first part of the *-LING* word"

hireling   'hī-ə(r)-liŋ   one who receives pay for work performed
starveling   'stärv-liŋ   one who is thin from lack of food
suckling   'sək-liŋ   child or animal that is nursed (sucks)
yearling   'yi-ə(r)-liŋ   one who is a year old

(b) "little"

duckling	ˈdək-liŋ	little duck
foundling	ˈfau̇n-dliŋ	infant found after being deserted by its unknown parents
gosling	ˈgäz-liŋ	young goose
stripling	ˈstrip-liŋ	lad (literally, "a little strip" from the main stem)

Also: **fledgling, princeling, sapling,** etc.

ANGLO-SAXON WORDS ENCOUNTERED IN LITERATURE

WORD		MEANING
anent	ə-ˈnent	about; concerning; in respect to
anon	ə-ˈnän	soon; presently
behest	bi-ˈhest	command; order
beholden	bi-ˈhōl-dən	bound in gratitude; indebted
behoove	bi-ˈhüv	be necessary for; be proper for
betimes	bi-ˈtīmz	early
heath	ˈhēth	tract of wasteland
wane	ˈwān	decrease gradually in size
warlock	ˈwȯr-ˌläk	sorcerer or wizard
warp	ˈwȯrp	the threads running lengthwise in the loom, crossed by the woof
wax	ˈwaks	to grow in size, as in "to wax and wane"
withal	with-ˈȯl	with it all; as well
woof	ˈwu̇f	the threads running from side to side in a woven fabric
yclept (or **ycleped**)	i-ˈklept	named; called

EXERCISE 1. In each sentence fill in the missing letters of the incomplete word. Each dash stands for one missing letter.

1. Do not b— — — — — — (*obscure, as with clouds*) the issue.
2. A n— — — — — — (*offensive to the sense of smell*) odor filled the chemistry laboratory.
3. Jim is friendly but his uncle holds himself a— — — — (*at a distance*).
4. Try as I might, I could not b— — — — — (*cause to be quiet*) the anxious mother.
5. In the fog we ran a— — — — of (*came in collision with*) a stalled car.
6. A public official should be cautious about accepting favors so as not to be b— — — — — — — (*bound in gratitude*) to anybody.
7. Don't you agree they make an attractive t— — — — — — (*group of two*)?
8. Present your passbook to the bank teller whenever you deposit or w— — — — — — — (*take back*) funds.
9. The monarch seemed not at all displeased by the obviously f— — — — — — (*offensively insincere*) compliments of his fawning subjects.
10. From her first performance it was obvious she was destined for s— — — — — — (*the state of being a star*).

EXERCISE 2. In the space provided, write the word of Anglo-Saxon origin that is equivalent to the italicized expression. The letters of each word appear in scrambled form in the parentheses. (The first answer has been filled in as an example.)

1. It *is necessary for* (VESHOOBE) students to be attentive. BEHOOVES _____

2. He rose before dawn and retired *early* (MESBETI). _____

3. Nothing was said *concerning* (TENNA) the proposal to grant a pardon. _____

4. The witches in Shakespeare's play MACBETH usually met on the *wasteland* (TEHAH). _____

5. We are *indebted* (HODNEBLE) to no one. _____

6. The moon *grows* (XESWA) and wanes. _____

7. With a small stone the *lad* (GRINPLITS) David slew the giant Goliath. _____

8. Richard I, *named* (PLETCY) the Lion-Hearted, was a twelfth-century king of England. _____

9. I'll be there *soon* (NANO). _____

10. The guard around the palace was doubled at the monarch's *command* (SETHEB). _____

LATIN ENRICHMENT OF ANGLO-SAXON

Because English has incorporated so many Latin words into its vocabulary, it often has two (or more) words for an idea: one from Anglo-Saxon (for example, *brotherly*) and another from Latin (for example, *fraternal*). The two words, however, are seldom exactly synonymous.

To illustrate, both *brotherly* and *fraternal* have the general meaning "pertaining to brothers." Yet, *brotherly* conveys greater warmth of feeling than *fraternal,* which is less intimate and more formal. Thus, we speak of "brotherly love," but "fraternal organizations." This is merely one example of how Latin has enriched our English vocabulary, enabling us to express varying shades of meaning.

In the pages that follow, Anglo-Saxon words will be presented side by side with similar words derived from Latin.

1. ADJECTIVES

ADJECTIVE FROM ANGLO-SAXON

fatherly
pertaining to a father (warmer than *paternal*)

motherly
pertaining to a mother (more tender than *maternal*)

brotherly
pertaining to a brother (more affectionate than *fraternal*)

ADJECTIVE FROM LATIN

paternal pə-'tərn-əl
1. fatherly
2. inherited from or related to the father's side

maternal mə-'tərn-əl
1. motherly
2. inherited from or related to the mother's side

fraternal frə-'tərn-əl
1. brotherly
2. having to do with a *fraternal* society (a group organized to pursue a common goal in brotherly union)

daughterly
pertaining to a daughter (less formal than *filial*)

childlike
of or like a child in a good sense, as *childlike* innocence

childish
of or like a child in a bad sense, as *childish* mentality

manly
having the finer qualities of a man, as *manly* independence

devilish
like a devil; mischievous

bearish
1. like a bear; rough
2. tending to depress stock prices

bullish
1. like a bull; obstinate
2. tending to cause rises in stock prices

catlike
like a cat; stealthy

cowlike
resembling a cow
oxlike
resembling an ox

doggish
doglike

donkeyish
like a donkey

fishy
like a fish in smell or taste

foxy
foxlike; wily; sly

filial   'fil-ē-əl
of or relating to a daughter or son, as *filial* respect

infantile   'in-fən-ˌtīl
of or like a very young child; babyish

puerile   'pyủ(-ə)r-əl
foolish for a grown-up to say or do, as a *puerile* remark

masculine   'mas-kyə-lən
1. denoting the opposite gender of feminine
2. having the strength and vigor of a man

virile   'vir-əl
having the qualities of fully developed manhood (stronger word than *masculine*)

diabolic(al)   ˌdī-ə-'bäl-ik(-i-kəl)
very cruel; wicked; fiendish (stronger word than *devilish*)

ursine   'ər-ˌsīn
of or like a bear

taurine   'tȯr-ˌīn
1. of or like a bull
2. relating to Taurus (a sign of the zodiac)

feline   'fē-ˌlīn
of or pertaining to the cat family (cat, lion, tiger, leopard, etc.); sly; stealthy

bovine   'bō-ˌvīn
1. of or like the cow or ox
2. sluggish and patient, as a *bovine* disposition

canine   'kā-ˌnīn
1. of or pertaining to the dog family (dog, wolf, jackal, etc.)
2. designating one of the four pointed teeth next to the incisors

asinine   'as-ᵊn-ˌīn
like an ass or donkey (the most stupid beast of burden); stupid; silly

piscine   'pi-ˌsēn
of or like a fish

vulpine   'vəl-ˌpīn
of or like a fox; crafty; cunning

goatish
  goatlike; coarse

horsy
  having to do with horses or horse racing, as *horsy* talk

piggish
  hoggish, swinish

sheepish
  1. like a sheep in timidity or stupidity
  2. awkwardly bashful or embarrassed

wolfish
  characteristic of a wolf; ferocious

bloody
  smeared with blood; involving bloodshed

hircine   'hər-ˌsīn
  goatlike, especially in smell

equine   'ē-ˌkwīn
  of or like a horse

porcine   'pȯr-ˌsīn
  of or like a pig

ovine   'ō-ˌvīn
  of or like a sheep

lupine   'lü-ˌpīn
  of or like a wolf; ravenous

sanguine   'saŋ-gwən
  1. having a ruddy color, as a *sanguine* complexion
  2. confident, as *sanguine* of success

sanguinary   'saŋ-gwə-ˌner-ē
  bloody, as a *sanguinary* battle

EXERCISE 3. Write the *letter* of the word or words that best completes the analogy.

1. *Canine* is to *dog* as *feline* is to ------.
   (A) ox   (C) bull   (E) donkey
   (B) wolf   (D) tiger

2. *Fraternal* is to *brother* as *filial* is to ------.
   (A) son   (C) daughter   (E) daughter-in-law
   (B) son-in-law   (D) son or daughter

3. *Neigh* is to *equine* as *bleat* is to ------.
   (A) horsy   (C) sanguinary   (E) ovine
   (B) bashful   (D) zodiacal

4. *Mature* is to *puerile* as *intelligent* is to ------.
   (A) paternal   (C) cunning   (E) infantile
   (B) asinine   (D) porcine

5. *Courageous* is to *mettle* as *sanguine* is to ------.
   (A) success   (C) battle   (E) hope
   (B) despair   (D) complexion

6. *Bullish* is to *bearish* as *up* is to ------.
   (A) above   (C) down   (E) beyond
   (B) under   (D) over

7. *Fiendish* is to *diabolical* as *mischievous* is to ------.
   (A) spoiled   (C) ruddy   (E) clever
   (B) impish   (D) cherubic

8. *Cow* is to *bull* as *feminine* is to _____.

    (A) masculine   (C) bovine   (E) virile

    (B) ferocity   (D) manly

9. *Bear* is to *ursine* as *fox* is to _____.

    (A) vulpine   (C) lupine   (E) stealthy

    (B) taurine   (D) wily

10. *Hircine* is to *goat* as *piscine* is to _____.

    (A) leopard   (C) lion   (E) swine

    (B) speed   (D) fish

EXERCISE 4. Fill each blank with the most appropriate word selected from the vocabulary list below.

VOCABULARY LIST

sanguinary	canine	puerile
diabolical	bearish	feminine
lupine	filial	bullish
fraternal	vulpine	feline
sheepish	masculine	maternal

1. Joe's only response when confronted with his blunder was a(an) _____ (*awkwardly bashful*) grin.

2. The little boy followed on the heels of his older brother, his idol, with a kind of _____ (*pertaining to the dog family*) devotion.

3. Don't discuss the change with Will; he's a(an) _____ (*unyielding in opinion*) opponent of anything new.

4. The blackmailer had devised a(an) _____ (*fiendish*) scheme for extorting money from his victim.

5. Some parents do not know how to cope with _____ (*of a son or daughter*) disobedience.

6. Rarely have we witnessed such _____ (*foolish*) behavior from a mature person.

7. The _____ (*used to denote a female*) form of "confidant" is "confidante."

8. My _____ (*on my mother's side*) grandfather was a Senator.

9. At the close of THE CALL OF THE WILD, the dog Buck gradually lapses into _____ (*wolfish*) characteristics.

10. The fratricidal Battle of Gettysburg was one of the world's most _____ (*bloody*) conflicts.

2. VERBS

FROM ANGLO-SAXON	FROM LATIN			
beget	procreate	'prō-krē-ˌāt	generate	'jen-ə-ˌrāt
begin	originate	ə-'rij-ə-ˌnāt	initiate	in-'ish-ē-ˌāt
behead	decapitate	di-'kap-ə-ˌtāt		
bless	consecrate	'kän-sə-ˌkrāt		
bow, stoop	condescend	ˌkän-di-'send	prostrate	'präs-ˌtrāt
break	disintegrate	dis-'int-ə-ˌgrāt	invalidate	in-'val-ə-ˌdāt
chew	masticate	'mas-tə-ˌkāt		
curse	execrate	'ek-sə-ˌkrāt		
drink	imbibe	im-'bīb		
eat	devour	di-'vaủ(ə)r	consume	kən-'süm
flay, fleece, skin	excoriate	ek-'skȯr-ē-ˌāt		
free	emancipate	i-'man-sə-ˌpāt	liberate	'lib-ə-ˌrāt
frighten	intimidate	in-'tim-ə-ˌdāt		
lie	prevaricate	pri-'var-ə-ˌkāt		
sail	navigate	'nav-ə-ˌgāt		
shorten	abridge	ə-'brij	abbreviate	ə-'brē-vē-ˌāt
show	demonstrate	'dem-ən-ˌstrāt		
soothe	assuage	ə-'swāj	pacify	'pas-ə-ˌfī
spit	expectorate	ek-'spek-tə-ˌrāt		
steal	peculate	'pek-yə-ˌlāt		
strengthen	corroborate	kə-'räb-ə-ˌrāt	invigorate	in-'vig-ə-ˌrāt
sweat	perspire	pər-'spī-ə(r)		
take (for oneself)	appropriate	ə-'prō-prē-ˌāt		
think	cogitate	'käj-ə-ˌtāt	ratiocinate	ˌrat-ē-'ōs-ᵊn-ˌāt
twinkle, sparkle	scintillate	'sint-ᵊl-ˌāt		
understand	comprehend	ˌkäm-pri-'hend		
withstand	resist	ri-'zist	oppose	ə-'pōz
worship	venerate	'ven-ə-ˌrāt	revere	ri-'vi-ə(r)
yield	capitulate	kə-'pich-ə-ˌlāt	succumb	sə-'kəm

EXERCISE 5. Replace the italicized Anglo-Saxon word with a Latin derivative from the verb pairs just presented.

1. Tell the truth. Don't *lie.* _____

2. The young acrobat gave a *sparkling* performance. _____

3. Dad will *flay* you for taking the car without permission. _____

4. We cannot *understand* how you can be intimidated by such a small dog. _____

5. Don't gulp down your food; take the time to *chew* it. _____

6. At the end of the play, Macbeth is *beheaded* by Macduff. _____

7. *Spitting* in a public place is an offense punishable by a fine. _____

8. I am not afraid of you; you can't *frighten* me. _____

9. Sir Toby Belch's excessive *drinking* got him into trouble with his niece. _____

10. We shall evict those who have illegally *taken* our homes and our land. _____

EXERCISE 6. Write the *letter* of the word that means the SAME as or the OPPOSITE of the italicized word.

------ 1. *Resist* pressure
(A) withdraw   (C) reduce   (E) withhold
(B) withstand   (D) raise

------ 2. Ready to *capitulate*
(A) yield   (C) flatter   (E) worship
(B) behead   (D) delay

------ 3. *Generate* confusion
(A) conceal   (C) beget   (E) employ
(B) show   (D) strengthen

------ 4. Newly *emancipated*
(A) promoted   (C) disgraced   (E) fleeced
(B) honored   (D) enslaved

------ 5. Deep *ratiocination*
(A) slumber   (C) devotion   (E) fright
(B) thought   (D) understanding

------ 6. *Abridged* version
(A) unfinished   (C) disconnected   (E) expanded
(B) official   (D) unreliable

------ 7. Hurl *execrations*
(A) accusations   (C) insinuations   (E) criticisms
(B) challenges   (D) curses

------ 8. *Unassuaged* complainants
(A) uninformed   (C) noisy   (E) alarmed
(B) soothed   (D) unreasonable

------ 9. Beyond *comprehension*
(A) recovery   (C) understanding (E) recall
(B) arrest   (D) suspicion

------ 10. *Corroborated* report
(A) unconfirmed (C) untested   (E) unwritten
(B) abbreviated (D) misunderstood

3. NOUNS

FROM ANGLO-SAXON	FROM LATIN			
breach	**infraction**	in-'frak-shən	**rupture**	''rəp-chə(r)
burden	**obligation**	ˌäb-lə-'ḡā-shən		
fire	**conflagration**	ˌkän-flə-'grā-shən		
food	**nutriment**	'n(y)ü-trə-mənt		
greed	**avarice**	'av-(ə-)rəs		
heaven	**firmament**	'fər-mə-mənt		
home	**domicile**	'däm-ə-ˌsīl		
mirth	**hilarity**	hil-'ar-ət-ē		
name	**appellation**	ˌap-ə-'lā-shən		
oath	**affirmation**	ˌaf-ə(r)-'mā-shən	**malediction**	ˌmal-ə-'dik-shən
shame	**ignominy**	'ig-nə-ˌmin-ē		
shard	**fragment**	'frag-mənt		
smear	**vilification**	ˌvil-ə-fə-'kā-shən		
snake	**reptile**	'rep-tᵊl		
sorrow	**contrition**	kən-'trish-ən	**remorse**	ri-'mȯrs
speed	**velocity**	və-'läs-ət-ē	**celerity**	sə-'ler-ət-ē
strength	**impregnability**	im-ˌpreg-nə-'bil-ət-ē		
theft	**larceny**	'lärs-ə-nē		
thread	**filament**	'fil-ə-mənt		
threat	**menace**	'men-əs		
truth	**verity** (of things)	'ver-ət-ē		
truthfulness	**veracity** (of persons)	və-'ras-ət-ē		
wedding	**nuptials**	'nəp-shəlz		

EXERCISE 7. If the italicized word is *correctly* used in the sentence, write *C* in the space provided. If *incorrectly* used, write *X*.

_____ 1. The Rock of Gibraltar is often cited as a symbol of *impregnability*.

_____ 2. As a result of his numerous prevarications, our informant acquired a reputation for *veracity*.

_____ 3. The "Bard of Avon" is an *appellation* often applied to William Shakespeare.

_____ 4. As soon as he noticed that the securities were missing from the vault, the executive notified the police of the *larceny*.

_____ 5. Our debating team's brilliant victories have brought great *ignominy* to our school.

_____ 6. During his hunger strike the prisoner took water but no *nutriment*.

_____ 7. To be sound, a structure should be built upon a solid *firmament*.

_____ 8. The problem in the physics textbook had to do with the *velocity* of a missile in outer space.

_____ 9. All that remained of the shattered vase were some scattered *shards*.

_____ 10. When the sad news came, everyone was thrown into profound *hilarity*.

EXERCISE 8. Which of the two terms makes the sentence correct? Write the *letter* of the correct answer in the space provided.

1. It is a well-known _____ that the early bird catches the worm.

    (A) verity   (B) veracity

2. The guillotine was an instrument of _____.

    (A) capitulation   (B) decapitation

3. The four-year-old tried to carry the _____ crowbar to his father.

    (A) lissome   (B) cumbersome

4. Cats, leopards, and tigers belong to the _____ family.

    (A) feline   (B) canine

5. Dan's brawl with the visiting player was a serious _____ of the rules of sportsmanship.

    (A) fragment   (B) infraction

6. Shares of stock are relatively cheaper in a _____ market.

    (A) bullish   (B) bearish

7. If you do your daily assignments and review regularly, you should feel _____ of passing.

    (A) sanguinary   (B) sanguine

8. Do not interfere in matters that are not your concern, or you will be called _____.

    (A) meddlesome   (B) mettlesome

9. The hungry hiker _____ his sandwiches quickly.

    (A) consumed   (B) imbibed

10. The drowning woman was saved not by a full-grown man but by a _____ of 16.

    (A) yearling   (B) stripling

CHAPTER VII

FRENCH WORDS IN ENGLISH

English has never hesitated to adopt useful French words. Any French expression that describes an idea better than the corresponding English expression may sooner or later be incorporated into English. The process has been going on for centuries.

This chapter will teach you how to use some of the more important French words and expressions that are today part of an educated person's English vocabulary.

1. TERMS DESCRIBING PERSONS

WORD	MEANING	TYPICAL USE
au courant ˌō-ˌkü-ˈrä^n	well-informed; up-to-date	By reading reviews, you can keep *au courant* with new developments in literature, films, television, and the theater.
blasé blä-ˈzā	tired of pleasures; bored	Edna has been attending too many parties during the holidays; she appears *blasé*.
chic ˈshēk	stylish	She looked very *chic* in her new hat.
debonair ˌdeb-ə-ˈne(ə)r	affable and courteous; gay; pleasant	The headwaiter was *debonair* with the guests but firm with the waiters.
maladroit ˌmal-ə-ˈdrȯit (*ant.* **adroit**)	unskillful; clumsy	Our new supervisor is clever in matters in which his predecessor was *maladroit*.
naive nä-ˈēv	simple in nature; artless; ingenuous	You are *naive* if you believe implacable foes can be reconciled easily.
nonchalant ˌnän-shə-ˈlänt	without concern or enthusiasm; indifferent	I am amazed that you can be so *nonchalant* about the coming test when everyone else is so worried.

EXERCISE 1. In each blank insert the most appropriate expression from group 1.

1. Some advertising is so exaggerated that only a(an) ---------------------------- person would believe it.

2. If every meal were a banquet, we should all soon become ----------------------------, bored with even the most delicious food.

3. Read a good daily newspaper to keep ---------------------------- with what is going on in the world.

4. The cuts on the teenager's face showed that he was still ---------------------------- in the use of his razor.

5. Unlike his discourteous predecessor, the new service manager is quite ----------------------------.

2. TERMS FOR PERSONS

attaché
ˌat-ə-'shā

member of the diplomatic staff of an ambassador or minister

We were unable to see the ambassador, but we spoke to one of the *attachés*.

bourgeoisie
ˌbu̇rzh-wä-'zē

the middle class

A virile *bourgeoisie* contributes to a nation's prosperity.

chargé d'affaires
'shär-ˌzhäd-ə-'fe(ə)r

temporary substitute for an ambassador

Whom did the President designate as *chargé d'affaires* when he recalled the ambassador?

connoisseur
ˌkän-ə-'sər

expert; critical judge

To verify the gem's value, we consulted a *connoisseur* of rare diamonds.

coterie
'kōt-ə-rē

set or circle of acquaintances; clique

Helen won't bowl with us; she has her own *coterie* of bowling friends.

debutante
'deb-yu̇-ˌtänt

girl who has just made her *debut* (formal entrance into society)

The *debutante's* photograph was at the head of the society page.

devotee
ˌdev-ə-'tē

ardent adherent; partisan

Samuel Adams was a passionate *devotee* of American independence.

elite
ā-'lēt

group of superior individuals; aristocracy; choice part

Fred likes to consider himself a member of the intellectual *elite*.

émigré
ˌem-ə-'grā

refugee

A committee was formed to find housing and employment for the anxious *émigrés*.

entrepreneur
ˌän-trə-prə-'nər

one who assumes the risks and management of a business

What *entrepreneur* will invest his capital unless there is some prospect of a profit?

envoy
'en-ˌvȯi

1. diplomatic agent
2. messenger

The President's *envoy* to the conference has not yet been chosen.

fiancé, *m*.
ˌfē-än-'sä
(**fiancée**, *f*.)

person engaged to be married

Madeline introduced Mr. Cole as her *fiancé*.

gendarme
'zhän-ˌdärm

policeman with military training

The chargé d'affaires requested that extra *gendarmes* be posted outside the embassy.

ingénue
'an-jə-ˌnü

1. actress playing the role of a naive young woman
2. naive young woman

She was as simple and pretty as a film *ingénue*.

maître d'hôtel
ˌmā-trə-dō-'tel
(or **maître d'**)

headwaiter

The *maître d'hôtel* supervises the waiters.

martinet
ˌmärt-ᵊn-'et

person who enforces very strict discipline

Our dean is an understanding counselor, not a *martinet*.

nouveaux riches
ˌnü-vō-'rēsh

persons newly rich

An unexpected inheritance catapulted him into the ranks of the *nouveaux riches*.

protégé, *m.* ˈprōt-ə-ˌzhā (**protégée,** *f.*)	person under the care and protection of another	The veteran first baseman passed on numerous fielding hints to his young *protégé.*
raconteur ˌrak-än-ˈtər	person who excels in telling stories, anecdotes, etc.	Mark Twain was an excellent *raconteur.*

EXERCISE 2. In each blank insert the most appropriate expression from group 2.

1. Rita's engagement was nearly broken when she quarreled with her _____.

2. Between the nobles on one extreme and the peasants on the other, a middle class known as the _____ emerged.

3. Bill can relate an anecdote better than I; he is a fine _____.

4. Though the Allens are friendly to everyone, they have rarely visited with anyone outside their tightly knit _____.

5. Anyone who flees his native land to escape political oppression is a(an) _____

3. TERMS FOR TRAITS OR FEELINGS OF PERSONS

éclat ā-ˈklä	brilliancy of achievement	The violinist performed with rare *éclat.*
élan ā-ˈlänⁿ	enthusiasm; eagerness for action	Because the cast had rehearsed with such *élan,* the director had few apprehensions about the opening-night performance.
ennui än-ˈwē	feeling of weariness and discontent; boredom; tedium	You too would suffer from *ennui* if you had to spend months in a hospital bed.
esprit de corps es-ˌprēd-ə-ˈkȯ(ə)r	feeling of union and common interest pervading a group; devotion to a group or to its ideals	The employees showed extraordinary *esprit de corps* when they volunteered to work Saturdays for the duration of the crisis.
finesse fə-ˈnes	skill	The adroit prosecutor arranged his questions with admirable *finesse.*
legerdemain ˌlej-ərd-ə-ˈmān	sleight of hand; artful trick	By a feat of *legerdemain,* the magician produced a rabbit from his hat.
malaise ma-ˈlāz	vague feeling of bodily discomfort or illness	After the late, heavy supper, he experienced a feeling of *malaise.*
noblesse oblige nō-ˌbles-ə-ˈblēzh	principle that persons of high rank or birth are obliged to act nobly	In the olden days, kings and other nobles, observing the principle of *noblesse oblige,* fought at the head of their troops.
rapport ra-ˈpȯ(ə)r	relationship characterized by harmony, conformity, or affinity	A common interest in gardening brought Molly and Loretta into closer *rapport.*

sangfroid 'sän-'frwä	coolness of mind or composure in difficult circumstances; equanimity	The quarterback's *sangfroid* during the last tense moments of the game enabled him to call the winning play.
savoir faire ,sav-,wär-'fe(ə)r	knowledge of just what to do; tact	You need both capital and *savoir faire* to be a successful entrepreneur.

EXERCISE 3. In each blank insert the most appropriate expression from group 3.

1. Joel is tactful; he has plenty of _____.

2. Your physician may help you to obtain some relief from the _____ that accompanies a severe cold.

3. Instead of reducing his subordinates' salaries, the executive acted more nobly by cutting his own compensation substantially, in accordance with the principle of _____

4. To do card tricks, you have to be good at _____.

5. If you get tired and bored on long train trips, try reading detective stories; they help to overcome _____.

4. TERMS DEALING WITH CONVERSATION AND WRITING

adieu ə-'d(y)ü	good-by; farewell	On commencement day we shall bid *adieu* to our alma mater.
au revoir ,ór-əv-'wär	good-by till we meet again	Since I hope to see you again, I'll say *au revoir* rather than adieu.
billet-doux ,bil-ā-'dü	love letter	A timely *billet-doux* can patch up a lovers' quarrel.
bon mot bōⁿ-'mō	clever saying; witty remark	The jester Yorick often set the table a-roaring with a well-placed *bon mot*.
brochure brō-'shu̇(ə)r	pamphlet; treatise	This helpful *brochure* explains social security benefits.
canard kə-'närd	false rumor; absurd story; hoax	It took a public appearance by the monarch to silence the *canard* that he had been assassinated.
cliché klē-'shā	trite or worn-out expression	Two *clichés* that we can easily do without are: "first and foremost" and "last but not least."
entre nous ,än-trə-'nü	between us; confidentially	The juniors expect to win, but, *entre nous,* their chances are not too good.
mot juste mō-zhu̅e̅st	the exactly right word	To improve your writing, try to find the *mot juste* for each idea and avoid clichés.

précis 'prā-sē	brief summary	Include only the essential points when you write a *précis*.
repartee ˌrep-ər-'tē	skill of replying quickly, cleverly, and humorously; witty reply	James Boswell admired Samuel Johnson's power of *repartee*.
résumé 'rez-ə-ˌmā	summary	The instructor asked for a *résumé* of the last lesson.
riposte ri-'pōst	1. quick retort or repartee 2. in fencing, a quick return thrust after a parry	Surprised to see him eating the apple core, I asked, "Won't it affect you?" "Pleasurably," was his *riposte*.
tête-à-tête ˌtāt-ə-'tāt	private conversation between two persons	Before answering, the witness had a *tête-à-tête* with his attorney.

EXERCISE 4. In each blank insert the most appropriate expression from group 4.

1. There are valuable hints on safe driving in this sixteen-page ---------------------------.

2. The expression "old as the hills" should be avoided because it is a(an) ---------------------.

3. Investigation proved that the story was unfounded; it was just a(an) ---------------------.

4. The manager went out to the mound for a brief -------------------------- with his faltering pitcher.

5. Everyone supposes this diamond is genuine but, --------------------------, it's only an imitation.

5. TERMS DEALING WITH SITUATIONS

bête noire ˌbāt-nə-'wär	object or person dreaded; bugbear	She enjoyed all her subjects except mathematics, her *bête noire*.
carte blanche 'kärt-'bläⁿsh	full discretionary power; freedom to use one's own judgment	The employer gave his secretary *carte blanche* in managing the routine affairs of the office.
cause célèbre ˌkōz-sā-'lebrᵉ	famous case in law that arouses considerable interest; an incident or situation attracting much attention	The trial of John Peter Zenger, a *cause célèbre* in the eighteenth century, helped to establish freedom of the press in America.
cul-de-sac ˌkəl-di-'sak	blind alley	Painting proved to be a *cul-de-sac* for Philip Carey, as he had no real talent.
debacle di-'bäk-əl	collapse; overthrow; rout	The *debacle* at Waterloo signaled the end of Napoleon's power.
fait accompli ˌfā-ta-kōⁿ-'plē	thing accomplished and presumably irrevocable	Since Mother couldn't decide whether or not to buy the dress for me, I planned to buy it myself and present her with a *fait accompli*.
faux pas (')fō-'pä	misstep or blunder in conduct, manners, speech, etc.	However, it turned out to be a *faux pas*, as Mother made me return the dress.

impasse		
'im-,pas	1. deadlock; predicament affording no escape 2. impassable road	The foreman reported that the jury could deliberate no further, as they had reached an *impasse*.
liaison		
'lē-ə-,zän	1. bond; linking up 2. coordination of activities	By joining the alumni association, graduates can maintain their *liaison* with the school.
mélange		
mā-'läⁿzh	mixture; medley; potpourri	Our last amateur show was a *mélange* of dramatic skits, acrobatics, ballet, popular tunes, and classical music.
mirage		
mə-'räzh	optical illusion	The sheet of water we thought we saw on the road ahead turned out to be only a *mirage*.

EXERCISE 5. In each blank insert the most appropriate expression from group 5.

1. Your flippant remark to Mrs. Lee about her ailing son was a(an) _____.

2. The inhabitants of the remote Eskimo village had practically no _____ with the outside world.

3. Mr. Briggs never concerned himself with hiring or dismissing employees, having given his plant manager _____ in these matters.

4. Despite seventeen hours of continuous deliberations, the weary negotiators still faced a(an) _____ over wages.

5. My position turned out to be a(an) _____, as it offered no opportunity for advancement.

REVIEW

EXERCISE 6. In the space before each word or expression in column I, write the *letter* of its correct meaning in column II.

COLUMN I	COLUMN II
_____ 1. refugee	(A) devotee
_____ 2. till we meet again	(B) debacle
_____ 3. well-informed	(C) bête noire
_____ 4. partisan	(D) au courant
_____ 5. brief summary	(E) sangfroid
_____ 6. hoax	(F) billet-doux
_____ 7. bugbear	(G) émigré
_____ 8. rout	(H) précis
_____ 9. love letter	(I) au revoir
_____ 10. equanimity	(J) canard

EXERCISE 7. Which of the three terms makes the sentence correct? Write the *letter* of the correct answer in the space provided. (Hint: For a clue to the missing term, study the italicized expression.)

1. In serving the soup, the _____ (*clumsy*) waitress spilled some of it on the guest of honor.
   (A) chic   (B) maladroit   (C) debonair

2. Monotonous repetition usually brings on _____ (*boredom*).
   (A) ennui   (B) éclat   (C) savoir faire

3. I'll be glad to give my opinion, but you must realize I am no _____ (*expert*).
   (A) raconteur   (B) martinet   (C) connoisseur

4. A bibliophile is usually a _____ (*ardent adherent*) of good literature.
   (A) protégée   (B) devotee   (C) repartee

5. We made a right turn into the next street, but it proved to be a _____ (*blind alley*).
   (A) mélange   (B) cul-de-sac   (C) canard

6. The President was represented at the state funeral in Paris by a special _____ (*diplomatic agent*).
   (A) ingénue   (B) bourgeoisie   (C) envoy

7. We had a _____ (*private conversation*) over a couple of ice-cream sodas.
   (A) bête noire   (B) tête-à-tête   (C) mirage

8. Do not commit the _____ (*blunder*) of coming unprepared to lessons.
   (A) faux pas   (B) impasse   (C) riposte

9. Today, my English teacher called on me for a _____ (*summary*) of yesterday's lesson.
   (A) rapport   (B) résumé   (C) brochure

10. Though awkward in sports, she has remarkable _____ (*skill*) at the piano.
    (A) sangfroid   (B) élan   (C) finesse

EXERCISE 8. In each sentence fill in the missing letters of the incomplete word or expression. Each dash stands for one missing letter.

1. Albert introduced us to his f____ ___ ___ ___ ___ ___ several weeks before they were to be married.

2. Try to find the m__ __   ___ ___ ___ ___ ___ for your idea; if a word only approximates what you wish to say, reject it.

3. Don't spoil your writing with such a c__ ___ ___ ___ ___ ___ as "the fly in the ointment" or "dumb as an ox."

4. Mae watched impatiently for the mailman; she was expecting a b__ ___ ___ ___ ___ ___ ___ ___ from her fiancé.

5. He is the kind of painter who is always surrounded by a c__ ___ ___ ___ ___ ___ of admirers and imitators.

6. She was as nervous as a d__ ___ ___ ___ ___ ___ ___ ___ at a coming-out party.

7. A good p__ ___ ___ ___ ___ should contain fewer than a third of the number of words in the original.

8. Some employees regard the manager as a m__ ___ ___ ___ ___ ___ ___, but I have found him not too strict.

9. The prosecutor, it was charged, had made the trial into a c_ _ _ _ _ _ _ _ _ _ _ _ to further his political ambitions.

10. My mispronunciation of our guest's name was an embarrassing f_ _ _ _ _ _.

6. TERMS DEALING WITH HISTORY AND GOVERNMENT

WORD	MEANING	TYPICAL USE
coup d'état ˌküd-ə-ˈtä (or **coup**)	sudden, violent, or illegal overthrow of a government	Napoleon seized power by a *coup d'état*.
démarche dā-ˈmärsh	course of action, especially one involving a change of policy	Hitler's attack on Russia, shortly after his pact with Stalin, was a stunning *démarche*.
détente dā-ˈtänt	a relaxing, as of strained relations between nations	An effective world disarmament treaty should bring a *détente* in international tensions.
entente än-ˈtänt	understanding or agreement between governments	Canada and the United States have a long-standing *entente* on border problems.
laissez-faire ˌles-ˌā-ˈfe(ə)r	absence of government interference or regulation	Adam Smith believed a policy of *laissez-faire* toward business would benefit a nation.
lettre de cachet ˌle-trə-də-ˌka-ˈshā	sealed letter obtainable from the King of France (before the Revolution) ordering the imprisonment without trial of the person named in the letter	Dr. Manette was imprisoned through a *lettre de cachet*.
rapprochement ˌrap-ˌrōsh-ˈmä^n	1. establishment or state of cordial relations 2. a coming together	The gradual *rapprochement* between these two nations, long traditional enemies, cheered all Europeans.
régime rā-ˈzhēm	system of government or rule	The coup d'état brought to power a *régime* that restored civil liberties to the oppressed people.

EXERCISE 9. In each blank insert the most appropriate expression from group 6.

1. Do you favor strict regulation of business or a policy of _____?

2. The tyrannical dictator was eventually overthrown by a(an) _____, effected by a strong military group.

3. The newly elected officials will face many problems left by the outgoing _____.

4. Our Bill of Rights protects us from such tyrannical abuses as were made possible by a(an) _____, a document ordering the imprisonment of a person without a trial.

5. Hopes for world peace rose sharply with reports of a(an) _____ in the strained relations between the two rulers.

7. TERMS DEALING WITH THE ARTS

avant-garde
ˌäv-ˌän-ˈgärd

experimentalists or innovators in any art

Walt Whitman was no conservative; his daring innovations in poetry place him in the *avant-garde* of nineteenth-century writers.

bas-relief
ˌbä-ri-ˈlēf

carving or sculpture in which the figures project only slightly from the background

The ancient Greek Parthenon is famed for its beautiful sculpture in *bas-relief*.

baton
ba-ˈtän

stick with which a conductor beats time for an orchestra or band

A downbeat is the downward stroke of the conductor's *baton*, denoting the principally accented note of a measure.

chef d'oeuvre
shā-ˈdəvrᵉ

masterpiece in art, literature, etc.

Many connoisseurs regard HAMLET as Shakespeare's *chef d'oeuvre*.

denouement
ˌdā-nü-ˈmäⁿ

1. solution ("untying") of the plot in a play, story, or complex situation
2. outcome; end

In the *denouement* of GREAT EXPECTATIONS, we learn that Pip's secret benefactor is the runaway convict whom Pip had once helped.

encore
ˈän-ˌkȯ(ə)r

repetition of a performance (or the rendition of an additional selection) in response to the demand from an audience

In appreciation of the enthusiastic applause, the vocalist sang an *encore*.

genre
ˈzhän-rə

1. kind; sort; category
2. style of painting depicting scenes from everyday life

The literary *genre* to which Poe contributed most is the short story.

musicale
ˌmyü-zi-ˈkal

social gathering, with music as the featured entertainment

At last night's *musicale* in my cousin's house, we were entertained by a string quartet.

palette
ˈpal-ət

thin board (with a thumb hole at one end) on which an artist lays and mixes colors

After a few canvas strokes, the artist reapplies his brush to his *palette* for more paint.

repertoire
ˈrep-ə(r)-ˌtwär

list of plays, operas, roles, compositions, etc., that a company or performer is prepared to perform

The guitarist apologized for not being able to play the requested number, explaining that it was not in his *repertoire*.

vignette
vin-ˈyet

short verbal description; a literary sketch

James Joyce's DUBLINERS offers some unforgettable *vignettes* of life in Dublin at the turn of the century.

EXERCISE 10. In each blank insert the most appropriate expression from group 7.

1. After viewing the oil paintings, we turned our attention to another _____, water colors.

2. A novel with a suspenseful plot makes the reader impatient to get to the _____.

3. If audience reaction is favorable, Selma is prepared to play a(an) ------------------------.

4. Beethoven's NINTH SYMPHONY is regarded by many as his ------------------------.

5. By diligent study the young singer added several new numbers to his ------------------------.

8. TERMS DEALING WITH FOOD

à la carte ˌal-ə-'kärt (*ant.* **table d'hôte**)	according to the bill of fare; dish by dish, with a stated price for each dish	If you order an *à la carte* dinner, you select whatever you wish from the bill of fare, paying only for the dishes ordered.
apéritif ˌap-ˌer-ə-'tēf	alcoholic drink taken before a meal as an appetizer	Select a nonalcoholic appetizer, such as tomato juice, if you do not care for an *apéritif*.
bonbon 'bän-ˌbän	piece of candy	For St. Valentine's Day, Mother received a heart-shaped box of delicious *bonbons*.
cuisine kwi-'zēn	style of cooking or preparing food	Around the corner is a restaurant specializing in French *cuisine*.
demitasse 'dem-ē-ˌtas	small cup for, or of, black coffee	Aunt Dorothy always takes cream with her coffee; she is not fond of *demitasse*.
entrée 'än-trā	main dish at lunch or dinner	We had a choice of the following *entrées:* roast beef, fried chicken, or baked mackerel.
filet fi-'lā	slice of meat or fish without bones or fat	Because they contain no bones or excess fat, *filets* are more expensive than ordinary cuts of meat.
hors d'oeuvres ȯr-'dərvz	light food served as an appetizer before the regular courses of a meal	Mother will need olives, celery, and anchovies for her *hors d'oeuvres*.
pièce de résistance pē-ˌes-də-rə-ˌzē-'stäns	1. main dish 2. main item of any collection, series, program, etc.	If you eat too much of the introductory dishes, you will have little appetite for the *pièce de résistance*.
table d'hôte ˌtäb-əl-'dōt (*ant.* **à la carte**)	describing a complete meal that bears a fixed price	If you order a *table d'hôte* dinner, you pay the price fixed for the entire dinner, even if you do not have some of the dishes.

EXERCISE 11. In each blank insert the most appropriate expression from group 8.

1. Before dinner, our hostess brought in a large tray of appetizing ------------------------.

2. Though this chef's style of cooking is quite interesting, it cannot compare with Grandmother's

------------------------.

3. When I do not care to have a complete dinner, I order a few dishes ------------------------.

4. My little sister was so fond of candy that she had to be restricted to one _____ after each meal.

5. If you like flounder but are worried about accidentally swallowing a fishbone, try _____ of flounder.

9. TERMS DEALING WITH DRESS

bouffant bü-'fänt	puffed out; full	School corridors and stairways would have to be widened considerably if all girls were to wear *bouffant* skirts.
chemise shə-'mēz	loose-fitting, sacklike dress	Though more comfortable than most other dresses, the *chemise* has often been ridiculed for its shapelessness.
coiffure kwä-'fyủ(ə)r	style of arranging the hair; head-dress	Sally's attractive new *coiffure* was arranged for her by my sister's hair stylist.
corsage kȯr-'säzh	small bouquet worn by a woman	At the Christmas season, ladies often adorn their coats with a holly *corsage*.
cravat krə-'vat	necktie	My cousin sent me a light blue shirt and a navy blue *cravat*.
flamboyant flam-'bȯi-ənt	1. flamelike 2. very ornate; showy	To add a touch of bright color to her outfit, Jane wore a *flamboyant* scarf.
toupee tü-'pā	wig	The actor's baldness was cleverly concealed by a very natural-looking *toupee*.
vogue 'vōg	fashion; accepted style	Women's fashions change rapidly; what is in style today may be out of *vogue* tomorrow.

EXERCISE 12. In each blank insert the most appropriate expression from group 9.

1. The excessive heat made George untie his _____ and unbutton his shirt collar.

2. After trying several elaborate hair styles, Marie has returned to a simple _____.

3. On your visit to Mount Vernon in Virginia, you will be able to see the furniture styles that were in

_____ in George Washington's time.

4. It was easy to identify the guest of honor because of the beautiful _____ at her shoulder.

5. The gowns in the dress salon range from sedate blacks to _____ reds and golds.

avoirdupois
ˌav-ərd-ə-ˈpȯiz

weight; heaviness

Dieters constantly check their *avoirdupois*.

bagatelle
ˌbag-ə-ˈtel

trifle

Pay attention to important matters; don't waste time on *bagatelles*.

coup de grâce
ˌküd-ə-ˈgräs

merciful or decisive finishing stroke

Ma Baxter had merely wounded the yearling; poor Jody himself had to administer the *coup de grâce*.

façade
fə-ˈsäd

face or front of a building, or of anything

The patient's cheerful smile was just a *façade;* actually, she was suffering from ennui.

fête
ˈfāt

1. festival; entertainment; party
2. to honor with a fête

Retiring employees are often *fêted* at a special dinner.

foyer
ˈfȯi(-ə)r

entrance hall; lobby

Let's meet in the *foyer* of the Bijou Theater.

milieu
mēl-ˈyə

environment; setting

David found it much easier to make friends in his new *milieu*.

parasol
ˈpar-ə-ˌsȯl

umbrella for protection against the sun

In summer when you stroll on the boardwalk in the noonday sun, it is advisable to take along a *parasol*.

par excellence
ˌpär-ˌek-sə-ˈläⁿs

above all others of the same sort (follows the word it modifies)

Charles Dickens was a raconteur *par excellence*.

pince-nez
paⁿs-ˈnā

eyeglasses clipped to the nose by a spring

Since they are held in place by a spring that pinches the nose, *pince-nez* may not be as comfortable as ordinary eyeglasses.

raison d'être
ˌrā-ˌzōⁿ-ˈdetrᵊ

reason or justification for existing

Abe is very fond of golf; he feels it is his chief *raison d'être*.

rendezvous
ˈrän-di-ˌvü

1. meeting place fixed by prior agreement
2. appointment to meet at a fixed time and place

We agreed to meet after the test at the corner ice-cream parlor, our usual *rendezvous*.

silhouette
ˌsil-ə-ˈwet

1. shadow
2. outline

I knew that Dad was coming to let me in because I recognized his *silhouette* behind the curtained door.

sobriquet
ˈsō-bri-ˌkā
(or **soubriquet**)

nickname

Andrew Jackson was known by the *sobriquet* "Old Hickory."

souvenir
ˈsü-və-ˌni(ə)r

reminder; keepsake; memento

To most graduates the senior yearbook is a treasured *souvenir* of high school days.

tour de force ˌtu̇(ə)rd-ə-ˈfȯrs	feat of strength or skill; adroit accomplishment	George's sixty-yard touchdown run was an admirable *tour de force* that won the game for us.
vis-à-vis ˌvē-zə-ˈvē	1. face to face; opposite 2. when confronted or compared with	At the banquet table, I had the good fortune to sit *vis-à-vis* an old school chum.

EXERCISE 13. In each blank insert the most appropriate expression from group 10.

1. Father brought me a print of the Lincoln Memorial as a(an) _____ of his visit to Washington.

2. When Paula was dieting, she would mount the scale morning and night in order to check her

   _____.

3. After school, I meet my friends at our _____ across the street.

4. Agnes is a mimic _____; no one in our club can do impersonations as well as she.

5. Because of his flaming hair, Harvey is popularly known by the _____ "Red."

6. The few small merchants who have survived the intense competition are fearful that the opening of another supermarket will be the _____ for them.

7. Our club is planning a(an) _____ to honor the outgoing president.

8. The first day at high school places the newly arrived pupil in a bewildering _____.

9. I did not recognize the hotel because its _____ and foyer had been modernized since my last stay there.

10. Winning the league pennant is an outstanding baseball achievement, but going on to capture the World Series in four straight victories is an even greater _____.

REVIEW

EXERCISE 14. In the space before each word or expression in column I, write the *letter* of its correct meaning in column II.

COLUMN I	COLUMN II
_____ 1. piece of candy	(A) silhouette
_____ 2. nickname	(B) coup d'état
_____ 3. relaxing of strained relations	(C) bouffant
_____ 4. full; puffed out	(D) coup de grâce
_____ 5. style of cooking	(E) détente
_____ 6. masterpiece	(F) bonbon
_____ 7. shadow	(G) chef d'oeuvre
_____ 8. weight	(H) cuisine
_____ 9. decisive finishing stroke	(I) avoirdupois
_____ 10. sudden overthrow of a régime	(J) sobriquet

EXERCISE 15. Write the *letter* of the expression NOT RELATED in meaning to the other expressions in each group.

1. (A) face to face   (B) up to date   (C) compared with   (D) vis-à-vis   _____

2. (A) setting   (B) milieu   (C) surroundings   (D) mélange   _____

3. (A) pamphlet   (B) treatise   (C) brochure   (D) silhouette   _____

4. (A) category   (B) style   (C) rate   (D) genre   _____

5. (A) par excellence   (B) exploit   (C) tour de force   (D) achievement   _____

6. (A) binoculars   (B) spectacles   (C) pince-nez   (D) camera   _____

7. (A) engagement   (B) rendezvous   (C) adieu   (D) appointment   _____

8. (A) précis   (B) encore   (C) résumé   (D) summary   _____

9. (A) entente   (B) understanding   (C) rapprochement   (D) régime   _____

10. (A) apéritif   (B) debut   (C) hors d'oeuvres   (D) dénouement   _____

EXERCISE 16. In the space provided, write the *letter* of the word or expression that has most nearly the SAME MEANING as the italicized expression.

_____ 1. Prosperous *bourgeoisie*   (A) elite   (C) middle class   (E) officialdom
   (B) entrepreneur   (D) citizenry

_____ 2. *Flamboyant* jacket   (A) debonair   (C) sanguinary   (E) stylish
   (B) warm   (D) showy

_____ 3. Happy *denouement*   (A) ending   (C) milieu   (E) episode
   (B) vignette   (D) event

_____ 4. Sudden *démarche*   (A) détente   (C) entrée   (E) aggression
   (B) reversal   (D) discovery

_____ 5. Attitude of *laissez-faire*   (A) boredom   (C) eagerness   (E) noninterference
   (B) equanimity   (D) cordiality

_____ 6. Enduring *entente*   (A) influence   (C) bitterness   (E) entrance
   (B) understanding   (D) cause célèbre

_____ 7. Serve *hors d'oeuvres*   (A) à la carte   (C) desserts   (E) table d'hôte
   (B) appetizers   (D) pièce de résistance

_____ 8. Join the *avant-garde*   (A) gendarmes   (C) devotees   (E) innovators
   (B) protégés   (D) underground

_____ 9. Request an *encore*   (A) cancellation   (C) repetition   (E) improvement
   (B) delay   (D) refund

_____ 10. Flavor *par excellence*   (A) new   (C) spicy   (E) inferior
   (B) unsurpassed   (D) mild

EXERCISE 17. Fill each blank with the most appropriate word or expression selected from the vocabulary list below.

VOCABULARY LIST

coiffure	chargé d'affaires	régime
au courant	pièce de résistance	raison d'être
envoy	éclat	avant-garde
genre	bagatelle	nouveaux riches
laissez-faire	façade	souvenir

1. At one time or another, some hobby or interest becomes so important to us that it is practically our only _____ (*reason for existence*).

2. This piece of driftwood is a(an) _____ (*something that serves as a reminder*) of last summer's camping trip.

3. The reason you didn't finish the English test yesterday is that you spent too much time on a mere _____ (*unimportant, trifling matter*).

4. What _____ (*style of arranging the hair*) is most in vogue today?

5. The _____ (*persons who had newly become rich*) felt ill at ease in their new social milieu.

6. In her letters Susan kept me _____ (*up to date*) with events at home.

7. The _____ (*main number on the program*) of the musicale was a medley of Gilbert and Sullivan airs.

8. It is an unwise father who follows a policy of _____ (*absence of interference*) in bringing up his children.

9. The United States has encouraged nations everywhere to adopt a democratic _____ (*system of government or rule*).

10. The _____ (*ambassador's substitute*) has had years of experience in the diplomatic service.

EXERCISE 18. If the italicized expression is *correctly* used in the sentence, write *C* in the space provided. If *incorrectly* used, write the expression that should replace it.

1. One of the piano pieces I have recently added to my *repertoire* is "Autumn Leaves." _____

2. My guest declined the *hors d'oeuvres*, as he does not usually take an alcoholic drink before dinner. _____

3. Only his closest friends know that he wears a *sobriquet* to cover his bald spot. _____

4. Most of Washington's political elite attended the *tête-à-tête* celebrating the President's inauguration. _____

5. There is an excellent *vignette* on the small-town mind in Sinclair Lewis' ARROWSMITH. _____

6. Recalled by tumultuous applause, the violinist played an *encore* to the delight of the audience. _____

7. There was a hushed silence in the auditorium as the conductor raised his *palette*.

      ----

8. By means of a *pièce de résistance,* a Frenchman in the Old Régime could be imprisoned without knowing the charges against him and without being brought to trial.

      ----

9. On her jacket she wore a fragrant *mirage* sent by her fiancé on the occasion of her birthday.

      ----

10. On the way out of the theater we passed through the *filet,* where a line of ticket-holders was awaiting the next performance.

EXERCISE 19. Write the *letter* of the expression that best completes the analogy.

1. *Parasol* is to *sun* as *souvenir* is to _____.

    (A) remembering   (C) forgetting   (E) enjoying
    (B) hoping   (D) returning

2. *Régime* is to *revolutionists* as *custom* is to _____.

    (A) elite   (C) devotees   (E) conservatives
    (B) connoisseurs   (D) avant-garde

3. *Scene I* is to *climax* as *hors d'oeuvres* is to _____.

    (A) entrée   (C) bonbon   (E) bagatelle
    (B) cuisine   (D) chef d'oeuvre

4. *Demitasse* is to *coffee* as *drum* is to ____.

    (A) orchestra   (C) drummer   (E) sugar
    (B) conductor   (D) oil

5. *Bottle* is to *neck* as *hotel* is to _____.

    (A) façade   (C) foyer   (E) table d'hôte
    (B) cul-de-sac   (D) suburb

6. *Nourished* is to *food* as *au courant* is to _____.

    (A) exercise   (C) news   (E) rumor
    (B) drink   (D) rest

7. *Entrepreneur* is to *employee* as *maître d'hôtel* is to _____.

    (A) patron   (C) manager   (E) guest
    (B) employer   (D) waiter

8. *Bas-relief* is to *sculpture* as *genre* is to _____.

    (A) palette   (C) sculptor   (E) art
    (B) painter   (D) baton

9. *Ingénue* is to *theater* as *maître d'* is to _____.

    (A) hotel   (C) government   (E) diplomacy
    (B) conductor   (D) instruction

10. *Ice* is to *thaw* as *hostility* is to _____.

    (A) coup de grâce   (C) coup d'état   (E) denouement
    (B) détente   (D) tour de force

CHAPTER VIII

ITALIAN WORDS IN ENGLISH

The Italian impact on English, though not as great as the French, is nevertheless important. Italy's rich contributions to the arts have profoundly influenced our cultural life. In our language, this influence shows itself by the presence of useful Italian loanwords dealing mainly with music, painting, architecture, sculpture, and other arts.

1. WORDS FOR SINGING VOICES
(arranged in order of increasing pitch)

WORD		MEANING
basso	'bas-ō	lowest male voice; bass
baritone	'bar-ə-ˌtōn	male voice between bass and tenor
tenor	'ten-ə(r)	adult male voice between baritone and alto
alto	'al-tō	1. highest male voice 2. lowest female voice, the contralto
contralto	kən-'tral-tō	lowest female voice
mezzo-soprano	ˌmet-sō-sə-'pran-ō	female voice between contralto and soprano
soprano	sə-'pran-ō	highest singing voice in women and boys
coloratura	ˌkəl-ə-rə-'t(y)ùr-ə	1. ornamental passages (runs, trills, etc.) in vocal music 2. soprano who sings such passages, i.e., a *coloratura* soprano
falsetto	fȯl-'set-ō	1. unnaturally high-pitched male voice 2. artificial voice

EXERCISE 1. In each blank insert the most appropriate expression from group 1.

1. For her superb rendering of ornamental passages, the ------------------------ soprano was wildly acclaimed.

2. The lowest singing voice is *contralto* for women and ------------------ for men.

3. Yodeling is a form of singing that requires frequent changes from the natural voice to a(an) ----------------------.

4. Since Oscar's singing voice is between baritone and alto, he is classified as a(an) -----------

5. The highest singing voice is *soprano* for women and ------------------ for men.

2. WORDS FOR TEMPOS (RATES OF SPEED) OF MUSICAL COMPOSITIONS
(arranged in order of increasing speed)

grave	'gräv-ā	slow (the slowest tempo in music); serious
largo	'lär-gō	slow and dignified; stately
adagio	ə-'däj-ō	slow; in an easy, graceful manner
lento	'len-ˌtō	slow
andante	än-'dän-'tā	moderately slow, but flowing
moderato	ˌmäd-ə-'rät-ō	in moderate time

allegro	ə-'leg-rō	brisk; quick; lively
vivace	vē-'väch-ā	brisk; spirited
presto	'pres-tō	quick
prestissimo	pre-'stis-ə-ˌmō	at a very rapid pace

EXERCISE 2. In each blank insert the most appropriate expression from group 2.

1. A piece of music marked _____ moves more rapidly than one marked *presto*.

2. The slowest tempo in music, _____, is used in the opening measures of Beethoven's SONATE PATHÉTIQUE.

3. ANNIE LAURIE should be sung at a moderately slow but flowing pace, for its tempo is _____.

4. The _____ movement of Dvorak's NEW WORLD SYMPHONY is played in a slow and dignified manner.

5. The term _____ over the opening notes of SWEET GEORGIA BROWN indicates that this tune should be played neither rapidly nor slowly, but in moderate time.

3. WORDS FOR DYNAMICS (DEGREE OF LOUDNESS)

crescendo *ant.* **decrescendo**	kri-'shen-dō	gradually increasing (or a gradual increase) in force or loudness
decrescendo *syn.* **diminuendo** *ant.* **crescendo**	ˌdā-krə-'shen-dō	gradually decreasing (or a gradual decrease) in force or loudness
dolce	'dōl-chā	soft; sweet
forte *ant.* **piano**	'for-ˌtā	loud
fortissimo *ant.* **pianissimo**	for-'tis-ə-ˌmō	very loud
pianissimo *ant.* **fortissimo**	ˌpē-ə-'nis-ə-ˌmō	very soft
piano *ant.* **forte**	pē-'än-ō	soft
sforzando	sfort-'sän-dō	accented

EXERCISE 3. In each blank insert the most appropriate expression from group 3.

1. The word _____ designates a familiar musical instrument, as well as a musical direction meaning "soft."

2. Ravel's BOLERO rises to a dramatic climax by a gradual increase in loudness; few pieces have such an electrifying _____.

3. When a composer wants a chord played with a strong accent, he uses the term _____.

4. Mendelssohn's SCHERZO has a _____ ending; it has to be played very softly.

5. A degree of loudness higher than *forte* is _____.

4. WORDS FOR MUSICAL EFFECTS

a cappella	‚äk-ə-'pel-ə	without musical accompaniment, as an *a cappella* choir
arpeggio	är-'pej-ō	1. production of the tones of a chord in rapid succession and not simultaneously 2. a chord thus played
legato	li-'gät-ō	smooth and connected
pizzicato	‚pit-si-'kät-ō	direction to players of bowed instruments to pluck the strings instead of using the bow
staccato	stə-'kät-ō	disconnected; abrupt; with breaks between successive notes
tremolo	'trem-ə-‚lō	rapid ("trembling") repetition of a tone or chord, without apparent breaks, to express emotion
vibrato	vē-'brät-ō	slightly throbbing or pulsating effect, adding warmth and beauty to the tone

EXERCISE 4. In each blank insert the most appropriate expression from group 4.

1. By plucking the strings with his fingers, a violinist achieves a(an) _____ effect.

2. In Tchaikovsky's 1812 OVERTURE, the rapid and prolonged repetition of two tones produces a "trembling," emotion-stirring effect known as _____.

3. Some beginning piano students strike all the correct notes but fail to achieve a smooth and connected effect because they do not play them _____.

4. It is surely much easier to play the tones of a chord simultaneously than to play them as a(an) _____.

5. In Schubert's AVE MARIA, the notes are smoothly connected, but in his MARCHE MILITAIRE they are mainly _____.

5. WORDS DEALING WITH MUSICAL COMPOSITIONS

aria	'är-ē-ə	air, melody, or tune; especially, an elaborate, accompanied melody for a single voice in an opera
bravura	brə-'v(y)ur-ə	1. piece of music requiring skill and spirit in the performer 2. display of daring or brilliancy
cantata	kən-'tät-ə	story or play set to music to be sung by a chorus, but not acted
concerto	kən-'chert-ō	long musical composition for one or more principal instruments
duet	d(y)ü-'et	1. piece of music for two voices or instruments 2. two singers or players performing together
finale	fə-'nal-ē	close or termination, as the last section of a musical composition
intermezzo	‚int-ər-'met-sō	1. short musical or dramatic entertainment between the acts of a play 2. short musical composition between the main divisions of an extended musical work 3. a short, independent musical composition

libretto	lə-'bret-ō	text or words of an opera or other long musical composition
opera	'äp-(ə-)rə	play mostly sung, with costumes, scenery, action, and music
oratorio	ˌȯr-ə-'tȯr-ē-ˌō	musical composition, usually on a religious theme, for solo voices, chorus, and orchestra
scherzo	'skert-sō	light or playful part of a sonata or symphony
solo	'sō-lō	1. piece of music for one voice or instrument 2. anything done without a partner
sonata	sə-'nät-ə	piece of music (for one or two instruments) having three or four movements in contrasted rhythms but related tonality
trio	'trē-ō	1. piece of music for three voices or instruments 2. three singers or players performing together

EXERCISE 5. In each blank insert the most appropriate expression from group 5.

1. To perform in a(an) _____, one must be gifted both as a singer and as an actor.

2. Roberta refuses to do a solo, but she is willing to join with another in a(an) _____.

3. From the opening selection to the _____, we enjoyed the concert thoroughly

4. Though there is orchestral accompaniment in a piano _____, the pianist is the principal performer.

5. The selection you played is unfamiliar to me, but its light and playful character leads me to believe that it's a(an) _____.

6. WORDS DEALING WITH ARTS OTHER THAN MUSIC

cameo *ant.* intaglio	'kam-ē-ˌō	stone or shell on which a figure, cut in relief, appears against a background of a different color
campanile	ˌkam-pə-'nē-lē	bell tower
canto	'kan-ˌtō	one of the chief divisions of a long poem; a book
chiaroscuro	kē-ˌär-ə-'sk(y)u̇(ə)r-ō	1. style of pictorial art using only light and shade 2. sketch in black and white
cupola	'kyü-pə-lə	1. rounded roof; dome 2. small dome or tower on a roof
fresco	'fres-ˌkō	1. art of painting with water colors on damp, fresh plaster 2. picture or design so painted
intaglio *ant.* cameo	in-'tal-yō	design engraved by making cuts in a surface
majolica	mə-'jäl-i-kə	enameled Italian pottery richly decorated in colors
mezzanine	'mez-ᵊn-ˌēn	intermediate story in a theater between the main floor and the first balcony
mezzotint	'met-sō-ˌtint	picture engraved on copper or steel by polishing or scraping away parts of a roughened surface
patina	'pat-ə-nə	film or incrustation, usually green, on the surface of old bronze or copper

portico	'pōrt-i-ˌkō	roof supported by columns, forming a porch or a covered walk
rotunda	rō-'tən-də	1. round building, especially one with a dome or cupola
		2. large round room, as the *rotunda* of the Capitol
stucco	'stək-ō	plaster for covering exterior walls of buildings
tempera	'tem-pə-rə	method of painting in which the colors are mixed with white of egg or other substances, instead of oil
terra cotta	'ter-ə-'kät-ə	1. kind of hard, brownish-red earthenware, used for vases, statuettes, etc.
		2. dull brownish-red
torso	'tȯr-sō	1. trunk or body of a statue without a head, arms, or legs
		2. human trunk

EXERCISE 6. In each blank insert the most appropriate expression from group 6.

1. Because it is a large round room, the _____ of the Capitol in Washington, D.C., is ideal for an impressive ceremony.

2. The _____ my aunt wears has a carved ivory head raised on a light brown background.

3. A(an) _____ actually becomes a part of the wall on whose damp, fresh plaster surface it is painted.

4. The head of the statue was discovered not far from the place where its _____ had been found.

5. An antique increases in artistic value when its surface becomes incrusted with a fine natural

   _____.

6. The white of egg, or a similar substance, is used for mixing colors in _____ painting.

7. Read the fifth _____ of Scott's MARMION for a stirring description of young Lochinvar's elopement with fair Ellen.

8. The _____ applied to exterior walls of buildings is a mixture of portland cement, sand, and lime.

9. In the morning we heard the sound of bells coming from the _____, a tall structure right next to the church.

10. The main building and the annex are connected by a(an) _____ that facilitates traffic between the two buildings, especially in bad weather.

7. WORDS DEALING WITH PERSONS

cognoscente	ˌkän-yō-'shent-ē	connoisseur
dilettante	ˌdil-ə-'tänt(-ē)	person who follows some art or science as an amusement or in a trifling way
maestro	mä-'e-strō	1. eminent conductor, composer, or teacher of music
		2. master in any art
virtuoso	ˌvər-chə-'wō-sō	one who exhibits great technical skill in an art, especially in playing a musical instrument

8. WORDS FOR SITUATIONS INVOLVING PERSONS

dolce far niente	'dōl-chē-,fär-nē-'ent-ē	delightful idleness
fiasco	fē-'as-kō	crash; complete or ridiculous failure
imbroglio	im-'brōl-yō	1. difficult situation 2. complicated disagreement
incognito	,in-,käg-'nēt-ō	1. with one's identity concealed 2. disguised state
vendetta	ven-'det-ə	feud for blood revenge

9. WORDS DEALING WITH FOOD

antipasto	,ant-i-'pas-tō	appetizer consisting of fish, meats, etc.; hors d'oeuvres
Chianti	kē-'änt-ē	a dry, red Italian wine
gusto	'gəs-,tō	liking or taste; hearty enjoyment
pizza	'pēt-sə	large flat pie of bread dough spread with tomato pulp, cheese, meat, anchovies, etc.

10. MISCELLANEOUS COMMON WORDS

gondola	'gän-də-lə	1. boat used in the canals of Venice 2. cabin attached to the under part of an airship
grotto	'grät-ō	cave
piazza	pē-'az-ə	1. open square in an Italian town 2. veranda or porch
portfolio	pȯrt-'fō-lē-,ō	1. briefcase 2. position or duties of a cabinet member or minister of state
salvo	'sal-vō	1. simultaneous discharge of shots 2. burst of cheers, as a *salvo* of applause
sotto voce	,sät-ō-'vō-chē	under the breath; in an undertone; privately, as a *sotto voce* remark

EXERCISE 7. In each blank insert the most appropriate expression from groups 7-10.

1. My old briefcase can hold more books and papers than this new _____.

2. The host filled his guests' wineglasses from a freshly opened bottle of _____

3. The complicated disagreement about this year's budget is similar to the _____ we had about last year's budget.

4. Philip's cold prevented him from eating his dinner with his usual _____.

5. The versatile young musician has won fame not only as a conductor and composer, but also as a(an) _____ at the piano.

6. Because of the ridiculous failure of last year's amateur show, we are determined that this year's performance will not likewise become a(an) _____.

7. All eyes were riveted on the _____ as he raised his baton to begin the concert.

8. I did not hear what the proprietor said to the salesman, for they conferred _____.

9. The tourist relies on the taxicab in New York City and on the _____ in Venice.

10. While in prison, Edmond Dantès learned of an immense fortune concealed in an underground _____ on the island of Monte Cristo.

REVIEW

EXERCISE 8. Write the *letter* of the word or expression that means the SAME as or the OPPOSITE of the italicized word.

_____ 1. *canto*   (A) pace   (C) solo   (E) cantata
                       (B) lore   (D) division

_____ 2. *piano*   (A) crescendo   (C) legato   (E) alto
                       (B) forte   (D) decrescendo

_____ 3. *grotto*   (A) cave   (C) crash   (E) veranda
                       (B) terra cotta   (D) trunk

_____ 4. *cameo*   (A) patina   (C) intaglio   (E) bagatelle
                       (B) tempera   (D) campanile

_____ 5. *imbroglio* (A) disagreeable (C) pianissimo   (E) agreement
                       (B) fiasco   (D) diminuendo

_____ 6. *sforzando* (A) unstressed   (C) brisk   (E) slow
                       (B) dignified   (D) sweet

_____ 7. *torso*   (A) armless   (C) trunk   (E) legless
                       (B) statue   (D) largo

_____ 8. *antipasto* (A) Chianti   (C) piazza   (E) apéritif
                       (B) hors d'oeuvres (D) gusto

_____ 9. *crescendo* (A) salvo   (C) applause   (E) soprano
                       (B) pizzicato   (D) diminuendo

_____ 10. *piazza*   (A) pizza   (C) town   (E) column
                       (B) square   (D) rotunda

EXERCISE 9. Which of the two terms makes the sentence correct? Write the *letter* of the correct answer in the space provided.

1. A(an) _____ choir performs without accompaniment.

    (A) a cappella   (B) cantata

2. A _____ is a musical composition requiring an entire orchestra, but featuring a solo instrument such as the piano or violin.

    (A) sonata   (B) concerto

3. When Ulysses returned _____ to his palace, he was recognized by his dog Argus.

    (A) incognito   (B) falsetto

4. The anchored fleet welcomed the chief of state with a thunderous _____.

      (A) salvo   (B) staccato

5. An impression made from an _____ results in an image in relief.

      (A) imbroglio   (B) intaglio

6. The overworked executive longed for the _____ of a Caribbean cruise.

      (A) sotto voce   (B) dolce far niente

7. With the orchestra and balcony seats completely sold out, only a few _____ tickets are available.

      (A) mezzanine   (B) mezzotint

8. To achieve a smooth and flowing effect, my teacher advised me to play the first two measures _____.

      (A) tremolo   (B) legato

9. For an example of a crescendo from pianissimo all the way to _____, listen to Grieg's IN THE HALL OF THE MOUNTAIN KING.

      (A) prestissimo   (B) fortissimo

10. A _____ sketch achieves its effects solely by shadings between black and white.

      (A) chiaroscuro   (B) terra cotta

EXERCISE 10. In the space provided, write the word of Italian origin that is equivalent to the italicized expression. The letters of each word appear in scrambled form in the parentheses.

1. While the spaghetti was boiling, our hostess served a delicious *appetizer* (SOPATTIAN) attractively arranged on a large platter. _____

2. The article stated that the *cave* (TOGORT) had once been used as a hiding place for stolen treasure. _____

3. Have you heard of the *feud* (DEENVATT) between the Hatfields and the McCoys? _____

4. Over the years a(an) *green film* (TAPANI) had formed on the surface of the copper vessel. _____

5. Responding to the *gradual increase in volume* (CODSCREEN) of applause, the violinist returned for an encore. _____

6. After having cried his fill, the child continued to punctuate the silence with occasional *disconnected* (CATOSCAT) sobs. _____

7. The ill-matched challenger's bid to dethrone the heavyweight champion ended in a(an) *ridiculous failure* (ISCOFA) in the opening seconds of the first round. _____

8. In their reports on the pianist's performance, most of the critics lauded his finesse and *display of brilliancy* (RARAVUB). _____

9. My uncle paints as a(an) *trifler* (NILETATTED), not as a serious artist. _____

10. Verdi composed the music for the opera AÏDA, and Ghislanzoni wrote the *words* (RITTOBEL). _____

EXERCISE 11. Write the *letter* of the word-pair that best expresses a relationship similar to that existing between the capitalized word-pair.

------ 1. DESSERT: ANTIPASTO

    (A) grave: prestissimo   (D) play: denouement
    (B) basso: soprano   (E) finale: overture
    (C) entrée: hors d'oeuvres

------ 2. STAR: FILM

    (A) composer: sonata   (D) drama: protagonist
    (B) soloist: concerto   (E) actress: cast
    (C) aria: vocalist

------ 3. COGNOSCENTE: DILETTANTE

    (A) uncle: aunt   (D) ignoramus: connoisseur
    (B) professional: amateur   (E) artist: patron
    (C) odor: aroma

------ 4. INCOGNITO: IDENTITY

    (A) novel: pen name   (D) fiction: real
    (B) masquerade: disguise   (E) anonymous: known
    (C) pseudonym: authorship

------ 5. TORSO: STATUE

    (A) trunk: tree   (D) atom: nucleus
    (B) dismember: intact   (E) violinist: orchestra
    (C) shard: vase

------ 6. PATINA: TIME

    (A) white: hair   (D) mellowing: cheese
    (B) aging: wine   (E) incrustation: dirty
    (C) burn: acid

------ 7. LENTO: TEMPO

    (A) gondola: canal   (D) piano: volume
    (B) papers: portfolio   (E) allegro: loudness
    (C) Chianti: meal

------ 8. ROTUNDA: CUPOLA

    (A) bottom: top   (D) room: building
    (B) dome: tower   (E) base: mountain
    (C) edifice: dome

------ 9. CANTO: LONG POEM

    (A) volume: encyclopedia   (D) pianist: concerto
    (B) sergeant: commander-in-chief   (E) incident: full-length play
    (C) music: poetry

------ 10. CHORD: ARPEGGIO

    (A) salvo: performer   (D) unit: series
    (B) simultaneously: successively   (E) presto: tempo
    (C) chorus: conductor

CHAPTER IX

SPANISH WORDS IN ENGLISH

It should not surprise you that English has adopted many Spanish words. For centuries Spain administered huge areas of this nation, including Florida and the vast Southwest. Despite Spain's diminished prestige, Spanish today is spoken in virtually all of Central and South America, the West Indies, the Philippines, and numerous other regions. As one of the world's principal languages, Spanish continues to exert its influence on English.

1. WORDS FOR PERSONS

WORD		MEANING
aficionado	ə-ˌfis-ē-ə-ˈnäd-ō	1. person very enthusiastic about anything 2. sports devotee
caballero	ˌkab-ə-ˈler-ō	1. gentleman or gallant 2. horseman
conquistador	kȯŋ-ˈkēs-tə-ˌdȯ(r)	conqueror
desperado	ˌdes-pə-ˈräd-ō	bold, reckless criminal
duenna	d(y)ü-ˈen-ə	elderly woman chaperon of a young lady; governess
gaucho	ˈgau̇-chō	Argentine cowboy of mixed Spanish and Indian descent
grandee	gran-ˈdē	1. nobleman of the highest rank 2. person of eminence
hidalgo	hid-ˈal-gō	nobleman of the second class (not so high as a *grandee*)
junta	ˈhu̇n-tə	1. council for legislation or administration 2. junto
junto	ˈjənt-ō	1. political faction 2. group of plotters; clique
matador	ˈmat-ə-ˌdȯ(r)	bullfighter assigned to kill the bull
mestizo	me-ˈstē-zō	person of mixed (usually Spanish and American Indian) blood
peon	ˈpē-ˌän	1. common laborer 2. worker kept in service to repay a debt
picador	ˈpik-ə-ˌdȯ(r)	horseman who irritates the bull with a lance
picaro	ˈpē-kä-ˌrō	1. rogue; knave 2. vagabond (A *picaresque* novel is one that has a *picaro*, a rogue or vagabond, as the hero.)
renegade	ˈren-i-ˌgād	1. apostate (deserter) from a religion, party, etc. 2. turncoat; traitor
señor	sān-ˈyȯ(r)	gentleman; Mr. or Sir
señora	sān-ˈyōr-ə	lady; Mrs. or Madam
señorita	ˌsān-yə-ˈrēt-ə	young lady; Miss
toreador	ˈtȯr-ē-ə-ˌdȯ(r)	bullfighter, usually mounted
torero	tə-ˈrer-ō	bullfighter on foot
vaquero	vä-ˈker-ō	herdsman; cowboy

EXERCISE 1. In each blank insert the most appropriate word from group 1.

1. The onetime Democrat who joined the Republican Party was regarded as a(an) _____ by some of his former Democratic colleagues.

2. In the Old West, it was common for a stagecoach to be robbed by a(an) _____.

3. A(an) _____ is a nobleman of higher rank than a hidalgo.

4. Without an education or a skilled trade, you may earn little more than the wages of a(an)

   _____.

5. The average fan attends two or three games a season, but the _____ goes to many more.

6. Columbus was not a(an) _____; he engineered no military conquests, as did Cortez in Mexico and Pizarro in Peru.

7. The _____ was chaperoned by her duenna.

8. The ruler ordered the arrest of all members of the _____ involved in the plot against his régime.

9. Before slaying the bull, the _____ thrills the spectators by gracefully evading its charges.

10. The Spanish expressions for "Mr." and "Mrs." are _____ and _____.

2. WORDS FOR STRUCTURES, CLOTHING, ETC.

adobe	ə-'dō-bē	1. brick of sun-dried clay or mud 2. structure made of such bricks
bolero	bə-'ler-ō	1. lively dance in ¾ time 2. the music for this dance 3. short, loose jacket
bonanza	bə-'nan-zə	accidental discovery of a rich mass of ore in a mine
bravado	brə-'väd-ō	1. boastful behavior 2. pretense of bravery
cabana	kə-'ban-(y)ə	beach shelter resembling a cabin
castanets	ˌkas-tə-'nets	hand instruments clicked together to accompany music or dancing
fiesta	fē-'es-tə	religious holiday; any festival or holiday
flotilla	flō-'til-ə	small fleet; fleet of small vessels
hacienda	ˌ(h)äs-ē-'en-də	1. large ranch 2. landed estate 3. country house
incommunicado	ˌin-kə-ˌmyü-nə-'käd-ō	deprived of communication with others
mantilla	man-'tē-(y)ə	1. woman's light scarf or veil 2. cloak or cape
olio	'ō-lē-ˌō	mixture; hodgepodge; medley
peccadillo	ˌpek-ə-'dil-ō	slight offense
poncho	'pän-chō	large cloth, often waterproof, with a slit for the head

pueblo	pü-'eb-lō	Indian village built of adobe and stone
siesta	sē-'es-tə	short rest, especially at midday
tortilla	tȯr-'tē-(y)ə	thin, flat, round corn cake

EXERCISE 2. In each blank insert the most appropriate word from group 2.

1. Have you ever seen graceful Spanish dancers do the bolero to the accompaniment of clicking _____?

2. For every prospector who struck a(an) _____, there were countless others whose finds were disappointing.

3. Cheating on an examination is no _____, but a serious infraction of ethics.

4. You may be surprised to learn that a house made of _____ can last for more than a hundred years.

5. The ruffian's defiant challenge turned out to be mere _____, for when I offered to fight him he backed down.

6. Our Latin American neighbors celebrate a(an) _____ by wearing brightly colored costumes and by singing and dancing.

7. By midafternoon, the whole _____ of fishing vessels had returned to port with the day's catch.

8. A gaucho often carries a(an) _____, which he uses as a blanket or wears as a cape.

9. When the afternoon heat is most intense, Carlos takes a short _____ before resuming his work.

10. Mexicans are very fond of the _____, a thin, flat, round cake made of corn.

3. WORDS FOR PLACES, ANIMALS, ETC.

arroyo	ə-'rȯi-ō	watercourse; small, often dry, gully
bronco (or broncho)	'bräŋ-kō	half-wild pony
burro	'bər-ō	small donkey used as a pack animal
canyon	'kan-yən	deep valley with high, steep slopes, often with a stream flowing through it; as the Colorado River in the Grand *Canyon*
indigo	'in-di-ˌgō	1. plant yielding a blue dye 2. deep violet blue
mañana	mən-'yän-ə	tomorrow
mesa	'mā-sə	flat-topped rocky hill with steeply sloping sides
mustang	'məs-ˌtaŋ	bronco
pampas	'pam-pəz	vast, treeless, grassy plains, especially in Argentina
sierra	sē-'er-ə	ridge of mountains with an irregular, serrated (saw-toothed) outline

EXERCISE 3. In each blank insert the most appropriate word from group 3.

1. A Hopi Indian village was secure against enemy attacks because it was built on top of a steeply sloping, flat-topped _____.

2. The blue dye formerly obtained from the _____ plant can now be made artificially.

3. Do today's work today; don't postpone it to _____.

4. In desert areas of Mexico and our own Southwest, the _____ is used for carrying heavy loads.

5. The _____ in Argentina are famous for their cattle, corn, and wheat.

REVIEW

EXERCISE 4. In the space provided, write the *letter* of the word or expression that means the SAME as or the OPPOSITE of the numbered word at the left.

_____ **1.** duenna (A) duet (C) chaperon (E) fiancé
                      (B) biennial (D) twosome

_____ **2.** indigo (A) needy (C) clay (E) blue
                      (B) sugar (D) native

_____ **3.** peccadillo (A) erroneous (C) alligator (E) serious offense
                          (B) groundhog (D) petty officer

_____ **4.** olio (A) grease (C) fuel (E) confusing
                    (B) mixture (D) page

_____ **5.** grandee (A) peon (C) niece (E) canyon
                       (B) river (D) dam

_____ **6.** aficionado (A) zeal (C) enthusiast (E) fictional hero
                          (B) connoisseur (D) trifler

_____ **7.** conquistadors (A) discoverers (C) explorers (E) unvanquished
                             (B) conquests (D) conquerors

_____ **8.** renegade (A) infidel (C) rogue (E) turncoat
                        (B) desperado (D) villain

_____ **9.** arroyo (A) dart (C) mesa (E) bronco
                      (B) gully (D) waterfall

_____ **10.** siesta (A) holiday (C) fiesta (E) awakened
                       (B) sojourn (D) vigil

EXERCISE 5. Write the *letter* of the word (or set of words) which, if inserted in the sentence, would agree most closely with the thought of the sentence.

1. The _____ has become an institution in climates where the oppressive midday sun makes activity difficult.

   (A) fiesta (C) bourgeoisie (E) bolero
   (B) vendetta (D) siesta

2. To maintain anonymity, the leader of the junto employed a _____.

    (A) lackey   (C) pseudonym   (E) peon
    (B) grandee   (D) mantilla

3. _____ are Argentine cowboys who inhabit the _____.

    (A) Gauchos . . . . . pampas   (D) Vaqueros . . . . . pueblos
    (B) Caballeros . . . . . mesas   (E) Picaros . . . . . adobes
    (C) Desperadoes . . . . . sierras

4. A famous painting by Murillo depicts a smiling señorita looking down from a window with her mantilla-clad _____ by her side.

    (A) protégée   (C) duenna   (E) fiancé
    (B) aficionado   (D) grandee

5. Benedict Arnold was the _____ American Revolutionary general whose plot to surrender West Point resulted in a _____.

    (A) patriotic . . . . . vendetta   (D) turncoat . . . . . fiasco
    (B) renegade . . . . . coup d'état (E) apostate . . . . . détente
    (C) brilliant . . . . . junto

EXERCISE 6. Write the *letter* of the word-pair that best expresses a relationship similar to that existing between the capitalized word-pair.

_____ **1.** MATADOR : PICADOR

    (A) bravado : courage   (D) preface : conclusion
    (B) coup de grâce : initial blow (E) toreador : torero
    (C) overture : finale

_____ **2.** BONANZA : MINER

    (A) legacy : heir   (D) jackpot : gambler
    (B) crop : farmer   (E) bull's-eye : marksman
    (C) diploma : student

_____ **3.** ADOBE : PUEBLO

    (A) settlement : Indian   (D) seaport : flotilla
    (B) cabana : beach   (E) concrete : turnpike
    (C) terra cotta : clay

_____ **4.** OLIO : INGREDIENT

    (A) concerto : instrument   (D) entrée : dessert
    (B) medley : air   (E) aria : opera
    (C) potpourri : confusion

_____ **5.** SIERRA : CANYON

    (A) soprano : bass   (D) grandee : hidalgo
    (B) arroyo : mesa   (E) monarch : retinue
    (C) indigo : red

CHAPTER X

EXPANDING VOCABULARY THROUGH DERIVATIVES

Suppose you have just learned a new word—*ostentatious,* meaning "showy; done to impress others." If you know how to form derivatives, you have in reality learned not one new word, but several: you have learned *ostentatious* and *unostentatious; ostentatiously* and *unostentatiously; ostentatiousness* and *unostentatiousness,* etc.

This chapter will help you to get the most out of each new word learned, by teaching you how to form and spell derivatives.

WHAT IS A DERIVATIVE?

A derivative is a word formed by adding a prefix, or a suffix, or both a prefix and a suffix, to a word or a root.

	PREFIX		WORD		DERIVATIVE
	re *(again)*	+	apply	=	reapply *(apply again)*

	PREFIX		ROOT		DERIVATIVE
	e *(out)*	+	ject *(throw)*	=	eject *(throw out)*

	WORD		SUFFIX		DERIVATIVE
	ostentatious *(showy)*	+	ly *(manner)*	=	ostentatiously *(in a showy manner)*

	ROOT		SUFFIX		DERIVATIVE
	ten *(defend)*	+	able *(capable of being)*	=	tenable *(capable of being defended)*

PREFIX		WORD		SUFFIX		DERIVATIVE
un *(not)*	+	ostentatious	+	ly	=	unostentatiously *(not in a showy manner)*

PREFIX		ROOT		SUFFIX		DERIVATIVE
un	+	ten	+	able	=	untenable *(not capable of being defended)*

See how many words you can form using only the prefixes, roots, and suffixes below. For example: ab + rupt = abrupt, cred + ible = credible, dis + tort + ion = distortion.

PREFIXES	ROOTS	SUFFIXES
ab	cred, credit	able
ad	flex, flect	ible
con	fract	ion
de	monit	ive
dis	rupt	or, er
e, ex	strict	ory
in	ten, tent	ure
inter	tort	
re	vict	

A score of 75 words or more is excellent, 65-74 very good, 55-64 good, 45-54 fair. A score below 45 is unsatisfactory.

TERMS USED IN THIS CHAPTER

A derivative may be either a noun, an adjective, an adverb, or a verb.

A **noun** is a word naming a person, place, thing, or quality. In the following sentences, all the italicized words are nouns:

1. The young *motorist* very slowly drove his badly damaged *car* to the nearest *garage*.
2. *Health* is *wealth*.

An **adjective** is a word that modifies (describes) a noun. The following words in sentence 1 above are adjectives: *young, damaged, nearest*.

A **verb** is a word that expresses (*a*) action or (*b*) a state of being. The verbs in the sentences above are *drove* (sentence 1) and *is* (sentence 2).

An **adverb** is a word that modifies a verb, an adjective, or another adverb. In sentence 1 above, *slowly* is an adverb because it modifies the verb "drove"; *badly* is an adverb because it modifies the adjective "damaged"; and *very* is an adverb because it modifies the adverb "slowly."

Vowels are the letters *a, e, i, o,* and *u.*

Consonants are all the other letters of the alphabet.

FORMING DERIVATIVES BY ATTACHING PREFIXES AND SUFFIXES

1. ATTACHING PREFIXES

Rule: Do not omit or add a letter when attaching a prefix to a word. Keep *all* the letters of the prefix and *all* the letters of the word.

PREFIX		WORD		DERIVATIVE
dis	+	similar	=	dissimilar
dis	+	organized	=	disorganized
un	+	natural	=	unnatural
un	+	acceptable	=	unacceptable
inter	+	related	=	interrelated
inter	+	action	=	interaction

EXERCISE 1. In column III write the required derivatives. Be sure to spell them correctly.

I. PREFIX		II. WORD		III. DERIVATIVE
1. micro	+	organism	=	-------------------------------
2. in	+	opportune	=	-------------------------------
3. dis	+	service	=	-------------------------------
4. extra	+	ordinary	=	-------------------------------
5. with	+	hold	=	-------------------------------
6. re	+	entry	=	-------------------------------
7. mis	+	shaped	=	-------------------------------
8. pre	+	monition	=	-------------------------------
9. semi	+	annually	=	-------------------------------
10. de	+	emphasis	=	-------------------------------

11.	mis	+	understood	=	----------------------------------
12.	re	+	election	=	----------------------------------
13.	dis	+	embark	=	----------------------------------
14.	pre	+	eminent	=	----------------------------------
15.	mis	+	statement	=	----------------------------------
16.	sub	+	basement	=	----------------------------------
17.	retro	+	actively	=	----------------------------------
18.	sub	+	ordinate	=	----------------------------------
19.	un	+	neighborly	=	----------------------------------
20.	pre	+	arrange	=	----------------------------------
21.	in	+	numerable	=	----------------------------------
22.	re	+	unify	=	----------------------------------
23.	inter	+	relationship	=	----------------------------------
24.	un	+	equal	=	----------------------------------
25.	mis	+	step	=	----------------------------------

2. ATTACHING THE PREFIX *UN* OR *IN*

You can give a negative meaning to a word by attaching the prefix UN or IN. Examples:

PREFIX		WORD		DERIVATIVE
un *(not)*	+	remunerative *(gainful)*	=	unremunerative *(not gainful)*
in *(not)*	+	tangible *(capable of being touched)*	=	intangible *(not capable of being touched)*

If you are not sure whether a word takes UN or IN, consult the dictionary.

Learn the different forms of IN:

1. Before *l*, IN changes to IL, as in *illegal, illiterate*, etc.
2. Before *b, m*, or *p*, IN changes to IM, as in *imbalance, immature, improper*, etc.
3. Before *r*, IN changes to IR, as in *irrational, irresistible*, etc.

Two less frequent negative prefixes are DIS, as in *disagreeable*, and A, as in *atypical*.

EXERCISE 2. Form the negative of the word in column II by writing *in, il, im*, or *ir* in column I. Then complete the new word in column III. (The first line has been done for you as an example.)

I. NEGATIVE PREFIX		II. WORD		III. NEGATIVE WORD
1. in	+	considerate	=	inconsiderate
2. -------	+	moral	=	----------------------------------
3. -------	+	legibly	=	----------------------------------
4. -------	+	redeemable	=	----------------------------------
5. -------	+	decisive	=	----------------------------------

6.	_____	+	patience	=	_____
7.	_____	+	regularity	=	_____
8.	_____	+	mobility	=	_____
9.	_____	+	convenience	=	_____
10.	_____	+	practical	=	_____
11.	_____	+	eligible	=	_____
12.	_____	+	responsibly	=	_____
13.	_____	+	mortal	=	_____
14.	_____	+	possible	=	_____
15.	_____	+	accuracy	=	_____
16.	_____	+	logical	=	_____
17.	_____	+	revocable	=	_____
18.	_____	+	perfection	=	_____
19.	_____	+	completely	=	_____
20.	_____	+	limitable	=	_____

3. ATTACHING SUFFIXES

Rule: Do not omit or add a letter when attaching a suffix to a word—unless the word ends in *y* or silent *e*. Keep *all* the letters of the word and *all* the letters of the suffix.

WORD		SUFFIX		DERIVATIVE
accidental	+	ly	=	accidentally
drunken	+	ness	=	drunkenness
banjo	+	ist	=	banjoist
ski	+	ing	=	skiing

EXERCISE 3. In column III write the required derivatives. Be sure to spell them correctly.

	I. WORD		II. SUFFIX		III. DERIVATIVE
1.	soul	+	less	=	_____
2.	ego	+	ism	=	_____
3.	room	+	mate	=	_____
4.	solo	+	ist	=	_____
5.	beach	+	head	=	_____
6.	barren	+	ness	=	_____
7.	convivial	+	ly	=	_____
8.	head	+	dress	=	_____
9.	Hindu	+	ism	=	_____
10.	book	+	keeper	=	_____

4. ATTACHING SUFFIXES TO WORDS ENDING IN Y

Rule 1: If a consonant precedes the *y*, change the *y* to *i* before adding a suffix.

WORD		SUFFIX		DERIVATIVE
hurry	+	ed	=	hurried
spicy	+	est	=	spiciest
heavy	+	ness	=	heaviness
greedy	+	ly	=	greedily

Exception 1: Except before *ing*.

hurry	+	ing	=	hurrying
falsify	+	ing	=	falsifying

Exception 2: Learn these special exceptions: dryly, dryness, shyly, shyness, babyish, ladylike.

Rule 2: If a vowel precedes the *y*, do *not* change the *y* before adding a suffix.

betray	+	al	=	betrayal
convey	+	ed	=	conveyed
joy	+	ful	=	joyful

Exceptions: daily, laid, paid, said.

EXERCISE 4. In column III write the required derivatives. Be sure to spell them correctly.

I. WORD		II. SUFFIX		III. DERIVATIVE
1. pacify	+	ing	=	_____
2. musty	+	ness	=	_____
3. arbitrary	+	ly	=	_____
4. controversy	+	al	=	_____
5. pray	+	ed	=	_____
6. calumny	+	ous	=	_____
7. accompany	+	ment	=	_____
8. vilify	+	ed	=	_____
9. earthy	+	est	=	_____
10. contrary	+	wise	=	_____
11. worry	+	some	=	_____
12. flay	+	ed	=	_____
13. colloquy	+	al	=	_____
14. vivify	+	ing	=	_____
15. pudgy	+	est	=	_____
16. cursory	+	ly	=	_____

17.	paltry	+	ness	=	_____
18.	coy	+	ly	=	_____
19.	burly	+	er	=	_____
20.	ignominy	+	ous	=	_____
21.	bloody	+	ly	=	_____
22.	mercy	+	less	=	_____
23.	refractory	+	ly	=	_____
24.	sully	+	ing	=	_____
25.	shy	+	ness	=	_____

EXERCISE 5. Four derivatives have been omitted from each line. Insert the missing words in the spaces provided. When completed, each line should correspond to the first.

	I. ADJECTIVE	II. ADJECTIVE ENDING IN ER	III. ADJECTIVE ENDING IN EST	IV. ADVERB	V. NOUN
1.	quiet	quieter	quietest	quietly	quietness
2.	_____	quicker	_____	_____	_____
3.	_____	_____	happiest	_____	_____
4.	_____	_____	_____	hastily	_____
5.	_____	_____	_____	_____	dizziness
6.	foxy	_____	_____	_____	_____
7.	_____	craftier	_____	_____	_____
8.	_____	_____	prettiest	_____	_____
9.	_____	_____	_____	readily	_____
10.	_____	_____	_____	_____	unsteadiness

5. ATTACHING SUFFIXES TO WORDS ENDING IN SILENT *E*

Rule 1: Drop the silent *e* before a suffix starting with a vowel.

WORD		SUFFIX		DERIVATIVE
love	+	able	=	lovable
use	+	age	=	usage
produce	+	er	=	producer

Exception 1: Words ending in *ce* or *ge* keep the final *e* before a suffix beginning with *a* or *o*.

notice	+	able	=	noticeable
advantage	+	ous	=	advantageous

Exception 2: Learn the following additional exceptions: acreage, mileage, singeing, canoeing, hoeing, shoeing.

Rule 2: Keep the final *e* before a suffix starting with a consonant.

WORD		SUFFIX		DERIVATIVE
excite	+	ment	=	excitement
care	+	ful	=	careful
fierce	+	ly	=	fiercely
complete	+	ness	=	completeness

Exceptions: acknowledgment, judgment, argument, awful, duly, truly, wholly, ninth.

EXERCISE 6. In column III write the required derivatives. Be sure to spell them correctly.

I. WORD		II. SUFFIX		III. DERIVATIVE
1. prosecute	+	or	=	_____
2. eulogize	+	ing	=	_____
3. induce	+	ment	=	_____
4. mature	+	ity	=	_____
5. blithe	+	ly	=	_____
6. contaminate	+	ion	=	_____
7. revive	+	al	=	_____
8. judge	+	ment	=	_____
9. avarice	+	ious	=	_____
10. remorse	+	ful	=	_____
11. convalesce	+	ent	=	_____
12. rationalize	+	ed	=	_____
13. trouble	+	some	=	_____
14. versatile	+	ity	=	_____
15. like	+	wise	=	_____
16. expedite	+	er	=	_____
17. dispute	+	able	=	_____
18. undulate	+	ion	=	_____
19. courage	+	ous	=	_____
20. nine	+	ty	=	_____
21. belittle	+	ing	=	_____
22. acre	+	age	=	_____
23. abridge	+	ment	=	_____
24. service	+	able	=	_____
25. naive	+	ly	=	_____

6. ATTACHING THE SUFFIX *LY*

You can change an adjective into an adverb by adding *ly*.

ADJECTIVE	SUFFIX		ADVERB
brave	+ ly	=	bravely
calm	+ ly	=	calmly

Exception: If an adjective ends in *ic*, add *al* before attaching *ly*.

heroic	+	*al*	+	ly	=	heroically
specific	+	*al*	+	ly	=	specifically

Note: Most adjectives ending in *ic* have an alternate form ending in *ical*. Examples: *philosophic* and *philosophical*, *historic* and *historical*, etc.

EXERCISE 7. Change the following adjectives to adverbs:

ADJECTIVE	ADVERB
1. fraternal	----------------------------------
2. diabolic	----------------------------------
3. solemn	----------------------------------
4. scientific	----------------------------------
5. fallacious	----------------------------------
6. nostalgic	----------------------------------
7. grave	----------------------------------
8. lethargic	----------------------------------
9. partial	----------------------------------
10. hermetic	----------------------------------

EXERCISE 8. For each noun in column I, write an adjective ending in *ic* in column II, and an adverb in column III. (As an example, the first question has been completed.)

I. NOUN	II. ADJECTIVE	III. ADVERB
1. biology	biologic	biologically
2. geology		
3. atheism		
4. sociology		
5. idealism		
6. comedy		
7. philanthropy		
8. geometry		
9. economics		

10. biography   ----------------------   ---------------------------------

11. egoism   ----------------------   ---------------------------------

12. psychology   ----------------------   ---------------------------------

13. meteorology   ----------------------   ---------------------------------

14. microbiology   ----------------------   ---------------------------------

15. socialism   ----------------------   ---------------------------------

16. technology   ----------------------   ---------------------------------

17. realism   ----------------------   ---------------------------------

18. tragedy   ----------------------   ---------------------------------

19. autobiography   ----------------------   ---------------------------------

20. physiology   ----------------------   ---------------------------------

7. DOUBLING FINAL CONSONANTS WHEN ATTACHING SUFFIXES

Rule 1: Double a final consonant in a one-syllable word before a suffix beginning with a vowel.

WORD		SUFFIXES		DERIVATIVES
run	+	ing, er	=	running, runner
stop	+	ed, age	=	stopped, stoppage
wet	+	er, est	=	wetter, wettest

Exception 1: If the final consonant is preceded by two vowels, no doubling occurs.

sail	+	ed, ing	=	sailed, sailing
kneel	+	ed, ing	=	kneeled, kneeling

Exception 2: If the final consonant is preceded by another consonant, no doubling occurs.

halt	+	ed, ing	=	halted, halting
ask	+	ed, ing	=	asked, asking

Rule 2: Double a final consonant in an *accented* syllable at the end of a word of two or more syllables before a suffix beginning with a vowel.

reFER′	+	ed, ing, al	=	referred, referring, referral
transMIT′	+	ed, ing, er	=	transmitted, transmitting, transmitter
readMIT′	+	ed, ing, ance	=	readmitted, readmitting, readmittance

Note: The rule does not apply when the final consonant is in an *unaccented* syllable.

CRED′it	+	ed, ing, or	=	credited, crediting, creditor
LIM′it	+	ed, ing	=	limited, limiting
OF′fer	+	ed, ing, er	=	offered, offering, offerer

Exception 1: The rule does not apply when the final consonant is preceded by two vowels.

contain	+	ed, ing, er	=	contained, containing, container
recoil	+	ed, ing	=	recoiled, recoiling
appeal	+	ed, ing	=	appealed, appealing

Exception 2: The rule does not apply when the final consonant is preceded by another consonant.

condemn	+	ed, ing, able	=	condemned, condemning, condemnable
conduct	+	ed, ing, or	=	conducted, conducting, conductor

Exception 3: The rule does not apply if the accent shifts back to the first syllable.

reFER′	+	ence	=	REF′erence
deFER′	+	ence	=	DEF′erence
inFER′	+	ence	=	IN′ference

However: exCEL′—EX′cellent.

EXERCISE 9. In column III write the required derivatives. Be sure to spell them correctly.

I. WORD		II. SUFFIX		III. DERIVATIVE
1. dispel	+	ing	=	------------------------------
2. occur	+	ence	=	------------------------------
3. accredit	+	ed	=	------------------------------
4. acquit	+	al	=	------------------------------
5. differ	+	ed	=	------------------------------
6. beget	+	ing	=	------------------------------
7. slip	+	ed	=	------------------------------
8. hot	+	est	=	------------------------------
9. suffer	+	ing	=	------------------------------
10. regret	+	able	=	------------------------------
11. confer	+	ence	=	------------------------------
12. excel	+	ing	=	------------------------------
13. gallop	+	ing	=	------------------------------
14. stoop	+	ing	=	------------------------------
15. defer	+	al	=	------------------------------
16. excel	+	ent	=	------------------------------
17. propel	+	er	=	------------------------------
18. inject	+	ed	=	------------------------------
19. commit	+	ee	=	------------------------------
20. libel	+	ous	=	------------------------------
21. fat	+	er	=	------------------------------
22. equip	+	ing	=	------------------------------
23. permit	+	ed	=	------------------------------
24. repel	+	ent	=	------------------------------
25. transmit	+	al	=	------------------------------

EXERCISE 10. For each word at the left, form four derivatives.

1. concur	_____ing	_____ed	_____ent	_____ence
2. defer	_____ing	_____ed	_____able	_____ence
3. retain	_____ing	_____ed	_____able	_____er
4. rebel	_____ing	_____ed	_____ious	_____ion
5. prefer	_____ing	_____ed	_____able	_____ence
6. ship	_____ing	_____ed	_____er	_____ment
7. differ	_____ing	_____ed	_____ent	_____ence
8. control	_____ing	_____ed	_____able	_____er
9. remit	_____ing	_____ed	_____al	_____ance
10. excel	_____ing	_____ed	_____ent	_____ence

8. TROUBLESOME SUFFIXES

There are no easy rules to tell you when to use *able* or *ible*, *er* or *or*, *ant* or *ent*, etc. Words ending in such troublesome suffixes must be studied individually. Develop the habit of consulting the dictionary when in doubt about which suffix is right.

1. Adding *able* or *ible*. Study the following adjectives:

ABLE	IBLE
demonstrable	credible
impregnable	fallible
indisputable	flexible
memorable	illegible
navigable	incontrovertible
returnable	invincible
serviceable	plausible
tenable	reprehensible
unmanageable	resistible

Note: Adjectives ending in *able* become nouns ending in *ability*. Adjectives ending in *ible* become nouns ending in *ibility*.

ADJECTIVE	NOUN	ADJECTIVE	NOUN
impregnable	impregnability	flexible	flexibility
venerable	venerability	invincible	invincibility

2. Adding *er* or *or*. Study the following nouns:

ER	OR
consumer	aggressor
defender	censor
foreigner	creditor
mariner	debtor
observer	governor
philosopher	originator
reporter	possessor
subscriber	progenitor
sympathizer	speculator

Note: Verbs ending in *ate* usually become nouns ending in *or*, rather than *er*.

VERB	NOUN
demonstrate	demonstrator
liberate	liberator

3. Adding *ant* or *ent*. Study the following adjectives:

ANT	ENT
brilliant	complacent
buoyant	decent
flamboyant	eloquent
flippant	eminent
fragrant	iridescent
malignant	obsolescent
nonchalant	pertinent
poignant	potent
relevant	recurrent
vacant	repellent

Note: Adjectives ending in *ant* become nouns ending in *ance* or *ancy*. Adjectives ending in *ent* become nouns ending in *ence* or *ency*.

ADJECTIVE	NOUN	ADJECTIVE	NOUN
nonchalant	nonchalance	eloquent	eloquence
vacant	vacancy	decent	decency
brilliant	brilliance, brilliancy	complacent	complacence, complacency

EXERCISE 11. Fill in the missing letter.

1. IRRESIST____BLE
2. MALIGN____NCY
3. EXCELL____NCE
4. DEBT____R
5. OMNIPOT____NT
6. INCRED____BLE
7. CONSUM____R
8. LEG____BILITY
9. UNNAVIG____BLE
10. SPECULAT____R

11. FLEX____BILITY
12. VAC____NCY
13. INFLEX____BLE
14. OBSOLESC____NCE
15. SERVICE____BILITY
16. SUBSCRIB____R
17. IMPERTIN____NCE
18. DISPUT____BLE
19. POIGN____NCY
20. IRRELEV____NT

EXERCISE 12. For each noun, write the corresponding adjective. (The first adjective has been filled in as an example.)

NOUN	ADJECTIVE
1. infrequency	infrequent
2. resistance	_____
3. visibility	_____

4. urgency   -------------------------------

5. dependability   -------------------------------

6. defiance   -------------------------------

7. negligence   -------------------------------

8. constancy   -------------------------------

9. unpredictability   -------------------------------

10. stringency   -------------------------------

11. self-reliance   -------------------------------

12. comprehensibility   -------------------------------

13. convalescence   -------------------------------

14. contingency   -------------------------------

15. diffidence   -------------------------------

16. preeminence   -------------------------------

17. hesitancy   -------------------------------

18. intangibility   -------------------------------

19. incompetence   -------------------------------

20. adolescence   -------------------------------

REVIEW

EXERCISE 13. In the following exercise, two derivatives have been omitted from each line. Insert the missing words in the spaces provided. When completed, each line should correspond to the first.

I. VERB	II. NOUN ENDING IN ER OR OR	III. NOUN ENDING IN ION
1. create	creator	creation
2. ------------	------------	production
3. ------------	elector	------------
4. pretend	------------	------------
5. ------------	------------	subscription
6. ------------	promoter	------------
7. abduct	------------	------------
8. ------------	------------	contribution
9. ------------	liberator	------------
10. violate	------------	------------

EXERCISE 14. In the following exercise, two derivatives have been omitted from each line. Insert the missing words in the spaces provided. When completed, each line should correspond to the first.

I. NOUN	II. ADJECTIVE	III. ADVERB
1. apathy	apathetic	apathetically
2. _____	vivid	_____
3. _____	_____	monotonously
4. fraternity	_____	_____
5. _____	hypersensitive	_____
6. _____	_____	lethargically
7. maladroitness	_____	_____
8. _____	unsavory	_____
9. _____	_____	controversially
10. euphemism	_____	_____
11. _____	pathetic	_____
12. _____	_____	eloquently
13. naiveté	_____	_____
14. _____	peripheral	_____
15. _____	_____	sheepishly
16. quarrelsomeness	_____	_____
17. _____	hypothetical	_____
18. _____	_____	avariciously
19. homogeneity	_____	_____
20. _____	heterogeneous	_____

EXERCISE 15. In the following exercise, five derivatives have been omitted from each set. Insert the missing derivatives in the spaces provided. When completed, each line should correspond to the first set.

ADJECTIVE AND OPPOSITE	ADVERB AND OPPOSITE	NOUN AND OPPOSITE
1. moral	morally	morality
immoral	immorally	immorality
2. _____	_____	_____
intemperate	_____	_____
3. _____	comprehensibly	_____
_____	_____	_____

4. _____
_____   dissimilarly   _____
                                             _____
5. _____ _____ fallibility
_____   _____
6. _____ _____ _____
_____   _____ unostentatiousness
7. flexible   _____ _____
_____   _____
8. _____ _____ _____
abnormal   _____ _____
9. _____ plausibly   _____
_____   _____
10. _____ _____ _____
_____   incontrovertibly   _____
11. _____ _____ pertinence
_____   _____ _____
12. _____ _____ _____
_____   _____ untenability
13. rational   _____ _____
_____   _____ _____
14. _____ _____ _____
incredible   _____ _____
15. _____ mortally   _____
_____   _____ _____
16. _____ _____ _____
_____   unconventionally   _____
17. _____ _____ retentiveness
_____   _____ _____
18. _____ _____ _____
_____   _____ irrelevance
19. credulous   _____ _____
_____   _____ _____
20. _____ _____ _____
incorruptible   _____ _____

CHAPTER XI

SAMPLE VOCABULARY QUESTIONS IN PRE-COLLEGE TESTS

Vocabulary questions play a prominent and decisive role in pre-college tests. You will probably take one or more of these tests as a junior or senior in high school if you expect to apply for college admission or compete for college scholarship awards. The makers of these tests rely heavily on vocabulary because of its demonstrated correlation with intelligence. Naturally, you will want to familiarize yourself with the types of vocabulary questions you are likely to encounter on such tests. For your guidance, therefore, this chapter will discuss and analyze the officially released sample vocabulary questions for four widely administered pre-college examinations:

1. Preliminary Scholastic Aptitude Test (PSAT)
2. Scholastic Aptitude Test (SAT)
3. National Merit Scholarship Qualifying Test
4. New York State Regents Scholarship Examination

The following sample PSAT questions and explanatory passages are reprinted from *Bulletin for Students—1963 Preliminary Scholastic Aptitude Test*. The sample SAT questions and explanatory passages starting on page 159 are reprinted from the 1963 edition of *A Description of the College Board Scholastic Aptitude Test*. Both booklets are published by the College Entrance Examination Board, which has graciously granted permission to reprint this material. The booklets, which contain many illustrative examples of the different kinds of questions used in the PSAT and SAT, are revised annually and supplied without cost to high schools for distribution to students before they take the test. These booklets may also be obtained on request by writing to the College Entrance Examination Board at either of these addresses: Box 592, Princeton, New Jersey 08540, or Box 1025, Berkeley, California 94701.

1. PRELIMINARY SCHOLASTIC APTITUDE TEST (PSAT)

ANTONYMS (OPPOSITES): These questions are designed to test the extent and quality of your vocabulary. In each question a word is given, and you are asked to select from the five choices that follow it the one most nearly opposite in meaning. The vocabulary used in this section includes words most high school students should have met in their general reading, although some of the words may not be ones you use in your everyday speech.

The test directions for this kind of question are as follows:

Each question below consists of a word printed in capital letters, followed by five words or phrases lettered A through E. Choose the lettered word or phrase which is most nearly *opposite* in meaning to the word in capital letters.

Since some of the questions require you to distinguish fine shades of meaning, be sure to consider all the choices before deciding which one is best.

1. AGILE: (A) humble (B) clumsy (C) useless (D) timid (E) ugly

Since "agile" means quick, dexterous, and easy in movement, the best answer is "clumsy" (B), which means slow, awkward, and ungainly in movement. If you know the meaning of this word, answers (A), (C), (D), and (E) are obviously incorrect. This is a relatively easy question.

2. ALLEVIATE: (A) lower (B) aggravate (C) finish (D) control (E) amuse

This is a relatively difficult question. "Alleviate" means to lighten or lessen (usually physical or mental troubles). The meaning most nearly opposite is "aggravate" (B). To one who understands the meaning of "alleviate," (C) and (E) are obviously incorrect. "Control" (D) can be thought of in relation to physical or mental troubles, but the act of controlling would not provide the opposite of "lightening or lessening"; the correct answer must imply increasing or magnifying. "Lower" (A) in a sense carries the same meaning as "alleviate" but is much more general and is certainly not the *opposite* of that word.

SENTENCE COMPLETIONS: Sentence completion questions require you to complete a sentence from which one or two words have been removed. They provide a measure of one aspect of reading comprehension: your ability to select a word or phrase that is consistent in logic and style with other elements in the sentence. If you understand the implications of the sentence, you will be able to select the one answer that best fulfills its meaning.

The sentences cover a wide variety of topics of the sort you are likely to have encountered in your general reading. Your understanding of the sentences will not depend on specialized knowledge in science, literature, music, philosophy, the social sciences, or other such fields. Still, a broad general knowledge of a wide range of topics should be helpful.

The directions given for sentence completion questions are as follows:

Each of the sentences below has one or more blank spaces, each blank indicating that a word has been omitted. Beneath the sentence are five lettered words or sets of words. You are to choose the one word or set of words which, when inserted in the sentence, *best* fits in with the meaning of the sentence as a whole.

3. Where the world is going is of no particular concern to him; that it ____ is sufficient.

(A) flourishes (B) acts (C) moves (D) grows (E) triumphs

The problem here is to select the word which most clearly conveys a lack of concern about "where the world is going." "Moves" (C) is the best choice, for it does not imply direction. Each of the other terms, by suggesting an interest in more than mere movement, indicates more concern than (C) does.

4. ____ makes it possible for us to profit by the experience of past generations as if this experience were our own.

(A) Language (B) Democracy (C) Progress (D) Truth (E) Economy

This relatively difficult sentence completion requires some understanding of one important function of language, namely, that it enables us to profit by the experience of past generations. Notice that if (B), (C), (D), or (E) were to be fitted into the blank space, they would fit no better than their opposites. That is, we can profit from the experience of past dictatorships as well as from past democracies. Falsehood has its lessons as well as Truth. Thus there is nothing particularly *fitting* about any of the choices except "Language" (A). Lacking a language, it would be almost impossible for one generation to communicate with another. Given a language, the experiences of Democracy, Progress, Truth, or Economy—or their opposites—of one generation can be used by a succeeding one.

ANALOGIES: Analogy questions test your understanding of relationships among words and ideas. They ask you to analyze such relationships and to recognize those that are similar or parallel in nature. Some of the questions will involve cause and effect relationships; in others you will be asked to carry an analogy from a concrete, tangible relationship to an abstract, less tangible one. You should consider each relationship critically and then select as your answer the choice that comes closest to satisfying all of the demands.

The directions given for analogy questions are as follows:

In each of the following questions, a related pair of words or phrases is followed by five lettered pairs of words or phrases. Select the lettered pair which best expresses a relationship similar to that expressed in the original pair.

5. FOOTBALL : SPORT ::

   (A) frame : picture   (B) clock : time   (C) gourmet : food
   (D) cherry : fruit   (E) intelligence : personality

This is a relatively easy analogy. Since football is one of a number of sports, the correct answer must involve some object that is included in a larger category described by the second part of the answer. The choice that best fits this description is (D), "cherry:fruit."

6. ILLEGIBLE : WRITING ::

   (A) obnoxious : odor   (B) iridescent : glass   (C) soundproof : wall
   (D) illusory : sight   (E) garbled : speech

This is an analogy of medium difficulty. Since writing that is illegible cannot be read, the correct answer must involve terms that result in an inability to comprehend something. Choice (E) is the only one that expresses a similar relationship: garbled speech cannot be understood.

2. SCHOLASTIC APTITUDE TEST (SAT)

ANTONYMS (OPPOSITES): Questions of this type test the extent and quality of your vocabulary. In each question a word is given, and you are asked to select, from the five choices that follow it, the word most nearly *opposite* in meaning. The vocabulary used in this section includes words that most high school students should have met in their general reading, although some words may not be of the kind that you use in everyday speech.

The directions given in the test for this type of question are approximately as follows:

Each question below consists of a word printed in capital letters, followed by five words or phrases lettered A through E. Choose the lettered word or phrase which is most nearly *opposite* in meaning to the word in capital letters.

Since some of the questions require you to distinguish fine shades of meaning, be sure to consider all the choices before deciding which one is best.

1. EXAGGERATION: (A) slight misunderstanding   (B) silence   (C) accurate representation (D) truth   (E) understatement

Since exaggeration means to overstate the truth about some matter, the most appropriate answer is (E). If you know the meaning of the word, answers (A), (B) and (D) are obviously inappropriate. Answer (C) is, in a sense, partially correct, but represents what may be called a midpoint between the extremes of "exaggeration" and "understatement." It can also be eliminated as a possible correct answer if you consider that (C) and (D) are almost identical in meaning. If you reason that (D) is incorrect, then (C), too, must be wrong.

2. SCHISM: (A) majority (B) union (C) uniformity (D) conference (E) construction

The word schism means "division" or "separation." Answers (A), (D), and (E) may be eliminated since they do not convey any meaning opposite to that required by the word "schism." The correct answer must therefore be either (B) or (C). Since "uniformity" is the state of being uniform, that is, always having the same form, manner, or degree, while "union" is the condition of being united, the correct answer is (B).

3. CHRONIC: (A) slight (B) temporary (C) wholesome (D) patient (E) pleasant

In order to answer this question correctly, you need to know that "chronic" describes something that continues for a long time. It will also be helpful if you realize that this word is usually used in describing a disease, and that the word usually used as an opposite in this specific sense is "acute." Since, however, "acute" does not appear as one of the choices, you must search further for the correct answer. (C), (D), and (E) may be readily eliminated. Of the remaining choices, the word most nearly opposite in meaning is (B) "temporary," since "slight" refers to quantity rather than to time.

SENTENCE COMPLETIONS: The second type of question requires you to complete a sentence from which one or two words have been removed. That is, you must identify, from a list of five choices, the word or words which would make the most sense if inserted in the sentence. Such questions provide a measure of one aspect of reading comprehension: your ability to recognize logical and stylistic consistency among the elements in a sentence. If you understand the implications of a sentence, you should be able to select the answer that best fulfills the meaning of the sentence, the element that makes the sentence lucid, logical, and stylistically consistent.

The sentences cover a wide variety of topics of the sort you are likely to have encountered in your general reading. Your understanding of any one sentence will inevitably depend to some degree on your knowledge of the subject matter involved: science, literature, music, philosophy, social studies, or other fields. But your success in answering each question will depend primarily on your ability to understand and use the English language.

The directions given for sentence completion questions are approximately as follows:

Each of the sentences below has one or more blank spaces, each blank indicating that a word has been omitted. Beneath the sentence are five lettered words or sets of words. You are to choose the one word or set of words which, when inserted in the sentence, *best* fits in with the meaning of the sentence as a whole.

4. High yields of food crops per acre accelerate the ____ of soil nutrients.
   - (A) depletion
   - (B) erosion
   - (C) cultivation
   - (D) fertilization
   - (E) conservation

The correct answer to this question is (A), since high yields of food crops per acre require more soil nutrients than would normally be the case; this of course means more rapid consumption of available nutrients, or accelerated depletion. Although "cultivation" (C) and "fertilization" (D) would probably be necessary in order to obtain continued high yields per acre, both processes refer to the soil rather than to the nutrients. By definition, "erosion" (B) is the washing or wearing away of the soil; therefore, one cannot properly refer to the erosion of nutrients. Answer (E) is illogical, since "accelerating conservation" is a contradiction in terms, meaning something like "more rapid saving" of the nutrients in the soil.

5. From the first the islanders, despite an outward ____, did what they could to ____ the ruthless occupying power.
   - (A) harmony . . assist
   - (B) enmity . . embarrass
   - (C) rebellion . . foil
   - (D) resistance . . destroy
   - (E) acquiescence . . thwart

An examination of this sentence should suggest to you that the answer will involve two words that are more or less opposite in meaning, since the word "despite" implies that the islanders acted in one fashion, while presenting a somewhat different impression to the "ruthless occupying power." If you bear this relationship in mind, you can eliminate (A), (B), (C), and (D) since all of these answers fail to give the sense of opposition that is required. If "outward harmony" existed, "to assist" the occupying power would probably contribute to this state of harmony and strengthen it. If "enmity" existed, embarrassing the occupying power would be one method of expressing this feeling. Should "rebellion" exist, then the islanders would be doing what they could to foil the occupying power; these terms do not imply opposition. The same logic holds for "resistance..destroy." The correct answer, the only one implying two opposed actions, is (E).

6. As warfare has come to engross an increasing proportion of the belligerent populations, so military ____ has grown far beyond the problems of varying terrain.

   (A) custom
   (B) life
   (C) history
   (D) strength
   (E) geography

This is a relatively difficult question. An analogy is drawn between the growth of whatever is indicated by the missing term and the general expansion of warfare. A careful examination of the sentence should indicate that the missing word is related in some fashion to "the problems of varying terrain," as it affects some aspect of military operations, and at some earlier time was limited to this topic. Of the five choices, (A) and (C) are obviously incorrect; military custom and military history have changed and grown, but were never limited in their concern to problems of varying terrain. (B) and (D) seem plausible; military life and strength do involve problems relating to terrain, but this is not their major concern. Of the five alternatives given, only (E) "geography" relates specifically to terrain, and is the correct answer.

ANALOGIES: Questions of this third type test your understanding of relationships among words and ideas. You are asked to analyze relationships and to recognize those that are similar or parallel in nature. Some of the questions involve cause and effect relationships; in others you are asked to carry an analogy from a concrete, tangible relationship to a more abstract and less tangible one. You should consider each relationship critically and then select as your answer the choice that comes closest to satisfying all the demands.

The directions given for analogy questions are approximately as follows:

In each of the following questions, a related pair of words or phrases is followed by five lettered pairs of words or phrases. Select the lettered pair which best expresses a relationship similar to that expressed in the original pair.

7. TRIGGER : BULLET ::

   (A) handle : drawer
   (B) holster : gun
   (C) bulb : light
   (D) switch : current
   (E) pulley : rope

This is a relatively easy question which involves the relationship between a mechanical object that is manipulated ("trigger") and a second object that is activated as a result of this action ("bullet"). The only choice which involves the relation between a mechanical object that is moved and something that is activated as a direct result of this action is (D).

It may help you if you verbalize each question in your head. For instance, in answering the above question, you would think, "Trigger is to bullet as ____ is to ____," the blanks being, in turn, the five pairs of words. Or, you might phrase it, "Trigger bears the same relationship to bullet as ____ to ____."

8. BICYCLE : LOCOMOTION ::

    (A) canoe : paddle
    (B) hero : worship
    (C) hay : horse
    (D) spectacles : vision
    (E) statement : contention

This analogy is of average difficulty. In order to answer this question correctly, you should analyze the relationship between a bicycle and locomotion. A bicycle is an object that provides some form of assistance to normal locomotion (that is, the act or power of moving from place to place). The correct answer should also involve an object that provides assistance to some normal function. The answer that meets this requirement is (D), the relationship of spectacles to vision, since spectacles are an object, the function of which is to assist vision.

9. WANDER : TRESPASS ::

    (A) eat : gorge
    (B) recline : sprawl
    (C) mar : destroy
    (D) narrate : perjure
    (E) glance : examine

This is a relatively difficult question requiring rather careful analysis. If you consider "wander: trespass" closely, you will see that "wander" means to move about without a fixed course or aim, while "trespass" means intrusion, especially one that is unwarranted or illegal. The correct answer will involve two actions that may be related; the second word in the answer should be some form of the action described by the first word—but conveying the idea of illegality. The correct answer, then, is (D). Narration and perjury both pertain to something that is spoken; perjury refers to the illegal act of telling what is false when one is sworn to tell the truth.

ADDITIONAL SAMPLE SCHOLASTIC APTITUDE TEST QUESTIONS

Now, try to answer the following 38 questions without assistance. When you have finished, check your answers by using the answer key on page 165.

Each question below consists of a word printed in capital letters, followed by five words or phrases lettered A through E. Choose the lettered word or phrase which is most nearly *opposite* in meaning to the word in capital letters.

Since some of the questions require you to distinguish fine shades of meaning, be sure to consider all the choices before deciding which one is best.

1. REFRAIN: (A) undertake (B) conceal (C) decide (D) identify (E) address

2. LABORIOUS: (A) stationary (B) free (C) automatic (D) common (E) easy

3. VIGILANT: (A) useless (B) skeptical (C) frantic (D) unwary (E) calculating

4. DEPRESS: (A) appreciate (B) allow (C) swell (D) elate (E) loosen

5. DEPRECATING: (A) obligatory (B) reasonable (C) approving (D) confounding (E) insensitive

6. SUBSEQUENT: (A) primary (B) contemporary (C) recent (D) prior (E) simultaneous

7. LAUD: (A) fight (B) silence (C) censure (D) question (E) exasperate

8. REPROACH: (A) commend (B) requite (C) reward (D) excuse (E) apologize

9. INCREDIBLE: (A) comprehensible (B) lessened (C) generous (D) truthful
(E) plausible

10. PLACATE: (A) destroy (B) demand (C) expose (D) deprive (E) enrage

11. ABATE: (A) add (B) increase (C) level (D) multiply (E) raise

12. VIRTUE: (A) regret (B) hatred (C) penalty (D) denial (E) depravity

Each of the sentences below has one or more blank spaces, each blank indicating that a word has been omitted. Beneath the sentence are five lettered words or sets of words. You are to choose the one word or set of words which, when inserted in the sentence, *best* fits in with the meaning of the sentence as a whole.

13. Science is always ____, expecting that modifications of its present theories will sooner or later be found necessary.
    (A) final
    (B) original
    (C) tentative
    (D) practical
    (E) improving

14. The voice has an advantage over the instrument. It can sing words as well as tones, thus stirring us through ____ as well as music.
    (A) intensity
    (B) personality
    (C) thoughts
    (D) harmony
    (E) sound

15. Since growth is not a ____ process for all people, the importance of studying the ____ growth pattern has been emphasized.
    (A) uniform . . individual
    (B) healthy . . normal
    (C) unique . . varying
    (D) simple . . fundamental
    (E) normal . . typical

16. Every point in which one tomb differs from another may prove to be evidence for relative dating and must be brought into the argument; because nothing is known at the outset, nothing must be ____.
    (A) saved
    (B) damaged
    (C) believed
    (D) disturbed
    (E) neglected

17. One of the advantages that a large investor should enjoy is the ability to take advantage of the ____ yields obtainable on certain "speculative" ____.
    (A) uncertain . . propositions
    (B) guaranteed . . securities
    (C) higher . . investments
    (D) flexible . . properties
    (E) limited . . occasions

18. Despite the popular feeling against ____ in college football, the major teams have found it difficult to ____ without encouraging outstanding athletes with scholarships.

   (A) competition . . win
   (B) favoritism . . be impartial
   (C) professionalism . . survive
   (D) academic standards . . discriminate
   (E) rivalry . . qualify

19. The average uneducated person does not distinguish between science and invention and lumps together people whose work is wholly directed toward ____ ends with those who are out to discover principles without much regard for their utility.

   (A) inevitable
   (B) theoretical
   (C) ideal
   (D) practical
   (E) obvious

20. ____ no physical basis for the disorder can be found with the tests now available, doctors refuse to say that the cause must be ____.

   (A) Although . . mental
   (B) Insofar as . . hereditary
   (C) Since . . unknown
   (D) When . . mysterious
   (E) Because . . serious

21. The Gothic church, with its open clerestory and soaring spire, was created as a ____ in stone of man's ____ for the divine.

   (A) symbol . . yearning
   (B) sermon . . consideration
   (C) parable . . affection
   (D) milestone . . quest
   (E) monument . . request

22. I destroyed all those papers, not then anticipating that I could ever feel any ____ about my first attempts at writing and reasoning.

   (A) antagonism
   (B) reluctance
   (C) timidity
   (D) shame
   (E) curiosity

23. The Indo-European group of languages is a relatively junior member of the Old World linguistic family, evolving at a time when such languages as Sumerian and those in the Hamitic and Semitic groups were of respectable ____.

   (A) origin
   (B) antiquity
   (C) usage
   (D) size
   (E) fluency

24. Though he was romantic and sensual in his aesthetic philosophy, his life was one of ____.

   (A) disillusionment
   (B) abandonment
   (C) creativity
   (D) naïveté
   (E) austerity

25. Plato's insistence on the all-pervading domination of the state, exaggerated though it be, is exaggerated on the actual lines of Greek practice, and ____ the ____ between their point of view and our idea of individual dignity.

    (A) evades . . inconsistency
    (B) prevents . . relationship
    (C) minimizes . . incongruity
    (D) indicates . . antithesis
    (E) resolves . . dispute

In each of the following questions, a related pair of words or phrases is followed by five lettered pairs of words or phrases. Select the lettered pair which best expresses a relationship similar to that expressed in the original pair.

26. KNIFE : INCISION :: (A) bulldozer : excavation   (B) tool : operation   (C) pencil : calculation   (D) hose : irrigation   (E) plow : agriculture

27. TORCH : LIBERTY :: (A) tray : waiter (B) scales : justice (C) candle : poverty (D) bars : punishment (E) lever : power

28. ADVERTISEMENT : PURCHASE :: (A) defense : conquest (B) attitude : conviction (C) electioneering : vote (D) offer : force (E) attempt : achievement

29. HEREDITY : MUTATION :: (A) authority : leadership (B) tradition : innovation (C) religion : heresy (D) obstinacy : persuasion (E) surprise : exclamation

30. TESTIMONY : OATH :: (A) future : prediction (B) advertisement : quality (C) decision : judgment (D) product : guarantee (E) confidence : promise

31. ISLAND : WATER :: (A) sand : desert (B) mountain : ocean (C) city : meadows (D) lake : land (E) river : banks

32. SONG : REPERTOIRE :: (A) score : melody (B) instrument : artist (C) solo : chorus (D) benediction : church (E) suit : wardrobe

33. HYBRID : SPECIES :: (A) alloy : metal (B) chip : block (C) flower : plant (B) blend : mixture (E) metal : rock

34. REQUEST : ENTREAT :: (A) control : explode (B) admire : idolize (C) borrow : steal (D) repeat : plead (E) cancel : invalidate

35. SNUB : CONTEMPT :: (A) praise : understanding (B) applause : approbation (C) injury : retaliation (D) scorn : superiority (E) grimace : amusement

36. REPETITION : MONOTONY :: (A) familiarity : recognition (B) interest : boredom (C) dissipation : depravity (D) attempt : achievement (E) callowness : inexperience

37. GROVE : TREE :: (A) monastery : monk (B) pond : stream (C) illumination : watt (D) peninsula : isthmus (E) archipelago : island

38. PARSIMONY : ECONOMY :: (A) prejudice : intolerance (B) asceticism : self-discipline (C) frugality : affluence (D) criticism : abuse (E) logic : philosophy

Answers

1. A	7. C	13. C	19. D	24. E	29. B	34. B
2. E	8. A	14. C	20. A	25. D	30. D	35. B
3. D	9. E	15. A	21. A	26. A	31. D	36. C
4. D	10. E	16. E	22. E	27. B	32. E	37. E
5. C	11. B	17. C	23. B	28. C	33. A	38. B
6. D	12. E	18. C				

3. NATIONAL MERIT SCHOLARSHIP QUALIFYING TEST

The word usage test below is reprinted from the *Student Information Bulletin* of the National Merit Scholarship Program: 1963-64.

Word Usage Test

For questions 18 through 20, decide which of the four suggested answers has most nearly the same meaning as the underlined word in the phrase preceding them.

18. A facetious remark   A. factual   C. sarcastic
                          B. plausible   D. jocose

19. A latent skill   A. potential   C. critical
                          B. lost   D. lagging

20. Inveterate behavior   A. ineradicable C. invertible
                          B. reversible   D. spineless

Answers

18. D   19. A   20. A

4. NEW YORK STATE REGENTS SCHOLARSHIP EXAMINATION

The thirty-five questions below are reprinted from *Opening the Door to College Study Through the New York State Regents Scholarship Examination*, the State Education Department, Albany, 1961.

You are advised to use these sample questions below as practice exercises so that you may become thoroughly familiar with the directions and the best methods for working out the answers to each type of question.

Write the question numbers on a separate sheet of paper and opposite each number write the number of the answer you think is correct. Then check your answers with those given in the key on page 169. If you chose the wrong answer, go back to the question and analyze it until you know why a different answer is correct.

Directions: Select the alternative that means the *same as* or the *opposite of* the italicized word.

		1	2	3	4	5
1	*acquire*	judge	identify	surrender	educate	happen
2	*begrudge*	envy	hate	annoy	obstruct	punish
3	*obsolete*	fatal	modern	distracting	untouched	broken
4	*inflexible*	weak	righteous	harmless	unyielding	secret
5	*nominal*	just	slight	factual	familiar	ceaseless
6	*deft*	insane	artificial	skillful	determined	humble
7	*censure*	focus	exclude	baffle	portray	praise
8	*nebulous*	imaginary	spiritual	distinct	starry-eyed	unanswerable
9	*impart*	hasten	adjust	gamble	address	communicate
10	*terminate*	gain	graduate	harvest	institute	paralyze

Directions: Select the word which, if inserted in the blank space, agrees most closely with the thought of the sentence.

11 Every good story is carefully contrived: the elements of the story are _____ to fit with one another in order to make an effect on the reader.

    1 read   3 emphasized   5 planned
    2 learned   4 reduced

12 Their work was commemorative in character and consisted largely of _____ erected upon the occasion of victories.

    1 towers   3 monuments   5 fortresses
    2 tombs   4 castles

13 Before criticizing the work of an artist one needs to _____ his purpose.

    1 understand   3 defend   5 change
    2 reveal   4 correct

14 Because in the administration it hath respect not to the group but to the _____, our form of government is called a democracy.

    1 courts   3 majority   5 law
    2 people   4 individual

15 Deductive reasoning is that form of reasoning in which the conclusion must necessarily follow if we accept the premise as true. In deduction, it is _____ for the premise to be true and the conclusion false.

    1 impossible   3 reasonable   5 unlikely
    2 inevitable   4 surprising

16 Mathematics is the product of thought operating by means of _____ for the purpose of expressing general laws.

    1 equations   3 words   5 science
    2 symbols   4 examples

17 A creditor is worse than a master. A master owns only your person, but a creditor owns your _____ as well.

    1 aspirations   3 ideas   5 wealth
    2 potentialities   4 dignity

18 People _____ small faults, in order to insinuate that they have no great ones.

    1 create   3 confess   5 reject
    2 display   4 seek

19 The latent period for the contractile response to direct stimulation of the muscle has quite another and shorter value, encompassing only a utilization period. Hence it is that the term *latent period* must be _____ carefully each time that it is used.

    1 checked   3 introduced   5 selected
    2 timed   4 defined

20 A man who cannot win honor in his own _____ will have a very small chance of winning it from posterity.

    1 right   3 country   5 age
    2 field   4 way

Directions: Select the word that best completes the analogy.

(As an aid to the student, questions 21-35, the analogy questions, have been analyzed at the end of this chapter. The analysis, on pages 169-173, was prepared by the author, not by the State Education Department.)

21 *Furniture* is to *period* as *wine* is to
1 vintage   3 bouquet   5 mellowness
2 aroma   4 proof

22 *Senile* is to *infantile* as *supper* is to
1 snack   3 dinner   5 evening
2 breakfast   4 daytime

23 *Synonym* is to *meaning* as *homonym* is to
1 purport   3 pronunciation 5 sameness
2 position   4 relationship

24 *Lawyer* is to *court* as *soldier* is to
1 battle   3 training   5 discipline
2 victory   4 rifle

25 *Taxes* is to *obligation* as *voting* is to
1 election   3 tally   5 privilege
2 campaign   4 restriction

26 *Wing* is to *airplane* as *hand* is to
1 finger   3 dish   5 work
2 applause   4 clock

27 *Chimney* is to *smoke* as *guide* is to
1 snare   3 hunter   5 wild game
2 compass   4 firewood

28 *Prodigy* is to *ability* as *ocean* is to
1 water   3 ships   5 current
2 waves   4 icebergs

29 *Apple* is to *potato* as *cherry* is to
1 plum   3 tomato   5 radish
2 blueberry   4 squash

30 *Sapphire* is to *emerald* as *sky* is to
1 storm   3 star   5 purity
2 world   4 grass

31 *Pour* is to *spill* as *lie* is to
1 deception   3 falsehood   5 fraud
2 misstatement   4 perjury

32 *Disparage* is to *despise* as *praise* is to
1 dislike   3 acclaim   5 compliment
2 adore   4 advocate

33 *Wall* is to *mortar* as *nation* is to

    1 family   3 patriotism   5 boundaries
    2 people   4 geography

34 *Aquarium* is to *fish* as *apiary* is to

    1 bees   3 flowers   5 cattle
    2 eagles   4 monkeys

35 *Fan* is to *air* as *newspaper* is to

    1 literature   3 information   5 reader
    2 reporter   4 subscription

Answers

1—3	6—3	11—5	16—2	21—1	26—4	31—2
2—1	7—5	12—3	17—4	22—2	27—3	32—2
3—2	8—3	13—1	18—3	23—3	28—1	33—3
4—4	9—5	14—4	19—4	24—1	29—5	34—1
5—2	10—4	15—1	20—5	25—5	30—4	35—3

AUTHOR'S ANALYSIS OF ANALOGY QUESTIONS 21-35

(The correct answer is preceded by an asterisk.)

21 *Furniture* is to *period* as *wine* is to

    *1 vintage   3 bouquet   5 mellowness
    2 aroma   4 proof

ANSWER EXPLAINED

FURNITURE : PERIOD   We classify *furniture* by the *period* in which it originally flourished; for example, Colonial furniture.

    Relationship: The second word (*period*) is used to classify the first (*furniture*) according to time.

WINE : VINTAGE   We classify *wine* by its *vintage* (the grape crop of the year in which the wine was made).

22 *Senile* is to *infantile* as *supper* is to

    1 snack   3 dinner   5 evening
    *2 breakfast   4 daytime

ANSWER EXPLAINED

SENILE : INFANTILE   *Senile* describes the last phase of life and *infantile* the first.

    Relationship: last to first

SUPPER : BREAKFAST   *Supper* is the last meal of the day and *breakfast* the first.

23 *Synonym* is to *meaning* as *homonym* is to
   1 purport   *3 pronunciation   5 sameness
   2 position   4 relationship

ANSWER EXPLAINED

SYNONYM : MEANING   A *synonym* is a word similar to another in *meaning;* for example, "crowd" and "throng" are synonyms.

    Relationship: The second word (*meaning*) tells the way in which the first word (*synonym*) is similar.

HOMONYM : PRONUNCIATION   A *homonym* is a word similar to another in *pronunciation;* for example, "hole" and "whole" are homonyms.

24 *Lawyer* is to *court* as *soldier* is to
   *1 battle   3 training   5 discipline
    2 victory   4 rifle

ANSWER EXPLAINED

LAWYER : COURT   *Lawyer* describes a specially trained person, and *court* the general area for which he has been trained.

    Relationship: specially trained person and the general area for which he has been trained

SOLDIER : BATTLE   *Soldier* describes a specially trained person, and *battle* the general area for which he has been trained.

25 *Taxes* is to *obligation* as *voting* is to
   1 election   3 tally   *5 privilege
   2 campaign   4 restriction

ANSWER EXPLAINED

TAXES : OBLIGATION   *Taxes* are an *obligation* since they must be paid. One has no choice.

    Relationship: The second word (*obligation*) accurately denotes a basic characteristic of the first (*taxes*).

VOTING : PRIVILEGE   *Voting* is a *privilege* since a citizen may or may not vote. There is no compulsion. The second word (*privilege*) accurately denotes a basic characteristic of the first (*voting*).

26 *Wing* is to *airplane* as *hand* is to
   1 finger   3 dish   5 work
   2 applause   *4 clock

ANSWER EXPLAINED

WING : AIRPLANE   A *wing* is a part of an *airplane*.

    Relationship: part to whole

HAND : CLOCK   A *hand* is part of a *clock*.

27 *Chimney* is to *smoke* as *guide* is to

    1 snare   *3 hunter   5 wild game
    2 compass   4 firewood

ANSWER EXPLAINED

CHIMNEY : SMOKE   A *chimney* conducts *smoke*.

   Relationship: conductor to conducted

GUIDE : HUNTER   A *guide* conducts a *hunter*.

28 *Prodigy* is to *ability* as *ocean* is to

    *1 water   3 ships   5 current
    2 waves   4 icebergs

ANSWER EXPLAINED

PRODIGY : ABILITY   A *prodigy* (extraordinary person) has a great deal of one basic ingredient—*ability*.

   Relationship: The second word (*ability*) denotes the basic ingredient abundantly present in the first (*prodigy*).

OCEAN : WATER   An *ocean* has a great deal of one basic ingredient—*water*.

29 *Apple* is to *potato* as *cherry* is to

    1 plum   3 tomato   *5 radish
    2 blueberry   4 squash

ANSWER EXPLAINED

APPLE : POTATO   The *apple* is a tree-grown fruit, whereas the *potato* is a vegetable grown beneath the soil's surface.

   Relationship: tree-grown fruit to vegetable growing beneath soil's surface

CHERRY : RADISH   The *cherry* is a tree-grown fruit, whereas the *radish* grows beneath the soil's surface.

30 *Sapphire* is to *emerald* as *sky* is to

    1 storm   3 star   5 purity
    2 world   *4 grass

ANSWER EXPLAINED

SAPPHIRE : EMERALD   *Sapphire* is blue; *emerald* is green.

   Relationship: blue to green

SKY : GRASS   The *sky* is blue; the *grass* is green.

31 *Pour* is to *spill* as *lie* is to

1 deception   3 falsehood   5 fraud
*2 misstatement   4 perjury

ANSWER EXPLAINED

POUR : SPILL   *Pour* describes an intentional, controlled action; *spill* describes an unintentional, accidental action.

Relationship: intentional vs. unintentional

LIE : MISSTATEMENT   A *lie* is an intentional falsification. A *misstatement*, on the other hand, is an unintentional, incorrect statement resulting from error or accident.

32 *Disparage* is to *despise* as *praise* is to

1 dislike   3 acclaim   5 compliment
*2 adore   4 advocate

ANSWER EXPLAINED

DISPARAGE : DESPISE   Both *disparage* and *despise* express disapproval. Disparage ("speak slightingly of") involves speaking. Despise ("look upon with contempt") involves feeling rather than words.

Relationship: use of a "speaking" word vs. use of a "feeling" word to express a similar idea

PRAISE : ADORE   *Praise* involves the use of words; you can't praise without using words. *Adore* ("regard with very great affection") involves feeling rather than words. Both *praise* and *adore* express approval.

33 *Wall* is to *mortar* as *nation* is to

1 family   *3 patriotism   5 boundaries
2 people   4 geography

ANSWER EXPLAINED

WALL : MORTAR   The bricks in a *wall* are held together by *mortar* (a mixture of sand, cement, and water).

Relationship: The second word (*mortar*) is the cementing agent that makes the first word (*wall*) strong.

NATION : PATRIOTISM   A *nation* is made strong by *patriotism*, the cementing force that holds a nation together.

34 *Aquarium* is to *fish* as *apiary* is to

*1 bees   3 flowers   5 cattle
2 eagles   4 monkeys

ANSWER EXPLAINED

AQUARIUM : FISH   An *aquarium* is a place where *fish* are kept.

Relationship: place to inhabitants

APIARY : BEES   An *apiary* is a place where *bees* are kept.

35 *Fan* is to *air* as *newspaper* is to

    1 literature   *3 information   5 reader

    2 reporter   4 subscription

ANSWER EXPLAINED

FAN : AIR   The function of a *fan* is to put *air* into motion.

Relationship: The first word (*fan*) is a means of circulating the second (*air*).

NEWSPAPER : INFORMATION   The function of a *newspaper* is to circulate *information*.

CHAPTER XII

DICTIONARY OF WORDS TAUGHT IN THIS TEXT

The following pages contain a partial listing of the words presented in this book. The words included are those likely to offer some degree of difficulty. The definitions given have in many cases been condensed.

Use this dictionary as a tool of reference and review. It is a convenient means of restudying the meanings of words that you may have missed in the exercises. It is also a useful device for a general review before an important vocabulary test. Bear in mind, however, that you will get a fuller understanding of these words from the explanations and exercises of the foregoing chapters.

abase: lower

abiogenesis: spontaneous generation

abject: deserving contempt; sunk to a low condition

abridge: shorten

abrupt: broken off; sudden

abstemious: sparing in eating and drinking

abstinent: sparing in eating and drinking

absurd: ridiculous

abyss: bottomless, immeasurably deep space

a cappella: without musical accompaniment

acclaim: welcome with approval

acclivity: upward slope

accredit: accept as worthy of belief; provide with credentials

acme: highest point

acrid: sharp in smell or taste

acrophobia: fear of being at a great height

adagio: slow; in an easy, graceful manner

adherent: supporter; follower

adieu: good-by

adjacent: lying near or next to

admonish: warn of a fault

admonition: counseling against a fault or error

admonitory: conveying a gentle rebuke

adobe: brick of sun-dried clay or mud; structure made of such bricks

adolescent: growing from childhood to adulthood

Adonis: very handsome young man

adroit: skillful

adulation: excessive praise

aegis: shield or protection; sponsorship

affinity: attraction; likeness; relationship

affirmation: declaration

aficionado: person very enthusiastic about anything; sports devotee

afield: out of the way; astray

afoul: in collision

aggressive: disposed to attack

agoraphobia: fear of open spaces

à la carte: dish by dish, with a stated price for each dish

alacrity: cheerful willingness

allegro: quick

aloft: on high; in the air

aloof: at or from a distance; withdrawn

alto: highest male voice; lowest female voice (contralto)

amazon: tall, strong, masculine woman

ambrosial: exceptionally pleasing to taste or smell

amoral: without sense of moral responsibility

amorphous: without definite form or shape

amphibious: able to live both on land and in water

analogy: likeness in some respects between things otherwise different

anarchy: total absence of rule or government; confusion

anatomy: dissection of plants or animals for the purpose of studying their structure; structure of a plant or animal

andante: moderately slow, but flowing

anecdote: short, entertaining account of some happening

anemia: lack of a normal number of red blood cells

anent: concerning

anesthesia: loss of feeling or sensation resulting from ether, chloroform, novocaine, etc.

Anglophile: supporter of England or the English

Anglophobe: one who dislikes England or the English

Anglophobia: dislike of England or the English

anguish: extreme pain

anhydrous: destitute of water

anomaly: deviation from the common rule

anon: soon

anonymous: nameless; of unknown or unnamed origin

anoxia: deprivation of oxygen

antediluvian: antiquated; belonging to the time before the Biblical Flood

anthropology: science dealing with the origin, races, customs, and beliefs of man

anthropomorphic: attributing human form or characteristics to beings not human, especially gods

antibiotic: antibacterial substance produced by a living organism

anticlimactic: strikingly or ridiculously less important than what precedes

anticlimax: abrupt decline in dignity or importance at the end

antidote: remedy for a poison or evil

antipasto: appetizer consisting of fish, meats, etc.; hors d'oeuvres

antipathy: strong dislike

antipodes: parts of the earth (or their inhabitants) diametrically opposite

anxious: fearful of what may come

apathy: lack of feeling, emotion, interest, or excitement

apéritif: alcoholic drink taken before a meal as an appetizer

apex: farthest point opposite the base, as in a triangle or pyramid

aphelion: farthest point from the sun in the orbit of a planet or comet

apiary: place where bees are kept

apogee: farthest point from the earth in the orbit of a man-made satellite or heavenly body; highest point

apostate: one who has forsaken the faith, principles, or party he supported earlier

appellation: name

appendectomy: surgical removal of the appendix

apprehend: seize or take into custody; understand

apprehensive: fearful of what may come

appropriate: take for oneself

approximate: nearly correct

aqueduct: artificial channel for conducting water from a distance

arbiter: a person having power to decide a dispute

arbitrary: proceeding from a whim or fancy

arbitrate: decide a dispute, acting as arbiter (judge); submit a dispute to an arbiter

archaic: no longer used, except in a special context; old-fashioned

aria: melody; an elaborate, accompanied melody for a single voice in an opera

aristocracy: class regarded as superior in some respect

aroma: pleasant odor

arpeggio: production of the tones of

a chord in rapid succession and not simultaneously; a chord thus played

arrogant: haughty

arroyo: watercourse; small, often dry, gully

arthropod: any invertebrate (animal having no backbone) with jointed legs

ascetic: self-denying; person who shuns pleasures

aseptic: free from disease-causing microorganisms

asinine: like an ass or donkey; stupid; silly

assertive: acting and speaking boldly

assuage: ease or lessen

astringent: drawing (the tissues) tightly together; stern; substance that shrinks tissues and checks flow of blood by contracting blood vessels

asymmetrical: lacking balanced proportions

atheism: godlessness

atlas: book of maps

atom: smallest particle of an element

atomizer: instrument for reducing to minute particles or a fine spray

atrophy: lack of growth from want of nourishment or from disuse

attaché: member of the diplomatic staff of an ambassador or minister

attenuate: make thin; weaken

atypical: unlike the typical

au courant: well-informed; up-to-date

auditory: pertaining to the sense of hearing

au revoir: good-by till we meet again

auroral: pertaining to or resembling the dawn; rosy

auspices: patronage and care

austere: stern

autarchy: rule by an absolute sovereign

autobiography: story of a person's life written by the person himself

avant-garde: experimentalists or innovators in any art

avarice: greed

averse: disinclined

aversion: strong dislike

avert: turn away; prevent

aviary: place where birds are kept

avoirdupois: weight

awe: veneration; dread; wonder

awesome: causing or expressive of awe

axiomatic: self-evident

bacchanalian: jovial or wild with drunkenness

bacchic: jovial or wild with drunkenness

bacteriology: science dealing with the study of bacteria

badger: nag

bagatelle: trifle

banter: playful teasing

baritone: male voice between bass and tenor

bas-relief: carving or sculpture in which the figures project only slightly from the background

bass: lowest male voice

basso: lowest male voice

bathos: abrupt decline in dignity or importance at the end

baton: stick with which a conductor beats time for an orchestra or band

bearish: like a bear; rough; tending to depress stock prices

becalm: hold motionless for lack of wind

becloud: obscure

bedevil: torment

bedim: make less bright or shiny

befog: obscure

beget: bring into life or into existence

begrime: make dirty

begrudge: give reluctantly; envy the pleasure or enjoyment of

behest: command

beholden: bound in gratitude; indebted

behoove: be necessary for; be proper for

belabor: beat; attack verbally

belie: misrepresent; be false or unfaithful to

belittle: cause to be little or unimportant; disparage

bemuddle: confuse

benign: not dangerous; gentle

beset: attack on all sides; surround

besiege: surround with armed forces

besmirch: soil

bête noire: object or person dreaded

betimes: early

bewitch: place under a spell; fascinate

bias: opinion formed before there are grounds for it; unthinking preference

bibliophile: lover of books

bigoted: narrow-minded

billet-doux: love letter

biochemistry: chemistry dealing with chemical compounds and processes in living plants and animals

biogenesis: development of life from preexisting life

biography: story of a person's life written by another person

biology: science dealing with the study of living organisms

biometry: calculation of the probable duration of human life

biopsy: diagnostic examination of a piece of tissue from the living body

biota: the living plants (flora) and living animals (fauna) of a region

biped: two-footed animal

blandishment: word or deed of mild flattery

blasé: tired of pleasures; bored

bliss: perfect happiness

blithe: cheerful

bluster: talk or act with noisy violence

boa constrictor: snake that crushes its prey in its coils

bolero: lively dance in ¾ time; the music for this dance; short, loose jacket

bombastic: using pompous language

bonanza: accidental discovery of a rich mass of ore in a mine

bonbon: piece of candy

bon mot: clever saying

bouffant: full; puffed out

bouquet: pleasant odor

bourgeoisie: the middle class

bovine: of or like the cow or ox; sluggish and patient

bow: forward part of a ship

bowdlerize: remove objectionable material from a book

bravado: boastful behavior; pretense of bravery

bravura: piece of music requiring skill and spirit in the performer; display of daring or brilliancy

brazen: shameless; made of brass or bronze; harsh-sounding

breach: a breaking; gap; violation

breadthwise: in the direction of the width

brine: salty water; ocean

brisk: lively

brochure: pamphlet

broncho: half-wild pony

bronco: half-wild pony

bugbear: object of dread

bullish: like a bull; obstinate; tending to cause rises in stock prices

buoyant: cheerful; able to float

burly: stout

burro: small donkey used as a pack animal

buxom: plump and attractive

caballero: gentleman or gallant; horseman

cabana: beach shelter resembling a cabin

cacophonous: harsh-sounding

cajole: persuade by pleasing words

callow: young and inexperienced

calumnious: falsely and maliciously accusing

calumny: false and malicious accusation

cameo: stone or shell on which a figure, cut in relief, appears against a background of a different color

campanile: bell tower

canard: false rumor

canine: of or pertaining to the dog family; designating one of the four pointed teeth next to the incisors

cantata: story or play set to music to be sung by a chorus, but not acted

canto: one of the chief divisions of a long poem; book

canyon: deep valley with high, steep slopes, often with a stream flowing through it

capitulate: yield

capricious: proceeding from a whim or fancy

cardiology: science dealing with the action and diseases of the heart

caricature: drawing, imitation, or description that ridiculously exaggerates peculiarities or defects

carnivorous: flesh-eating

carousal: drinking party

carrion: decaying flesh of a carcass

carte blanche: freedom to use one's own judgment

castanets: hand instruments clicked together to accompany music or dancing

cause célèbre: famous case in law that arouses considerable interest

celerity: speed

celestial: of the heavens

censurable: blamable

censure: adverse criticism

centipede: small wormlike animal with many pairs of legs

chagrin: embarrassment; disappointment

chargé d'affaires: temporary substitute for an ambassador

chasm: wide gap

chef d'oeuvre: masterpiece in art, literature, etc.

chemise: loose-fitting, sacklike dress

cherub: angel in the form of a baby or child

cherubic: chubby and innocent-looking

Chianti: a dry, red Italian wine

chiaroscuro: style of pictorial art using only light and shade; sketch in black and white

chic: stylish

childish: of or like a child in a bad sense

childlike: of or like a child in a good sense

chimerical: fantastic

chiropodist: one who specializes in the care of the feet

circumlocution: roundabout way of speaking

clamorous: noisy

claustrophobia: fear of confined spaces

cliché: trite or worn-out expression

climactic: arranged in order of increasing force and interest; of or constituting a climax

climax: point of highest interest

clique: small and exclusive set of persons

cogitate: consider with care

cognoscente: connoisseur

coiffure: style of arranging the hair; headdress

coincide: happen together

colloquy: conversation; conference

coloratura: ornamental passages (runs, trills, etc.) in vocal music; soprano who sings such passages

commence: begin

commendable: praiseworthy

compassion: pity combined with a desire to aid

complacent: self-satisfied

comprehensible: understandable

comprehensive: including very much

compunction: regret; misgiving

concave: curved inward, creating a hollow space

concerto: long musical composition for one or more principal instruments

concise: expressing much in a few words

concur: agree; happen together

concurrent: running together; occurring at the same time

condescend: stoop or descend to a less formal or stately attitude

conducive: tending to lead to

confidant(e): one to whom secrets are entrusted

confidential: communicated in trust

conflagration: fire

conformity: agreement; similarity

congratulate: express pleasure at another's success

coniferous: bearing cones

conjectural: of the nature of a guess or assumption

conjecture: a guess

connoisseur: expert

conquistador: conqueror

consecrate: bless

consecutive: following in order

consequence: result; importance

constrict: bind

consummate: perfect

contaminate: make impure by mixture

contemporary: of the same period

contiguous: touching; near

contingent: dependent on something else; accidental

contort: twist out of shape

contortionist: person who can twist or bend his body into odd postures

contour: outline of a figure

contralto: lowest female voice

contrariwise: on the contrary

contrite: showing regret for wrongdoing

contrition: regret for wrongdoing

controversy: dispute

convalesce: recover health after illness

conventional: generally accepted

convex: curved or rounded, as the exterior of a circular form viewed from without

convict: prove guilty; person serving a prison sentence

convince: persuade or show conclusively by argument or proof

convivial: fond of dining with friends; jovial

cordial: hearty

corporal: bodily

corps: organized body of persons; branch of the military

corpulent: very fat

corpus: general collection of writings, laws, etc.

corpuscle: blood cell; minute particle

corpus delicti: facts proving a crime has been committed

corroborate: confirm

corrupt: change from good to bad

corsage: small bouquet worn by a woman

coterie: set or circle of acquaintances

countermand: issue a contrary order

coup de grâce: merciful or decisive finishing stroke

coup d'état: sudden, violent, or illegal overthrow of a government

coy: pretending to be shy

cravat: necktie

credence: belief

credentials: documents, letters, references, etc., that inspire belief or trust

credit: trust

credulous: too ready to believe

creed: summary of principles believed in or adhered to

crescendo: gradually increasing (or a gradual increase) in force or loudness

criminology: scientific study of crimes and criminals

criterion: standard

crone: withered old woman

crux: essential part

cuisine: style of cooking

cul-de-sac: blind alley

culmination: highest point

culpable: blamable

cumbersome: burdensome

cupola: rounded roof; small dome or tower on a roof

current: now in progress; a running or flowing, as of water

curriculum: specific course of study in a school or college

curry favor: seek to gain favor by flattery

cursive: running or flowing

cursory: running over hastily

deadlock: stoppage produced by the opposition of equally powerful persons or groups

debacle: collapse

debonair: affable and courteous

debut: formal entrance into society; first public appearance

debutante: girl who has just made her debut

decapitate: behead

deceased: dead

deception: act of deceiving

deceptive: misleading

declivity: downward slope

decrepit: weakened by old age

decrescendo: gradually decreasing (or a gradual decrease) in force or loudness

deduce: derive by reasoning

deduction: subtraction; reasoning from the general to the particular
defamatory: harming or destroying a reputation
defile: make filthy
deflect: turn aside
defunct: dead; extinct
degrade: lower
dejected: in low spirits
delectable: very pleasing
deliberate: think long and carefully
démarche: course of action, especially one involving a change of policy
demise: death, especially of a monarch or other important person
demitasse: small cup for, or of, black coffee
demure: falsely modest or serious; grave
denouement: solution of the plot in a play, story, or complex situation
denunciation: public condemnation
dermatology: science dealing with the skin and its diseases
derogatory: expressing low esteem
desperado: bold, reckless criminal
despotic: unjustly severe
détente: a relaxing, as of strained relations between nations
detention: act of keeping back or detaining
devilish: like a devil; mischievous
devotee: ardent adherent
devour: eat greedily or ravenously; seize upon and destroy
diabolic(al): devilish; very cruel; wicked
dichotomy: cutting or division into two
diffident: lacking self-confidence
digressive: rambling
dilemma: situation requiring a choice between two equally bad alternatives
dilettante: person who follows some art or science as an amusement or in a trifling way
dimeter: line of poetry consisting of two feet
diminuendo: gradually decreasing (or a gradual decrease) in loudness
dimorphous: occurring under two distinct forms
dipody: verse (line of poetry) consisting of two feet
dipsomania: abnormal, uncontrollable craving for alcohol
disclose: make known
disconsolate: cheerless
discredit: cast doubt on; disgrace
discretionary: left to individual judgment
discursive: wandering from one topic to another
disgruntled: in bad humor
disintegrate: break up
disparage: speak slightingly of
disrupt: break apart
distort: twist out of shape; change from the true meaning
divert: turn aside; amuse
docile: easily led

dogmatic: asserting opinions as if they were facts
dolce: soft; sweet
dolce far niente: delightful idleness
doldrums: calm, windless part of the ocean near the equator; listlessness·
doleful: full of sorrow
dolorous: full of sorrow
domicile: home
dour: gloomy
Draconian: harsh
Draconic: harsh
dregs: most worthless part; sediment at the bottom of a liquid
droll: odd and laughter-provoking
dross: waste; scum on the surface of melting metals
duct: tube or channel for conducting a liquid, air, etc.
ductile: able to be drawn out or hammered thin (said of a metal); easily led
duenna: elderly woman chaperon of a young lady; governess
duet: piece of music for two voices or instruments; two singers or players performing together
dukedom: the territory of a duke; the title or dignity of a duke
dysentery: inflammation of the large intestine
dyspepsia: difficult digestion; indigestion
dysphagia: difficulty in swallowing
dysphasia: speech difficulty resulting from brain disease
dystrophy: faulty nutrition

earldom: realm or dignity of an earl
earthy: coarse; worldly
éclat: brilliancy of achievement
eclectic: choosing (ideas, methods, etc.) from various sources
ecology: science dealing with the relation of living things to their environment and to each other
ecstasy: state of overwhelming joy
ectoparasite: parasite living on the exterior of an animal
egoism: conceit
egress: exit
eject: throw out
élan: enthusiasm
elate: lift up with joy
elated: in high spirits
elite: group of superior individuals
elocution: art of speaking or reading effectively in public
eloquent: speaking with force and fluency
Elysian: blissful; heavenly
emaciate: make unnaturally thin
emancipate: free
émigré: refugee
eminence: high rank; lofty hill
emissary: person sent on a mission
emit: send out; give off
empathy: the complete understanding of another's feelings, motives, etc.

encomium: speech or writing of high praise
encore: repetition of a performance; rendition of an additional selection
encumbrance: burden that impedes action
endocarditis: inflammation of the lining of the heart
endocrine: secreting internally
endoderm: membranelike tissue lining the greater part of the digestive tract
endogamy: marriage within the tribe, caste, or social group
endogenous: produced from within; due to internal causes
endomorphic: occurring within
endoparasite: parasite living in the internal organs of an animal
endophyte: plant growing within another plant
endoskeleton: internal skeleton or supporting framework in an animal
endosmosis: osmosis inward
ennui: boredom
entente: understanding or agreement between governments
entrée: main dish at lunch or dinner
entre nous: between us
entrepreneur: one who assumes the risks and management of a business
environs: districts surrounding a place; suburbs
envoy: diplomatic agent; messenger
equanimity: evenness of mind
equine: of or like a horse
erupt: burst or break out
esoteric: private; difficult to understand
esprit de corps: feeling of union and common interest pervading a group
ethereal: of the heavens; delicate
ethnology: science dealing with the races of mankind, their origin, distribution, culture, etc.
eugenics: science dealing with improving the hereditary qualities of the human race
eulogistic: expressing praise
eulogize: write or speak in praise of someone
eupepsia: good digestion
euphemism: substitution of a "good" expression for an unpleasant one
euphonious: pleasing in sound
euphoria: sense of well-being
euthanasia: illegal practice of painlessly putting to death a person suffering from an incurable, painfully distressing disease
euthenics: science dealing with improving living conditions
evict: expel
evince: show clearly
exalt: lift up with joy, pride, etc.; raise in rank, dignity, etc.
excoriate: censure severely
execrate: curse
execute: follow through to completion; put to death
exocrine: secreting externally

exogamy: marriage outside the tribe, caste, or social group

exogenous: produced from without; due to external causes

exoskeleton: hard protective structure developed outside the body

exosmosis: osmosis outward

exoteric: external; readily understandable

exotic: introduced from a foreign country; excitingly strange

expectorate: spit

expedite: accelerate or speed up; make easy

expurgate: remove objectionable material from a book; purify

extinct: no longer in existence

extol: praise

extort: wrest (money, promises, etc.) from a person by force

extrovert: person more interested in what is going on around him than in his own thoughts and feelings

façade: face or front of a building, or of anything

facetious: in the habit of joking; said in jest without serious intent

facilitate: make easy

fait accompli: thing accomplished and presumably irrevocable

fallacious: based on an erroneous idea

fallacy: erroneous idea

fallible: liable to be mistaken

falsetto: unnaturally high-pitched male voice; artificial voice

farcical: exciting laughter

fatal: causing death

fathom: get to the bottom of; ascertain the depth of

faux pas: misstep or blunder in conduct, manners, speech, etc.

fawning: slavishly attentive

fearsome: frightful

felicitate: wish one joy or happiness

feline: of or pertaining to the cat family; sly; stealthy

fester: form pus; rot

fête: to honor with a party; festival

fetid: ill-smelling

fiancé(e): person engaged to be married

fiasco: crash; complete or ridiculous failure

fidelity: faithfulness to a trust or vow; accuracy

fiduciary: held in trust; confidential

fiesta: religious holiday; any festival or holiday

filament: thread

filet: slice of meat or fish without bones or fat

filial: of or like a son or daughter

finale: close or termination, as the last section of a musical composition

finesse: skill

firmament: heaven

flamboyant: flamelike; showy

flay: strip off the skin

fledgling: young bird that has just acquired feathers; an immature person

fleece: strip

flex: bend

flexible: capable of being bent

flexor: muscle that serves to bend a limb

flippant: treating serious matters lightly

flotilla: small fleet; fleet of small vessels

flotsam: wreckage of a ship or its cargo found floating on the sea; driftage

forebear: ancestor

forefather: ancestor

forte: loud

fortissimo: very loud

foundling: infant found after being deserted by its unknown parents

foxy: foxlike; wily; sly

foyer: lobby; entrance hall

fractious: apt to break out into a passion

fracture: break or crack; breaking of a bone

fragment: part broken off

fragrant: having a pleasant odor

Francophile: supporter of France or the French

Francophobe: one who dislikes France or the French

fraternal: brotherly; having to do with a fraternal society

fratricide: act of killing (or killer of) one's own brother

fresco: art of painting with water colors on damp, fresh plaster; picture or design so painted

frivolity: trifling gaiety

frolicsome: full of gaiety

fulsome: offensive because of excessive display or insincerity

fusty: stale-smelling; old-fashioned

gala: characterized by festivity

gallant: man of fashion; lover

garrulous: talkative

gaucho: Argentine cowboy of mixed Spanish and Indian descent

gaunt: excessively thin

gendarme: policeman with military training

genealogy: account of the descent of a person or family from an ancestor

generate: cause; bring into existence

genocide: deliberate extermination of a racial or cultural group

genre: kind; style

gentility: good manners; membership in the upper class

genuflect: bend the knee; touch the right knee to the ground, as in worship

geocentric: measured from the earth's center

geodesy: mathematics dealing with the earth's shape and dimensions

geodetic: pertaining to geodesy

geology: science dealing with the earth's history as recorded in rocks

geometry: mathematics dealing with lines, angles, surfaces, and solids

geomorphic: pertaining to the shape of the earth or the form of its surface

geophysics: science treating of the forces that modify the earth

geopolitics: study of government and its policies as affected by physical geography

geoponics: art or science of agriculture

georgic: agricultural; poem on husbandry (farming)

geotropism: response to earth's gravity, as the growing of roots downward in the ground

Germanophobe: one who dislikes Germany or the Germans

Germanophobia: dislike of Germany or the Germans

germicide: substance that kills germs

glee: joy

glum: gloomy

goatish: goatlike; coarse

gondola: boat used in the canals of Venice; cabin attached to the under part of an airship

gosling: young goose

gracious: courteous

gradation: a change by steps or stages

gradient: rate at which a road, railroad track, etc., rises; slope

gradual: by steps or degrees

graduated: arranged in regular steps, stages, or degrees

grandee: nobleman of the highest rank; person of eminence

grandiloquent: using lofty or pompous words

graphic: clear-cut and lifelike

gratis: out of kindness or favor; free

gratitude: thankfulness

gratuitous: given freely; unwarranted

gratuity: present of money in return for a favor or service

grave: deserving serious attention

grave: slow (the slowest tempo in music); serious

grime: dirt

grotto: cave

gruesome: horrifying and repulsive

gully: gorge excavated by running water

gustatory: pertaining to the sense of taste

gusto: liking or taste; hearty enjoyment

hacienda: large ranch; landed estate; country house

haggard: careworn

halcyon: calm

harlequin: clown

heath: tract of wasteland

hector: to bully; to bluster

herbivorous: dependent on plants as food

Herculean: very difficult; having or requiring the strength of Hercules

herdsman: one who owns, keeps, or tends a herd

heretical: rejecting regularly accepted beliefs or doctrines

hermetic: airtight
heterochromatic: having different colors
heteroclite: deviating from the common rule; person or thing deviating from the common rule
heterodox: rejecting regularly accepted beliefs or doctrines
heterogeneous: dissimilar
heterology: lack of correspondence between parts
heteromorphic: exhibiting diversity of form
heteronym: word spelled like another, but differing in sound and meaning
hidalgo: nobleman of the second class
hierarchy: body of rulers or officials grouped in ranks, each being subordinate to the rank above it
hilarity: noisy gaiety
hircine: goatlike, especially in smell
hireling: one who receives pay for work performed
hoary: white or gray with age; ancient
hoax: deception; joke
hodgepodge: mixture
homeopathy: system of medical practice that treats disease by administering minute doses of a remedy which, if given to healthy persons, would produce symptoms of the disease treated
homicide: killing of one human by another
homochromatic: having the same color
homogeneous: similar
homology: fundamental similarity of structure
homomorphic: exhibiting similarity of form
homonym: word that sounds like another but differs in meaning
homophonic: having the same sound
hors d'oeuvres: light food served as an appetizer before the regular courses of a meal
horsy: having to do with horses or horse racing
humble: of low position or condition; modest
humiliate: lower the pride, position, or dignity of
humility: freedom from pride
hydrophobia: rabies
hyperacidity: excessive acidity
hyperactive: overactive
hyperbole: extravagant exaggeration of statement
hypercritical: overcritical
hyperemia: superabundance of blood
hyperopia: farsightedness
hypersensitive: excessively sensitive
hypertension: abnormally high blood pressure
hyperthyroid: marked by excessive activity of the thyroid gland
hypertrophy: enlargement of a part or organ, as from excessive use
hypoacidity: weak acidity
hypoactive: underactive

hypochondriac: person morbidly anxious about his health or suffering from imagined illness
hypodermic: injected under the skin
hypotension: low blood pressure
hypothesis: theory or supposition assumed as a basis for reasoning
hypothetical: pertaining to a supposition made as a basis for reasoning or research
hypothyroid: marked by deficient activity of the thyroid gland

ignominy: shame
ignoramus: ignorant person
illusion: false impression
imbibe: drink
imbroglio: difficult situation; complicated disagreement
immaculate: absolutely clean
immortality: eternal life; lasting fame
immunity: resistance to a disease; freedom from an obligation
impasse: predicament affording no escape; impassable road
impede: hinder
impediment: hindrance; defect
impersonation: assuming the appearance or manners of another person
impertinent: inappropriate; rude
impregnability: state of being unconquerable
impudent: insolent
imputation: insinuation; accusation
incense: substance yielding a pleasant odor when burned
incognito: with one's identity concealed; disguised state
incommunicado: deprived of communication with others; in solitary confinement
inconsequential: unimportant
incontrovertible: certain
incorporate: combine so as to form one body
incorruptible: incapable of being corrupted or bribed
incredible: not believable
incredulity: disbelief
incrustation: crust or coating
incur: meet with something undesirable; bring upon oneself
incursion: a rushing into; raid
indigo: plant yielding a blue dye; deep violet blue
indisputable: too evident for doubt
indubitable: certain
induce: move by persuasion
induction: reasoning from the particular to the general
inebriated: drunk
infanticide: act of killing (or killer of) an infant
infantile: of or like a very young child; babyish
infer: derive by reasoning
inference: conclusion
infernal: pertaining to the realm of the dead; hellish

infidel: one who does not accept a particular faith
infinite: without end; without limits
inflexibility: rigidity
infraction: violation
ingénue: naive young woman; actress playing such a role
ingenuous: artlessly frank
ingrate: ungrateful person
ingratiate: work (oneself) into another's favor
initiate: begin
inject: force or introduce a liquid, a remark, etc.
innovator: one who introduces a change or something new
insatiable: incapable of being satisfied
insecticide: preparation for killing insects
insectivorous: dependent on insects as food
intact: kept or left whole
intaglio: design engraved by making cuts in a surface
intangible: not capable of being touched
interject: throw in between
interlocutor: one who participates in a conversation; questioner
intermezzo: short musical or dramatic entertainment between the acts of a play; short musical composition between the main divisions of an extended musical work; a short, independent musical composition
intermittent: coming and going at intervals
interpose: place between
intimidate: make fearful
intolerant: narrow-minded
intoxicated: drunk
intractable: hard to manage
intricate: complicated
introvert: person more interested in his own thoughts than in what is going on around him
invalidate: make valueless
invert: turn upside down
inveterate: firmly established by age; habitual
invigorate: give vigor, life, or energy to
invincible: incapable of being conquered
iridescent: having colors like the rainbow
irksome: wearisome; tedious
irony: type of humor whose intended meaning is the opposite of the words used
irrational: senseless

jetsam: goods cast overboard to lighten a ship in distress
jettison: throw (goods) overboard to lighten a ship or plane; discard
jocose: given to jesting; playfully humorous
jocular: given to jesting; done as a joke
jocund: merry
jovial: jolly
jubilation: rejoicing

junta: council for legislation or administration

junto: political faction; group of plotters

juvenile: of or for youth; immature

juxtaposition: close or side-by-side position

kith and kin: friends and relatives

knave: tricky, deceitful fellow

labyrinthine: full of confusing passageways; complicated like the Labyrinth

lackey: slavish follower

laconic: using words sparingly

laissez-faire: absence of government interference or regulation

lamentable: pitiable

lank: long and thin

larceny: theft

largo: slow and dignified

laudable: praiseworthy

laudatory: expressing praise

lax: careless

leeward: in the direction away from the wind

legato: smooth and connected

legerdemain: sleight of hand

lento: slow

lesion: injury

lethargic: unnaturally drowsy; sluggish

lettre de cachet: sealed letter obtainable from the King of France (before the Revolution) ordering the imprisonment without trial of the person named in the letter

levity: lack of proper seriousness

liaison: bond; coordination of activities

libel: false and defamatory written or printed statement

libretto: text or words of an opera or other long musical composition

lineage: descent in a line from a common ancestor

lionize: treat as highly important

lissom(e): lithesome; nimble

lithe: slender and agile

lithesome: capable of bending and twisting with ease

loath: disinclined

lobotomy: type of brain surgery

longevity: long life; length of life

loquacious: talkative

Lucullan: luxurious

ludicrous: exciting laughter

lupine: of or like a wolf; ravenous

macrocosm: great world; universe

macron: horizontal mark indicating that the vowel over which it is placed is long

macroscopic: large enough to be visible to the naked eye

maestro: eminent conductor, composer, or teacher of music; master in any art

maître d'hôtel: headwaiter

majolica: variety of enameled Italian pottery richly decorated in colors

maladroit: unskillful; clumsy

malaise: vague feeling of bodily discomfort or illness

malediction: curse

malign: speak evil of

malignant: threatening to cause death; very evil

malleable: capable of being shaped by hammering; adaptable

malodorous: ill-smelling

mañana: tomorrow

mandate: authoritative command; a territory administered by a trustee (supervisory nation)

mandatory: required by command

mantilla: woman's light scarf or veil; cloak or cape

marine: of the sea or shipping

maritime: of the sea or shipping

martial: pertaining to war; warlike

martinet: person who enforces very strict discipline

martyrdom: state of being a martyr

masticate: chew

matador: bullfighter appointed to kill the bull

maternal: motherly; inherited from or related to the mother's side

matriarchy: form of social organization in which the mother rules the family or tribe, descent being traced through the mother

matricide: act of killing (or killer of) one's own mother

mature: full-grown; carefully thought out

maudlin: weakly sentimental and tearful

mean: without distinction

medley: mixture

melancholy: sad

mélange: mixture

memento: keepsake; reminder

menace: threat

menial: low

mentor: wise and trusted adviser; athletic coach

mercurial: vivacious; changeable; crafty; eloquent

mesa: flat-topped rocky hill with steeply sloping sides

mestizo: person of mixed (usually Spanish and American Indian) blood

metamorphosis: change of form

meteorology: science dealing with the atmosphere and weather

mettlesome: courageous; spirited

mezzanine: intermediate story in a theater between the main floor and the first balcony

mezzo-soprano: female voice between contralto and soprano

mezzotint: picture engraved on copper or steel by polishing or scraping away parts of a roughened surface

microbe: very minute organism; microorganism

microbicide: agent that destroys microbes

microcosm: little world

microdont: having small teeth

microfilm: film of very small size

micrometer: instrument for measuring very short distances

microscopic: invisible to the naked eye

microwave: very short electromagnetic wave

milieu: environment

militant: given to fighting

mirage: optical illusion

mirth: merriment

misanthrope: hater of mankind

misanthropy: hatred of mankind

misconception: erroneous belief

misogamy: hatred of marriage

misogyny: hatred of women

misology: hatred of argument or discussion

misoneism: hatred of anything new

missile: weapon propelled to hit a distant object

missive: letter

mocking: ridiculing

moderato: in moderate time

modest: humble; decent

modesty: humbleness

molt: shed feathers, skin, hair, etc.

momentous: very important

monarchy: state ruled over by a single person, as a king or queen

monitor: one who admonishes

monochromatic: of one color

monocle: eyeglass for one eye

monogamy: marriage with but one mate at a time

monogram: two or more letters interwoven to represent a name

monograph: written account of a single thing or class of things

monolith: single stone of large size

monolog(ue): long speech by one person in a group

monomania: derangement of mind on one subject only

monomorphic: having but a single form

monophobia: fear of being alone

monopode: one-footed creature

monosyllabic: having but one syllable

monotheism: belief that there is but one God

monotonous: continuing in an unchanging tone; wearying

morbid: having to do with disease; gruesome

moribund: near death

morose: ill-humoredly silent

morphology: branch of biology dealing with the form and structure of animals and plants

mortal: destined to die; human; causing death

mortality: death rate; mortal nature

mortification: embarrassment

mortify: humiliate; embarrass

mortuary: morgue

mot juste: the exactly right word

mournful: full of sorrow

musicale: social gathering, with music as the featured entertainment

mustang: bronco
musty: moldy or stale
myopia: nearsightedness
myrmidon: obedient and unquestioning follower
mythology: account or study of myths

nadir: lowest point
naive: simple; unsophisticated
nautical: of the sea or shipping
necrology: register of persons who have died
nemesis: due punishment for evil deeds; one who inflicts such punishment
nepotism: favoritism to relatives by those in power
neurology: scientific study of the nervous system and its diseases
nimble: quick and light in motion
noblesse oblige: principle that persons of high rank or birth are obliged to act nobly
noisome: offensive to the sense of smell; unwholesome
nonage: legal minority; period before maturity
nonagenarian: person in his 90's
nonchalant: without concern or enthusiasm
nostalgia: homesickness; yearning for the past
notwithstanding: despite the fact that
nouveaux riches: persons newly rich
nowise: in no way
noxious: harmful
nugatory: worthless
nuptials: wedding
nutriment: nourishment; food

obese: very fat
obligatory: required
obloquy: a speaking against; public reproach
obsequious: slavishly attentive
obsolescent: going out of use
obsolete: no longer in use
obverse: front of a coin, medal, etc.
octogenarian: person in his 80's
odoriferous: yielding an odor, usually fragrant
odorous: having an odor, especially a sweet odor
odyssey: any long series of wanderings or travels
offal: waste parts of a butchered animal; refuse
officialdom: those having the authority of officials; officials collectively
olfactory: pertaining to the sense of smell
oligarchy: form of government in which a few people have the power
olio: mixture
omnibus: bus; book containing a variety of works by one author; covering many things at once
omnifarious: of all varieties, forms, or kinds
omnific: all-creating

omnipotent: unlimited in power
omnipresent: present everywhere at the same time
omniscient: knowing everything
omnivorous: eating everything; fond of all kinds
opinionated: unduly attached to one's own opinion
oratorio: musical composition, usually on a religious theme, for solo voices, chorus, and orchestra
ornate: elaborate
ornithology: study of birds
orthodox: generally accepted, especially in religion
ostentatious: done to impress others
osteopath: practitioner of osteopathy
osteopathy: treatment of diseases by manipulation of bones, muscles, nerves, etc.
oust: expel
overweening: thinking too highly of oneself
ovine: of or like a sheep

pacify: calm
paean: song or hymn of praise, joy, or triumph
paleontology: science dealing with life in the remote past as recorded in fossils
palette: thin board on which an artist lays and mixes colors
palladium: safeguard or protection
paltry: practically worthless
pampas: vast, treeless, grassy plains, especially in Argentina
pang: attack of severe pain
panic: unreasoning, sudden fright that grips a multitude
paradox: self-contradictory statement which may nevertheless be true
paradoxical: self-contradictory, yet possibly true
paramount: chief
parasite: animal, plant, or person living on others
par excellence: above all others of the same sort
parody: humorous imitation of a serious writing
parrot: repeat mechanically
parry: a warding off of a thrust or blow
partiality: special taste or liking
partisan: supporter; follower
paternal: fatherly; inherited from or related to the father's side
pathetic: arousing pity
pathogenic: causing disease
pathological: due to disease
pathology: science dealing with the nature and causes of disease
pathos: quality in speech, writing, music, events, etc., that arouses a feeling of pity or sadness
patina: film or incrustation, usually green, on the surface of old bronze or copper

patriarch: venerable old man; father and ruler of a family or tribe; founder
patriarchy: form of social organization in which the father rules the family or tribe, descent being traced through the father
patricide: act of killing (or killer of) one's own father
peccadillo: slight offense
peculate: steal
pedestal: support or foot of a column or statue; foundation
pedestrian: foot traveler; commonplace
pedigree: an ancestral line
penitent: feeling regret for wrongdoing
pensive: thoughtful in a sad way
peon: common laborer; worker kept in service to repay a debt
perfidious: false to a trust; faithless
perfidy: violation of a trust
pericardium: membranous sac enclosing the heart
perigee: nearest point to the earth in the orbit of a man-made satellite or heavenly body
perihelion: nearest point to the sun in the orbit of a planet or comet
perimeter: the whole outer boundary or measurement of a surface or figure
periphery: outside boundary
periphrastic: expressed in a roundabout way
periscope: instrument permitting those in a submarine a view of the surface
peristalsis: wavelike contraction of the intestines which propels contents onward
peristyle: row of columns around a building or court; the space so enclosed
peritoneum: membrane lining the abdominal cavity and covering the organs
peritonitis: inflammation of the peritoneum
persistence: perseverance
pert: saucy
pertinacious: adhering firmly to a purpose or opinion
pertinent: bearing on the matter in hand
pervade: pass or spread through
pervert: turn away from right or truth; person who has turned from what is normal or natural
pesticide: substance that kills rats, insects, bacteria, etc.
pestiferous: infected with or bearing disease; evil
pestilential: morally harmful; pertaining to a pestilence
petrology: scientific study of rocks
petty: trifling
philanthropist: lover of mankind
philanthropy: love of mankind
philately: collection and study of stamps
philharmonic: pertaining to a musical organization

philhellenism: support of Greece or the Greeks

philippic: bitter denunciation

philogyny: love of women

philology: study of language

philosopher: lover of wisdom

phlebotomy: opening of a vein for the purpose of diminishing the supply of blood

phobia: fear; dislike

photophobia: morbid aversion to light

physiology: science dealing with the functions of living things or their organs

pianissimo: very soft

piano: soft

piazza: open square in an Italian town; veranda or porch

picador: horseman who irritates the bull with a lance at the beginning of a bullfight

picaro: rogue; vagabond

piddling: trifling

pièce de résistance: main dish; main item of any collection, series, program, etc.

pince-nez: eyeglasses clipped to the nose by a spring

pinnacle: highest point

piscine: of or like a fish

pizzicato: direction to players of bowed instruments to pluck the strings instead of using the bow

plaudit: applause; enthusiastic praise

plausible: apparently trustworthy

pliable: easily bent or molded; capable of adaptation

plight: unfortunate state

plumb: get to the bottom of; ascertain the depth of

plutocratic: having great influence because of one's wealth

podiatrist: chiropodist

podium: dais; low wall serving as a foundation

poignant: painfully touching

pollute: make unclean

polyarchy: rule by many

polychromatic: showing a variety of colors

polygamy: marriage to several mates at the same time

polyglot: speaking several languages

polygon: closed plane figure having many angles, and hence many sides

polymorphic: having various forms

polyphonic: having many sounds or voices

polysyllabic: having more than three syllables

polytechnic: dealing with many arts or sciences

polytheism: belief that there is a plurality of gods

poncho: large cloth, often waterproof, with a slit for the head

ponder: weigh in the mind

porcine: of or like a pig

port: left-hand side of a ship when one faces forward

portfolio: briefcase; position or duties of a cabinet member or minister of state

portico: roof supported by columns, forming a porch or a covered walk

portly: imposing, especially because of size

posthumous: published after the author's death; occurring after death

potpourri: mixture

precipice: cliff

precipitous: steep as a precipice; overhasty

précis: brief summary

precursor: forerunner

predecessor: one who precedes another

predicament: unfortunate state

predilection: inclination to like or choose something

preeminent: standing out above others

prehensile: adapted for seizing

prejudice: unreasonable preference or objection

premonition: forewarning

premonitory: conveying a forewarning

preposterous: senseless

prestissimo: at a very rapid pace

presto: quick

presumptuous: taking undue liberties

pretentious: done to impress others

prevaricate: lie

prim: formal and precise in manner or appearance

primeval: pertaining to the world's first ages

primitive: characteristic of the original state of the world or of man

primordial: existing at the very beginning; first in order

princeling: small or petty prince

pristine: in original state; uncorrupted

procreate: beget

procrustean: cruel or inflexible in enforcing conformity

profound: very deep

progenitor: forefather

progeny: children; descendants

progressive: going forward to something better

projectile: object designed to be shot forward; anything thrown forward

propinquity: kinship; nearness of place

prosecute: follow to the end or until finished; conduct legal proceedings against

prospector: person who searches for precious minerals, oil, etc.

prostrate: lie with face down

protean: exceedingly variable; readily assuming different forms or shapes

protégé(e): person under the care and protection of another

prow: forward part of a ship

proximity: nearness

psychology: science of the mind

psychopathic: pertaining to mental disease; insane

puberty: physical beginning of manhood or womanhood

pudgy: short and fat

pueblo: Indian village built of adobe and stone

puerile: foolish for a grown-up to say or do; childish

pungent: sharp in smell or taste; biting

purge: cleanse; rid of undesired element or person

putrefy: rot

putrid: stinking from decay; extremely bad

Pyrrhic: gained at too great a cost

qualm: misgiving

quarrelsome: disposed to quarrel

raconteur: person who excels in telling stories, anecdotes, etc.

raillery: pleasantry touched with ridicule

raison d'être: reason or justification for existing

rancid: unpleasant to smell or taste from being spoiled or stale

rank: having a strong, bad odor or taste; extreme

rankle: cause inflammation

rapport: relationship characterized by harmony, conformity, or affinity

rapprochement: establishment or state of cordial relations; a coming together

rapture: state of overwhelming joy

rash: overhasty

ratiocinate: reason

rational: able to think clearly; based on reason

rationalize: devise excuses for one's actions, desires, failures, etc.

ravine: deep, narrow gorge worn by running water

recompense: payment

recuperate: recover health after illness

recur: happen again

reek: emit a strong, disagreeable smell; be permeated with

reflect: throw back light, heat, sound, etc.; think

reflex: involuntary response to a stimulus

refract: bend a ray of light, heat, sound, etc., from a straight course

refractory: hard to manage

regicide: act of killing (or killer of) a king

régime: system of government or rule

regimen: set of rules to improve health

regressive: disposed to move backward

reject: refuse to take

relevant: bearing upon the matter in hand

reluctant: disinclined

remand: send back; recommit

remiss: negligent

remit: send money due; forgive

remorse: regret for wrongdoing

rendezvous: meeting place; appointment to meet at a fixed time and place

renegade: deserter from a religion, party, etc.; traitor

repartee: skill of replying quickly, cleverly, and humorously; witty reply

repentant: showing regret for wrongdoing

repertoire: list of plays, operas, roles, compositions, etc., that a company or performer is prepared to perform

reprehensible: blamable

reproof: rebuke

reprove: disapprove or criticize

repugnance: strong dislike

repulsive: offensive

restrict: keep within limits

résumé: summary

retentive: able to retain or remember

retinue: group of followers accompanying a distinguished person

retort: reply quickly or sharply in kind; quick, sharp reply

retrograde: going backward; becoming worse

retrogression: act of going from a better to a worse state

retrogressive: disposed to move backward

revere: regard with reverence

reverse: back of a coin, medal, etc.

revert: go back

revive: bring back to life

rift: crack or opening

riposte: quick retort or repartee; in fencing, quick return thrust after a parry

rogue: tricky, deceitful fellow

rotund: rounded-out; full-toned

rotunda: round building, especially one with a dome or cupola; large round room

rout: state of confusion

rueful: pitiable

rupture: break; hostility

Russophobe: one who dislikes Russia or the Russians

salubrious: healthful

salvo: simultaneous discharge of shots; burst of cheers

sangfroid: coolness of mind or composure in difficult circumstances

sanguinary: bloody

sanguine: having a ruddy color; confident

sapling: young tree

sarcasm: sneering language intended to hurt a person's feelings

sardonic: bitterly sarcastic

satire: language or writing that exposes follies or abuses by holding them up to ridicule

saturnine: gloomy

savoir faire: knowledge of just what to do

scavenger: animal or person removing refuse, decay, etc.

scent: smell; get a suspicion of

scherzo: light or playful part of a sonata or symphony

scintillate: sparkle; twinkle

sebaceous: secreting fatty matter

sedate: of settled, quiet disposition

seduction: act of leading astray into wrongdoing

senile: showing the weakness of age

señor: gentleman; Mr. or Sir

señora: lady; Mrs. or Madam

señorita: young lady; Miss

septuagenarian: person in his 70's

sequel: something that follows

sequence: the following of one thing after another

serf: person bound to the soil and more or less subject to the will of the owner

serfdom: the condition or status of a serf

serpentine: winding in and out

servile: befitting a slave or servant

sforzando: accented

shard: fragment

sheepish: like a sheep in timidity or stupidity; awkwardly bashful or embarrassed

sheikdom: region under a sheik's rule

sibling: one of two or more children of a family

sierra: ridge of mountains with an irregular (saw-toothed) outline

siesta: short rest, especially at midday

silhouette: outline; shadow

simultaneously: at the same time

sinuous: bending in and out

siren: dangerous, attractive woman; woman who sings sweetly; apparatus for sounding loud warnings

slander: false and defamatory spoken statement

slanderous: falsely and maliciously accusing

slattern: untidy, slovenly woman

sloven: person habitually untidy, dirty, or careless in dress, habits, etc.

sober: not drunk; free from excitement or exaggeration

sobriquet: nickname

sociology: study of the evolution, development, and functioning of human society

sojourn: temporary stay

solo: piece of music for one voice or instrument; anything done without a partner

solon: legislator; wise man

somniferous: inducing sleep

sonata: piece of music (for one or two instruments) having three or four movements in contrasted rhythms but related tonality

sophistry: clever but deceptive reasoning

soprano: highest singing voice in women and boys

sorcerer: one who practices witchcraft

sordid: filthy

sororicide: act of killing (or killer of) one's own sister

sot: drunkard

sotto voce: in an undertone; privately

soubriquet: nickname

souvenir: keepsake

specious: apparently reasonable, but not really so

speculate: reflect; buy or sell with the hope of profiting by price fluctuations

squalid: filthy from neglect

staccato: disconnected; with breaks between successive notes

staid: of settled, quiet disposition

starboard: right-hand side of a ship when one faces forward

stardom: the status or position of a star

starveling: one who is thin from lack of food

stentorian: very loud

stern: rear end of a ship

stigma: mark of disgrace

stigmatize: brand with a mark of disgrace

stricture: adverse criticism

stringent: strict

stripling: lad

stucco: plaster for covering exterior walls of buildings

Stygian: dark; gloomy; infernal

sublimate: redirect the energy of a person's bad impulses into socially and morally higher channels; purify

sublime: uplifting

subservient: useful in an inferior capacity; servile

succession: the following of one thing after another

successive: following in order

succumb: yield

suckling: child or animal that is nursed

sullen: ill-humoredly silent

sully: soil

summit: highest point

sumptuous: luxurious

superannuated: retired on a pension; too old for work

supersensitive: excessively sensitive

supposition: a guess

supreme: above all others

survive: remain alive after

svelte: slender

sycophant: parasitic flatterer

symbiosis: the living together in mutually helpful association of two dissimilar organisms

symmetrical: balanced in arrangement

table d'hôte: describing a complete meal that bears a fixed price

tact: sensitive mental perception of what is appropriate on a given occasion

tactful: having or showing tact

tactile: pertaining to the sense of touch; able to be touched

tactless: lacking tact

tangent: touching; line or surface meeting a curved line or surface at one point, but not intersecting it

tantalize: excite a hope but prevent its fulfillment; tease

tarnish: soil or dull

taurine: of or like a bull; relating to Taurus (a sign of the zodiac)

technology: industrial science

tedium: boredom

teetotaler: person who totally abstains from intoxicating beverages

telepathy: transference of the thoughts and feelings of one person to another with no apparent communication

tempera: method of painting in which the colors are mixed with white of egg or other substances, instead of oil

temperate: moderate in eating and drinking

tenable: capable of being maintained or defended

tenacious: inclined to hold fast

tenacity: quality of holding fast

tenancy: period of a tenant's temporary holding of real estate

tenor: adult male voice between baritone and alto

tenuous: without substance

tenure: period for which an office or position is held

terpsichorean: pertaining to dancing

terra cotta: kind of hard, brownish-red earthenware, used for vases, statuettes, etc.; dull brownish-red

terse: free of unnecessary words

tête-à-tête: private conversation between two persons

theology: study of religion and religious ideas

theory: a supposition supported by considerable evidence

therapeutic: curative

thespian: pertaining to the drama or acting

throes: pangs

titanic: of enormous strength, size, or power

tonsillectomy: surgical removal of the tonsils

toothsome: pleasing; especially to the taste

toreador: bullfighter, usually mounted

torero: bullfighter on foot

torsion: act of twisting; twisting of a body by two equal and opposite forces

torso: trunk or body of a statue without a head, arms, or legs; human trunk

tortilla: thin, flat, round corn cake

tortuous: full of twists or curves; tricky

torture: inflict severe pain upon

toupee: wig

tour de force: feat of strength or skill

toxic: poisonous

tractable: capable of being controlled

traduce: expose to contempt or shame by a false report

transgress: step beyond the limits; break a law

travesty: imitation that makes a serious thing seem ridiculous

treatise: written account

tremolo: rapid repetition of a tone or chord without apparent breaks, to express emotion

tribulation: suffering

tribute: speech or writing of high praise

trio: piece of music for three voices or instruments; three singers or players performing together

tripod: utensil, stool, or caldron having three legs

trite: stale

truckle: submit servilely to a superior

turncoat: apostate

tyrannicide: act of killing (or killer of) a tyrant

unfledged: without feathers; immature

unguent: ointment

unipod: one-legged support

unrestricted: not confined within bounds; open to all

unsavory: unpleasant to taste or smell; morally offensive

untenable: incapable of being held or defended

ursine: of or like a bear

vagabond: one who wanders from place to place, having no fixed dwelling

vain: conceited; worthless

vainglorious: excessively proud or boastful

vanquish: conquer

vaquero: cowboy

velocipede: child's tricycle

velocity: speed

vendetta: feud for blood revenge

venerable: worthy of respect because of advanced age, religious association, or historical importance

venerate: regard with reverence

veracity: truthfulness

verity: truth

versatile: having many aptitudes

verse: line of poetry

vertex: farthest point opposite the base, as in a triangle or pyramid

viaduct: bridge for conducting a road or railroad over a valley, river, etc.

vibrato: slightly throbbing or pulsating effect, adding warmth and beauty to the tone

vignette: a literary sketch; short verbal description

vile: unclean; hateful

vilification: defamation

vilify: speak evil of

virile: having the qualities of fully developed manhood

virtuoso: one who exhibits great technical skill in an art, especially in playing a musical instrument

virulent: extremely poisonous; very bitter

virus: disease-causing organism; corruptive force

vis-à-vis: face to face; in comparison with; in relation to

vivace: spirited

vivacious: lively in temper or conduct

vivid: full of life; sharp and clear

vivify: enliven

vivisection: operation on a living animal for scientific investigation

vociferous: producing a loud outcry

vogue: fashion

volition: will

voracious: greedy in eating; incapable of being satisfied

vulpine: of or like a fox; crafty; cunning

wane: decrease gradually in size

warlock: sorcerer

warp: the threads running lengthwise in a loom

wax: to grow in size

wheedle: persuade by pleasing words

windward: in the direction from which the wind blows

winsome: full of a winning quality; cheerful

withal: with it all; as well

wolfish: characteristic of a wolf; ferocious

woof: the threads running from side to side in a woven fabric

wrench: twist violently

wretched: sunk to a low condition

writ of mandamus: written order from a court to enforce the performance of some public duty

xenophobia: aversion to foreigners

yclept: named

yearling: one who is a year old

yore: long ago

zenith: highest point; point in the heavens directly overhead